Ad

"In this book, Margo Mateas, through her own ~~~~
others, helps answer the questions that we all have throughout our lives... w~~~
that the world we live in is not what it seems. I highly recommend this book to anyone
who is searching for those answers."
Jimmy Church, Los Angeles, CA., 2017
Host "Fade 2 Black"
Fill in Host "Coast to Coast AM"
Host "Hanger One" History Channel

"If there is one intriguing book to read, THIS IS IT!
You will feel like you are watching a sci-fi movie or stepped into another galaxy.
Margo revives your hope in something greater than yourself and helps you regain hope
for a future full of joy and happiness. She offers unique classes and workshops on ways
we can grow spiritually and protect ourselves from things that are REAL and UNSEEN.
Finally, if you are suffering and are searching to the ends of the earth for relief, then
this is the book for you. There are no coincidences, so please stop your search and let
the words of this book change your perception about what is happening on a level far
beyond what your own eye can see. You will learn to connect with your soul and be able
to let your own light shine."
Regina Shiroma

"OMG I am LOVING this book! Margo is such a talented and gifted writer.
It really feels so personal and conversational, and I really sense that this book is going
to be so helpful for so many people. She provides so much information in digestible
amounts, and in clear, easy to follow language."
Rachel Miller

"O...M....G!!! Just had a chance to proofread this wonderful, incredible book!
This is going to light the world on fire! Margo has captured and expressed so much
important information. The world needs this right now!"
Angela Keller

"This is such an important work. Margo pulls back the veil and reveals the supernatural
world to us in ways we can understand. Through personal accounts, medical histories
and truly astounding before and after photos, we see for ourselves that the unseen world
is real – and how profoundly it affects us. We all need this knowledge so that we can be
fully supported by the Light during our time here on Earth. Stock up, because you're
going to want to share this book with everyone you know."
Lisa Barnett
#1 Int'l Best Selling Author of "The Infinite Wisdom of the Akashic Records" and
"From Questioning to Knowing – 73 Prayers To Transform Your Life"

Gay,

Thanks!

Mayo

FREED BY THE LIGHT

True Stories of How The Supernatural Affects Our Lives

By
Margo M. Mateas

Published by Silver Wolf Publishing, Topanga, Ca.

For permissions contact the publisher at info@freedbythelight.com

Freed By The Light Concept & Design	Margo M Mateas
Freed By The Light Cover Design	Margo M Mateas
Freed By The Light Cover Photo Credit	Kim Becker
Freed By The Light Back Cover Photo Credit	Margo Mateas
Illustrations	Basia Christ
Author Photo	Tiffany Mateas
Book Layout	Pamela Hawkins
Editorial Assistant	Rachel Miller

Printed in Hong Kong

ISBN 978-0-98-49113-3-2

Library of Congress number available upon request
1. Spirituality 2. Self-Help 3. Religion 4. Inspiration 5. Paranormal 6. Occult

Silver Wolf Publishing
Topanga, CA. 90290

To those who are suffering and to those who seek

TABLE OF CONTENTS

Disclaimer

ACKNOWLEDGEMENTS

A sincere soul thank you to God, Jesus, the angels and Ganesha for selecting me for this work, and giving me the gifts to do it. Thank you for your tremendous love for humanity. I follow where you lead, and this has been an amazing journey.

Thanks to all the people who graciously agreed to share their stories in this book so that others will know they are not alone. You are living proof that healing, grace and happiness are possible, no matter what. You are my inspiration. Thanks to everyone who bought the book early and waited so long to get it, while it grew a hundred pages more than anticipated.

To Kim Becker, thank you for the miraculous cover photo and the "birth" photo, too. You are a true angel, soul-sister and the "Keeper of the Skies!"

Many Volcanic thanks to Jimmy Church, Rita Kumarayan and the entire Fadernaut family for your warm acceptance of me and my work. Jimmy Church, you are the "Patron Saint of Margo." Thanks for having me on your shows. Fade To Black (www.jimmychurchradio.com), and Coast to Coast AM. Thanks to you and Rita for just being you. Thank you to Coast to Coast AM listeners for your overwhelming support for this subject matter. The hundreds of sessions I conducted with you gave this book so much more richness, strength and depth.

Thanks to Javier Sandoval for seeing the Light in me and helping to bring it to the world through your Awareness Life Expo. Thank you to Joseph Ernest Martin for having me on your award-winning TV show, Paranormal Insights.

Many thanks to Rev. Danielle Marie Hewitt and everyone at the Temple of Light in Irvine, CA for really opening your hearts to myself and Tiffany and the LPAC course in so many ways. We will never forget your many kindnesses.

Special thanks to Basia Christ for bringing my inner visions to life through your amazing illustrations. They add so much to the book, and you captured each one perfectly!

A very special shout-out to my dear Temple of Light "LPACers," Tony,

Rhonda and Regina. Tony, thank you for sharing your beautiful heart and letting us love you. Thank you, Regina Shiroma, for bravely deciding to share your story, diligently proofreading every line of this book and supporting me during the process. Rhonda, thank you for generously sharing your experiences and for always having my heart. I love you all.

Thanks to Amy Blackmore for reminding me what my "real" job is. This book would not be what it is without you and your steadfast courage and support.

To Pamela Hawkins, book designer and creative "midwife," thank you for bringing my visions to life with such patience and love and for making it through the nano and vaccines chapters! We did it! Thank you, Renee Duran, for creating this amazing book cover and my websites. Thank you, Rachel Miller, for coming in at the eleventh hour and proofreading with such insight and and love. You made the book so much better. Thanks to Denise Willis for your love and support.

Thanks to my "Fairy Book Mother" Karen Price at New Leaf who will bring this book to the world.

To my Facebook friends and fans around the world, thank you. We may be miles apart, but I feel your love in my heart. You make a huge difference in my life. Thanks to Katie Keeley and Trisha Gelder for bringing my books to the UK!

Thanks to my beloved sister, Jan Myers, for always loving, accepting and supporting me. Thank you for reading the book through the eyes of a skeptic and giving me such priceless feedback. You made the book the best it can be. I love you.

To Angela Keller, thank you for proofreading the book and coming out to send Rose off to Heaven. We love you.

Tom Ballas, thanks for understanding what I do, always listening to my media appearances and encouraging me to keep helping people. This book would not have made it into the world without your support. Thank you! I love you.

Finally, to Tiffany Mateas, thank you for your eagle-eye in proofreading, making meals, bringing tea, rubbing my neck, reminding me it's all going to be okay, shipping out books, talking to customers and basically living without me for eight months while I did sessions and worked nonstop on this book. I love you. You are the kindest person I know, and I am blessed to have you as my partner in love and life.

"Don't think about why you question,
simply don't stop questioning.

Don't worry about what you can't answer, and
don't try to explain what you can't know.

Curiosity is its own reason.

Aren't you in awe when you contemplate the mysteries of eternity,
of life, of the marvelous structure behind reality?

And this is the miracle of the human mind—to use its
constructions, concepts, and formulas as tools to explain what man
sees, feels and touches.

Try to comprehend a little more each day.

Have holy curiosity."

—Albert Einstein

1

EVERYTHING CHANGED THE DAY I MET TRAVIS

Everything changed the day I met Travis.

Travis smiled and happily played with his toys around his mother's desk. His second-grade teacher just told his mom what a great week he'd had in school. At home, he was helpful and cooperative. He even did chores on his own without being asked or reminded, and beamed with pride at his good behavior.

Three days earlier, Travis's mother told me she feared her son was going to grow up to become a mass murderer. He often talked about how he was going to kill people. He said it was his mission. He complained of incessant buzzing in his head, suffered from horrific night terrors, and could not focus at school. At home, he had frequent outbursts and could not do his homework or chores. He said he felt like worms were crawling around in his head, and had nightmares about robots coming to launch a world invasion.

His mother was terrified—and hopeless. She had no clue what was wrong with her son or how to help him. She planned to get him a psychiatrist. Deeply religious, she prayed for him daily, and they prayed together every night before bed. Still, many nights he came to his parents in the middle of the night because of nightmares "or the things in my room."

Like every parent, she wanted to reassure him that what he was experiencing was not real. She thought perhaps it was his imagination gone wild or some sort of autism disorder.

Except it wasn't.

Everything Travis experienced was absolutely <u>real.</u>

This sweet, seven year old little boy had been doing his best to withstand a full-fledged assault on his mind, body and spirit. No one knew what was going on, much less how to help him.

When I discovered what was really plaguing Travis and interceded for him, his life changed instantly.

He doesn't talk about being a soldier any more. He no longer has nightmares. He spends his time playing, not wrestling with unseen enemies. Travis's physical appearance changed, too. He shot up from a size 8 to a 10 and a small dent filled in along his jawline. His chin became rounder and shorter. I know that seems hard to believe. But it's true. You'll read his story later.

Everything Presented In This Book Is Real

Everything in this book really happened. Travis's mother signed an affidavit attesting that everything you see and read here is the absolute truth. So did everyone else mentioned in a major story. They did it because they want to share their joy at being freed and to encourage others to have hope. They have not been compensated in any way. Photos have not been altered, either.

Some of these accounts are absolutely mind-blowing, but they're true. As an investigative journalist, respected Fortune 500 trainer and former newspaper editor, the truth is very important to me. I've included actual before-and-after photos, Facebook posts and other evidence in each story so you can make up your own mind.

Amazing Transformations

Travis's transformation is amazing on its own. Yet, he is just one of thousands of people all over the world who've experienced these kinds of changes, including: doctors, nurses, teachers, attorneys, therapists, scientists, farmers, truck drivers, police officers, stay-at-home moms, construction and iron workers, bankers, famous artists and musicians, Hollywood designers, architects, authors, religious leaders, government workers, military personnel and retirees. They range from three months to 85 years old, and encompass many races, religions and income levels.

Instantly Freed

They were delivered from drugs, alcoholism, gambling, sex addiction and smoking. Tumors and other physical aliments just vanished. A dying infant was renewed from the inside out. Lifelong guilt, shame and fears lifted away instantaneously. Anxiety and depression left them. They gained new vitality and happiness. They all reconnected with some understanding of God and spirituality, which renewed their hope and gave them a new sense of purpose.

Some lost weight or instantly shot up in height. In fact, many of them changed so radically that they now look like completely different people.

I played a role in each person's healing, but this book is not about me.

The Great Awakening

The purpose of this book is to let you know that the supernatural plays a much larger role in your life than you may realize, and that many of the physical and emotional problems you encounter may actually have a supernatural cause.

There are powerful supernatural forces at work on you. It is time you understand the truth about these hidden influences so that you can deal with them appropriately.

This truth has been hidden for too long.

My goal is to awaken you to the unseen reality of this world so you can take charge of your own sacred life force and stop letting other things manipulate you. I also want you to be able to rid yourself of any supernatural invaders that may be making you sick or holding you back. You deserve to have complete sovereignty over your own body and soul.

It's also time that you realize there is a tremendous amount of spiritual help available to you—and why you may not have been able to receive it until now.

Discover Your Own Truth

As you read through these accounts, you may get chills, a knowing in your heart or a thudding in your gut that says, *"Wow. I just know this is real."* You may be dealing with these kinds of things, or know someone who is. In that case, believe yourself. Your body and spirit are encoded to respond to truth, so pay attention.

I invite you to explore the outer edges of what you consider to be possible while you begin to listen to your own inner truth. You will learn, from these people's fascinating accounts, that the world you live in is so much more amazing and complex than you can even comprehend.

To start with, reality is not what you think it is.

It is *so* much more.

———————————

We'll start our case studies with a truly astounding, medically documented story of a mother who used intuition and prayer to not only save her son's life, but to completely rebuild his body from the inside out.

HEALTH
AND
HEALING

2

MONIQUE AND GRANT
A MOTHER SAVES HER SON BY
REBUILDING HIS BODY FROM THE INSIDE OUT

Three-month-old Grant Alvarez fell ill on April 13, 2015. "The minute I looked at him, I knew something was terribly wrong," his mother, Monique, recalls. "He was lethargic. He was not my Grant. We rushed him over to Tucson Medical Center. At first, the nurse assured me that everything was fine, that his diarrhea was normal. But I still had no peace. She said they would run tests to double-check, but she really thought I was overreacting."

An hour later, the nurse came back with Grant's blood work. "She told me it was a good thing that I followed my motherly intuition. She said, 'You have a very sick little boy.' My heart sank. The doctors said he wasn't digesting his food, and that he had some genetic issue."

The vomiting and diarrhea made it impossible for him to retain any fluids or nutrition. Grant's liver and kidneys were failing. In fact, all his organs were shutting down. He weighed only eight pounds. He was immediately admitted into Intensive Care.

The next day, Monique took to Facebook and asked for prayers. I only knew Monique through my Career Cards oracle deck and was not a close friend of the family. Yet somehow, her post about Grant found its way to me. My heart broke when I saw him, so grey and withered. I knew he was dying. I didn't want to intrude, but I didn't want to hold back if I could help. I decided I would contact Monique when the time was right.

That night, Monique posted an encouraging update. *"…Over a thousand people around the world are praying, meditating, chanting, singing, dancing this sweet boy back to health. God has heard us! Update your circles and let's continue to hold him in perfect health. Our next step to getting out of ICU is continued good feedings, him metabolizing his fats and proteins and his kidneys, liver and gall bladder functioning as they were created to."*

The following day, though, things took an ominous turn. Again, Monique turned to her friends around the world to help with Grant's condition.

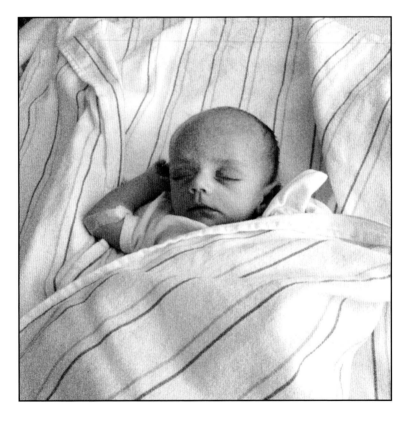

April 15th FB

We need prayer for two specific things today. First that his bowels would slow down and that his electrolytes would come into balance.

He needs an IV to assist with this, but he does not have any good veins at this time. In the next two hours a decision will be made on what to do about this. We need a miracle friends, we really do! Go call your circles, share this in all the prayer groups on Facebook etc. Let's stand in the gap for Grant. He's so precious and he needs us today. Thank you!!!

This time, I really felt compelled to reach out. I messaged Monique at 4:30 that afternoon and asked if she would like me to talk with Grant. She told me that he pulled out his IVs and screamed violently any time anyone approached him with a needle. Hopelessly dehydrated, his tiny veins were collapsing, one by one. Doctors did not know what to do to help him. He seemed determined to die—and she had absolutely no idea why. She hoped perhaps I could give her some answers.

Talking With Grant

I bent my head in prayer, as I always do before assisting anyone, and asked that I be allowed to connect with Grant's spirit. I asked that I only receive information that was for his highest and best good.

Grant's spirit was eagerly waiting. His energy and voice were that of a full-grown man, not a frail infant. He was calm, clear and grounded. He began by telling me that everything was "rushed" about him coming here, and that this body was "ill-prepared" for him. He said, "This body is frail and weak, and always will be." He did not want to be in a body like that.

"I'm supposed to climb mountains," he said, and showed me images of himself in his twenties, hiking happily through forests in his role as an environmentalist. He said his "health issues" would keep him from doing what he wanted to do, and he did not want to feel that unfulfilled and frustrated. He said this body was sick and would always be sick, and he didn't want to be in it. He wanted to be strong and healthy.

"I want a body that matches my spirit," he told me emphatically.

A Permanent Problem

I tried to feel further into the situation to see if what was afflicting him could be cured, or if it would pass, like a virus. The answer was no. Whatever was wrong with him went all the way through his entire body, through all of his cells. It seemed permanent.

His solution was to simply leave now and come back later, "when everyone is stronger." I had no idea what that meant. Grant told me he wanted to speak to his mother, so that they could come to a decision together. He didn't want to break her heart and promised he would not leave without her permission. But how do you tell a mother her baby is determined to die? I swallowed hard and prayed for the right words.

Monique was remarkably calm and focused. She told me that until now, the family had been fighting two battles: one to save Grant's physical body, and the other to persuade his spirit to work with them. No one understood why Grant was fighting so hard against treatment. When I explained that Grant did not want to live in a damaged body, suddenly everything made sense.

A Rare Genetic Disorder

Monique told me that Grant had been diagnosed with a rare genetic disorder called Lysinuric Protein Intolerance. This is a permanent condition that threatened to leave him with shortened stature, brittle bones and chronic kidney, lung and liver problems his entire life. This is why the problem seemed unchangeable—and why Grant kept saying that his body would *always* be sick.

A Mother's Decision

When I explained Grant's plan to "come back later when everyone was stronger," Monique revealed that she had almost bled to death giving birth to Grant and his older brother, Sam. Each time, a problem with the placenta caused massive bleeding, requiring multiple blood transfusions. Monique confided that she had to have emergency surgery to stop the bleeding right after Grant's birth. It took months for her to regain her strength. She also told me that that one-year-old Sam was still anemic. Grant was right: somehow he knew that his family was still recovering from a very traumatic time, and he didn't want to burden them with more health problems.

But there was a problem with Grant's plan. Doctors forbade Monique from ever becoming pregnant again because of the extreme risk. She couldn't have any more children. It was now, or never.

Daring To Believe In The Impossible

Monique held Grant close and dared to believe in the impossible.

She looked deep into his soul and asked him, *"If you are given a brand new body and perfect health, will you stay?"* She promised him that he would have the body he wanted: strong, athletic and perfect in every way.

To her great relief, she felt his spirit say, "yes." Right then, Monique asked God to give her son a brand new body. She turned to her husband and family for support. "I asked my Mom, Dad, Derek and my brother to pray for a brand new body. I knew they could believe with me and not let their rational brain get in the way. I prayed that every single cell of his body would be different from what he was born with.

"I held him and visualized perfectly round cells. I saw each organ being replaced. I told him that he was perfect in every way. I told him my love was giving him perfect DNA; that every single thing was brand new. I told him he knew how to digest his food, and that he knew how to heal and how to gain weight and be strong. I told him it was his nature. I reminded him that he was a warrior. I prayed that he would never need to go to the doctor again, and that nothing would ever linger or affect him again."

The Family's Faith Is Tested

Monique's faith was tested later that night when things reached a crisis point. Grant was so dehydrated that all his veins collapsed. The only way to get him the lifesaving fluids he needed was to insert the large IV needle right into his tiny, thin head. The idea was violently appalling. On the other hand, without the fluids, he would surely die.

Monique looked down at her boy and decided to believe in the promise they'd made to each other. "I didn't listen to a word the doctors said. I only focused on our conversation." She told the doctors to take the IV away, and to only give him oral fluids.

"I felt peace instantly. I felt his relief at not having more needles." Her intuition proved right again. *Now that Grant was on a mission to live, he kept down all his oral fluids and medication.*

In fact, he gained so much weight that night that he was <u>released</u> from Intensive Care the very next morning!

April 16th

~New Update On Baby Grant~Guess who is moving out of ICU? We have orders out to the main floor. As soon as a bed opens up we are out of here!!! Keep praying, it's working. This little boy is being renewed from the inside out. Thank you for standing with us!!!

"I felt him changing," Monique said. She insisted the doctor and nurses give him all the milk he wanted. "I knew it was happening. He really smiled at me, and I could feel him relaxing and healing."

She maintained her vigil, praying for him and visualizing all his cells as absolutely perfect. Grant continued to eat like a champion, gaining as much as an entire pound overnight. He gained two and half pounds over the next four days.

No Trace Of The Genetic Disorder

Grant was released from Tucson Medical Center on April 21, 2015 with absolutely no trace of Lysinuric Protein Intolerance anywhere in his body. All of his systems and organs came up perfect, test after test.

The genetic abnormality had completely vanished.

Monique Alvarez with Derek Alvarez.
22 hrs · 🌐

Two years ago I was getting ready to leave for the hospital to have Grant. My dad was driving in from Colorado. Derek and my mom were taking care of Sam so I could rest.

The second baby is different. You can't be naive. You know every baby is unique, but you certainly know more than you did the first time.

💜 What I didn't know was what sweet and happy boy would come into my world.

💜 What I didn't know was that I would almost lose him 12 weeks later.

💜 What I didn't know was that he would be completely renewed thanks to the prayers he received from around the world.

💜 What I didn't know was what I warrior mama I was.

You've heard that mothers can lift a car off their baby to save their lives. What no one tells you is that you do more than seems humanly possible on a daily basis when you're a mother.

I get so emotional in January because it's when I gave birth, 12 months apart to my "twins". I love them so much it hurts. I think of them 24 hours a day.

I didn't know the depth of my physical, emotional and spiritual capacities until I became a mother.

It's almost your birthday miracle boy! I love you forever! 💜

Monique and her family thanked me for my role in helping identify Grant's issue. "Margo, thank you so much! If we hadn't known why he wasn't trying to live, we really might have lost him. Your help was essential in us being able to turn everything around!"

Later that year, with Grant in perfect health, the family decided to relocate from Tucson to Mexico, where I'm sure he'll be climbing mountains in no time.

The photo on the previous page was taken on his second birthday. As you can see, not only is he perfectly healthy, but he's actually *stronger and more dextrous* than other children his age. According to doctors' charts, he is actually *twice* as big as an average two year old.

The Impossible Is Possible

Grant reminds us that the impossible IS possible, if we dare to believe in who we really are and the amazing spirit that resides within each of us. Grant's miraculous healing affected both of his parents profoundly. His mother has written about it many times on Facebook and his father Derek wrote a piece in the Huffington Post about what he learned from the experience.

It's easy to sum up this extraordinary event by thinking, "Wow! What a miracle!" and falsely believing that *you* could never do anything like that. But when we really look at what happened, we see that many other supernatural forces were at work here, too: *forces that you use every day, often without realizing it.*

DEFINITION OF A MIRACLE

"An effect or extraordinary event in the physical world that surpasses all known human or natural powers and is ascribed to a *supernatural* cause.

or

Such an effect or event manifesting or considered *as a work of God.*

—*Dictionary.com*

You may think Monique and Grant are unusual; that they have some kind of extrasensory perception that you don't. That's not so. *Every human being is wired with these senses—and you use them all the time.*

You've probably heard of Extra Sensory Perception or ESP. When I was a child growing up in the 1970's, the supernatural was mainstream. Books like *"Chariots of the Gods"* and the TV show, "In Search Of" were hugely popular. Author Taylor Caldwell penned a best-selling series of highly detailed books, including *"Dear and Glorious Physician,"* that were based on her past lives. People were open and curious about the unknown then. Today, though, the "supernatural" is most often associated with "paranormal," when it shouldn't be. The realm of the supernatural includes angels *and* ghosts. Miracles happen every day, in many ways. God is present in everything.

Extra-Sensory Senses

Clairvoyance	Clear seeing
Claircognition	Clear knowing
Clairaudience	Clear hearing
Clairsentience	Clear feeling
Clairalience	Clear smelling
Clairgustance	Clear tasting
Telepathy	Talking with your mind
Intuition	Knowing something
Premonition	Knowing something just before it happens
Prophecy	Predicting future events
Deja Vu	Feeling that what is happening right now has happened before, like a memory
Getting Vibes	Sensing a person's energy or spirit

Ever had a gut feeling? You used "clairsentience" or "clear feeling." Ever know something was going to happen just before it did? You had a *premonition*. Know who's calling before you pick up the phone? That's *"claircognition"*—otherwise known as *"intuition."*

You Have Supernatural Powers

Do you ever sense that you're reliving a moment that's happened before? That's called *Deja Vu*. The French coined all these terms. The "clair" means "clear" in French. Ever heard a bell ringing in your ear, or a voice giving you a warning? That's *clairaudience*. Ever "pick up a vibe" about someone? You're actually reading and sensing their energy field through "clairsentience" or "clear feeling." Do you ever know what your pet is thinking or feeling? That's *telepathy,* a way of communicating soul to soul, without words. Have you ever been in a situation where a friend asks what you want for dinner, say Chinese food—and you suddenly find yourself stopping and imagine yourself eating Chinese food? *You actually get a sense of what it would taste like to eat it*. Based on that, you make your decision. That is *Clairgustance*, or "clear tasting."

See how many supernatural superpowers you have?

Every human being has these heightened sensory abilities. It's hardwired into our architecture by the Divine. If we think of our five senses as what we perceive on the *outside*, ESP is perceiving those same things on the *inside*. We are given these channels so that our Creator can communicate with us. We are also given these abilities so we can help each other.

This book is going to show you more about how ordinary the "supernatural" is, so that you will be more aware of your gifts and how to use them more often. Contrary to what you may have been taught to believe, there is absolutely nothing wrong or bad about using the senses that have been built into you. Using your intuition is no different than using your arms or legs. They're all part of you and are there to help you.

The Supernatural Power of Intuition

Let's examine Monique's miraculous story in more detail and see just how many "supernatural superpowers" she used to heal her son. First, there was a mother's intuition: she knew something was wrong with her child. This is *claircognition:* clear knowing. She listened to her intuition even when the nurses initially assured her Grant was fine; she continued to listen to her intuition by refusing the final IV; and she continued to listen again when she told his doctors and nurses to give him as much milk as he wanted, so that he could quickly gain weight.

The Supernatural Powers of Clairvoyance, Telepathy and Clairaudience

The supernatural also came into play when I saw Grant's spirit slipping in and out of his body. *Clairvoyance* is a supernatural way to see things that are outside the range of normal vision. I've used this sense thousands of times to help people all over the world. It may be a little more advanced than the supernatural tools you use every day, but you have this ability, too.

I then used *telepathy*, a way of speaking soul-to-soul without words, when I spoke with Grant to find out why he was dying. I used *clairaudience* to hear his words and the sound of his soul's voice. Monique then used her own *telepathy* to talk with Grant and ask him if he would stay if she could ensure he would have a perfectly healthy body.

The Supernatural Power of Prayer

She then incorporated the divine *power of prayer* for Grant. As soon as his mother told him she would give him the body he wanted, Grant started healing and even gained an entire pound overnight. Monique also used the power of intention and visualization, seeing his cells as perfect in every way.

Grant's Spirit Knew Things He Could Not Have Known As An Infant

Monique recalled having a telepathic conversation with Grant while he was still in the womb. He told her that he and Sam were so close that they wanted to be born as twins, but decided to come "in two installments" to make it easier on her. This is why Grant initially complained that everything was so "rushed" with his being born. However, when Monique mentally reminded him that he wanted to be born so soon after Sam, he calmed down immediately. "I felt him relax and remember," Monique said.

That is using *Clairsentience: clear feeling.*

Grant Spoke To Monique From The Womb

Grant's ability to communicate from the womb actually impacted his parents' decision to move from Colorado to Tucson just before he was born. They had been considering the move, but weren't sure whether to do it before or after the birth. One morning around Thanksgiving of 2014, Monique awoke to a booming voice within her that said, "Go now!" She intuitively knew it was Grant. Even though they did not understand the need to move quickly, they complied and relocated to Tucson shortly thereafter.

Why did Grant tell them to leave Cortez? Well, just as three-month-old Grant somehow knew his entire family's medical troubles, he also knew that the tiny Colorado town they'd been living in had no hospital of its own. Critically-ill patients must be airlifted to Denver, which is at least a 45-minute flight. His mother would surely have bled to death—and he may have not survived, either.

In contrast, the home they found in Tucson was only ten minutes away from the Tucson Medical center. Also interesting? The Tucson Medical Center is located at 5301 *Grant* Street.

Intuition Leads To A Career Change

Grant's story is so inspiring. A little boy, his determined family and loving people all around the world came together to help him beat a terrible genetic disorder. *But more than that, his story shows us how powerful each and every one of us are—if we use the "supernatural" abilities inherent within us.*

I use these same "superpowers" on a daily basis to help people with all kinds of problems. One of the hidden secrets to my success as a trainer and executive coach is my well-honed ability to quickly read people and help them overcome their internal obstacles. I never marketed it as such, but now you know that I was simply using my intuition and ability to see what is hidden.

Before I met Grant, I created an oracle deck called *"The Career Cards: A Practical Guide to Life,"* to help people understand and live their life's purpose. I realized that my clients needed a tangible tool to help them understand what they were truly meant to do.

The Career Cards were an instant success, and are now used in 14 countries. I created them with nothing but my intuition and experience as a guide. Many people comment on how beautiful and elegant they are, even though I designed them myself, despite not being an artist and creating everything in a limited design program. I asked for guidance every step of the way. I did it all on faith, because I felt so strongly led to make them.

Career Cards Lead To Angelic Soul Clearing

Little did I know that the Career Cards themselves would lead me into my true calling, just as they have done for so many thousands around the world. I did my first workshop on spiritual healing in 1988. I never guessed that path would lead me here.

One day in late 2012, I did a Career Card reading for a woman in Australia. She was very depressed and stuck after a divorce. I knew she needed more help, but didn't know what else to do. As always, even in my work with corporate clients, I asked my angels and guides to direct me. I was surprised when my angels showed up and simply reached into her heart and took out the pain. *They just removed it.* She was a changed woman from that moment forward.

That was my first Angelic Soul Clearing.™ Since then, I've conducted more than 2,500 clearings and helped people over the world heal from physical, emotional and spiritual suffering. I'm always so humbled by these experiences, because they reveal so much about the true nature of our world, and how much we are truly loved by a power much greater than ourselves.

———————

I was so impressed with the way that Monique and her family healed Grant. At the time, I didn't know that I would be challenged to do the same thing for myself, less than a month later.

3

ANGELS HEAL MY CEREBRAL SPINAL FLUID LEAK

few weeks after helping Grant, I decided to have an epidural procedure to treat a lingering back injury. I was in pain and this was the least invasive form of treatment available. I was hesitant, because of the risks of developing a cerebral spinal fluid leak after the procedure. I talked with my angels about it. They actually told me that something *would* happen, but that I would be okay after a couple of weeks. I trusted them, so I went ahead and had the spinal injection.

During the end of the procedure, a man came into the room to retrieve something. As he left, an empty five gallon water bottle rolled over and jarred the table I was on. I felt the gurney rock, although I felt no pain, because I was numb at the time. I thought, *"Oh no. This is it. I bet this is what goes wrong."*

I hoped I would be fine. However, when I sat up, my head felt like it was in a vice. It was intensely painful and debilitating. The nurse told me to lay flat and rest quietly for about 15 minutes to see if it would pass. Unfortunately, it didn't.

I did have a cerebral spinal fluid leak. They sent me home and told me to lay completely flat and drink fluids for five days, and that it would resolve. I followed the instructions, but nothing changed. Each time I was upright for more than a few minutes, my head felt like it was being squeezed like a grape. The pain was excruciating and sent shooting pains into my temples. I lived like this for more than a week, each day praying it would heal.

The doctor's remedy was to bring me in to do a "blood patch"—a procedure in which they would inject me again, draw some of my blood, allow it to clot, then inject the clot in the spinal fluid in hopes that it would act as a patch and block the hole. The last thing I wanted was to let them put another needle in me.

Excruciating Pain and A Frantic Phone Call

My condition was so bad thirteen days later on May 8, 2014, that my partner, Tiffany and I interviewed a nurse from a home health service. Tiffany had to go out of town, and I could not stand long enough to make meals or care for the dogs. After the nurse

Margo Mateas
May 8, 2014

Hi everyone, I really appreciate the support and prayers. An update... since I am not getting better, the doctor really wants me to come in and do a blood patch tomorrow... I can only sit up for about 3 hours at a time and my BP today was very high just sitting up... I would appreciate any intuition / guidance you may have as to whether this will be helpful... I do have the feeling (now) that it will help. They say it can cure this within 24 hours. I really appreciate your feedback. Thank you so much! 💜 💜 💜

Mandy Vass Johnston, Tami Kotinek and 5 others   7 Comments   Seen by 132

left, I began to panic. The pain was intense. Desperate and crying, I gave in and called the doctor's office. They said they would make room for an emergency Blood Patch procedure the next day at 2 p.m. I also asked for prayer from an online spiritual support group (above). I still did not want the procedure, but didn't know what else to do.

I laid back down on the couch and tried to soothe myself. My angels had warned me that things would go wrong for a few weeks, but they had assured me that I would completely recover soon after. That hadn't happened yet, and this was seriously impacting my life. I've known people who had cerebral spinal fluid leaks for years, and it completely destroyed their lives.

Later that day I had an Angelic Soul Clearing™ scheduled for a client. We'd planned it prior to the procedure and I had completely forgotten about it. I decided to try and do the session laying flat on the sofa, where I could function normally, with no pain. The session went fine. When it was over, my client asked me how things were going. I told her about the leak.

She said, "Well, why don't you do an angelic soul healing on yourself?" I had never thought of it for healing any physical issues.

However, it was my only option, so I decided to give it a try.

Healing Myself For The First Time

I stayed on the couch and prepared for my own session the same way I do for my clients: I prayed and invoked my angelic guides and helpers and asked them to help me. However, instead of seeing within my clients' energy centers, I found myself in the middle of a warm, opaque river that gently pulsed with a small, steady current. At first I was surprised that the water was moving, then realized that *I must be inside the flow of cerebral spinal fluid, which constantly moves throughout the body.*

I looked around and saw layers of thin tissues surrounding this river. I realized this must be the dura, the thin membrane that holds the spinal fluid. As I traced its flow, I saw two holes in it: one up near the left side of my neck, and another at the injection site at the base of my spine.

Next, I saw a clot of blood flow past me and get absorbed into the river. Apparently the Blood Patch procedure scheduled for the next day was not going to work. This was the angels' way of letting me know that the blood patch would just get swallowed up in the spinal fluid and would not act as a plug at all. It was up to the angels and I to heal this, somehow.

We started by filling the holes in the dura with a gossamer-like substance infused with Light to plug the flow. Then we wrapped all of that in multiple layers of Light and other connective tissues until it felt and looked solid.

Then, I went around the entire outer edges of the dura with more layers of Light, and made sure that it was completely strong and healed. The holes were thoroughly gone, and everything felt and looked fine. I had never done this before. I hoped I wasn't deluding myself.

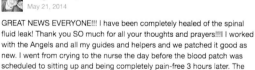

Margo Mateas
May 21, 2014

GREAT NEWS EVERYONE!!! I have been completely healed of the spinal fluid leak! Thank you SO much for all your thoughts and prayers!!!! I worked with the Angels and all my guides and helpers and we patched it good as new. I went from crying to the nurse the day before the blood patch was scheduled to sitting up and being completely pain-free 3 hours later. The Angels told me to rest for another 10 days, so I did and now I am good as gold! Thank you for praying for me, and for reminding me to look within for healing. The lesson I had to promise to learn was to honor my vulnerability and fragility and to not be so judgmental of myself and others. Thank you again!!! 💜 xoxoxoxo

Morag Hislop, George English and 23 others   15 Comments   Seen by 133

No Pain

I sat up. To my amazement, there was no pain at all. I leaned from

FREED BY THE LIGHT

side to side. Still, no pain. Finally, I stood up, preparing for the shooting pain in my temples. But miraculously, there was no pain at all! I got up off that couch at 7:30 p.m. on May 8, 2014, and have been utterly fine ever since. Obviously, I didn't show up for the Blood Patch procedure the next day.

I was astonished. How could the angels and I have repaired something that actually *had holes in it* without doing *anything* in the physical world? How was this possible?

I posted an update to the spiritual group (see previous page) and rested for the next 10 days, as the angels instructed. I did as they suggested, and have had no pain ever since. *They were right: I did have a problem, but it was completely resolved within two weeks—13 days, to be exact.*

The angels and I really did heal my spinal fluid leak. It was hard for me to grasp, but why would it be? I'd just witnessed Monique and Grant transform his entire body from death to life in less than a week's time. But I am very skeptical. It takes a lot of evidence to convince me.

Still, I was walking evidence that I had actually gone inside my own body with the healing guidance and power of angels, and repaired two holes in the spinal membrane. My chiropractor was astonished when she saw me walk in the next week, smiling from ear to ear, and heard the story.

These two physical healings were the beginning of my understanding of how the physical body is affected by spirit, and how many things actually affect our physical health.

When we realize that all matter is made out of energy, though, it makes sense. Many great doctors and metaphysicians know about the mind/body connection. Some classics for you to check out are Louse L. Hay's groundbreaking book, *"You Can Heal Your Body,"* about how the body reacts to emotions, and *"Love, Medicine and Miracles,"* by Dr. Bernie Segal about how he is able to heal cancer patients by helping them release repressed emotions. There are thousands of books and articles available.

Energy And How It Affects You

We are able to affect matter through spiritual or supernatural means because every living thing on this planet is made of energy, right down to the cellular level. Your molecules contain energy. Your body emits an electro-magnetic energy field known as an "aura" or "corona" which can be captured by electrical equipment. You even put out a certain amount of electrical voltage.

While electricity runs through your system, spiritual energy runs through your body, too. Many cultures refer to this life essence as "life force," "chi," "prana" and other names. More than 5,000 years ago these energy centers were mapped out in tremendous detail by both Hindu and Chinese religions and medicine, who understood their function in everyday life and the importance of keeping them in balance.

Human Battery

I had the opportunity to learn more about energy and how it works when I was scientifically tested and verified as a healer in April of 2016. Dr. Melinda Connor, a respected researcher and author on subtle energies, measured the amount of electricity put out by the palms of each of my hands with a standard Extremely Low Frequency Meter (ELF,) the same one used by electricians. While I was sitting there literally thinking about doing laundry, my hands emitted AC voltage of 8 volts in one and 10 in the other. When she asked me to send healing energy through my hands, the voltage more than doubled in both of my palms.

Next, she put two probes in the palms of my hands like jumper cables to see if my body produced DC current. It's extremely rare for a human being to be able to do this, but I do. I've always been able to help people start cars when it needs a little boost (I often help start my partner's antique car), but didn't know it was because I actually function as a battery!

Capturing the Aura

Next, Dr. Connor mapped out my electromagnetic field on the GDV (Gas Discharge Visualization) machine. It is the same machine used on Russian cosmonauts before they send them into space. It can detect weaknesses in the electrical and energetic bodies that may later translate into physical illnesses.

On the following pages, you'll see that my "corona" or energy field,

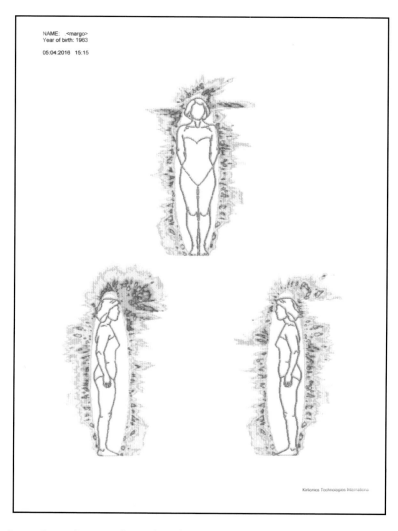

NAME: <margo>
Year of birth: 1963

05:04:2016 15:15

Kirlionica Technologies International

is quite enlarged around my head and stretches out in all directions, like an antenna. I have always felt like I have an antenna that is continuously scanning and capturing data, but it was very interesting to actually see it mapped out on a scientific machine. Even though I've been a certified massage therapist since 1988, I'd never seen energy mapped out like this. The dark blue color indicates strong, solid energy. The yellow is weaker energy output. Dr. Connor pointed out that empty spot at the back of my head in the image on the low right in the image above. In order to become

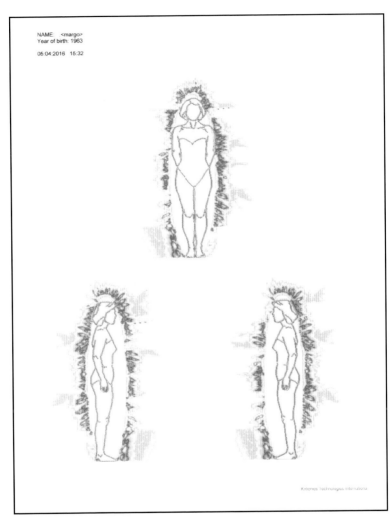

scientifically verified, I had to actually change my energy field. I had to pull in my "antenna," repair the weak spots, strengthen my energy and pull it in more tightly around my body. The scan above was taken 17 minutes later. You can see the changes. The energy field is darker and closer to my body. I pulled in the antenna and repaired the missing place at the back of my head. Dr. Connor also discovered that I output oscillating frequencies in the same range as FM radio stations and cell phones. One of my friends jokingly calls me "KMRGO." Each of us is an energetic being, but many don't really know anything about energy or how it works in our bodies. My session with Dr. Connor was really eye-opening.

Chakras Are Like Systems In Your Car

Though there are many energy centers throughout the body, the term most commonly used for these is "chakra" from the Indian Sanskrit. This refers to the seven spiritual power centers in the body. These contain energy. When they are open and properly balanced, we are healthy and happy. When they are clogged, we are unhealthy and unhappy.

Whether or not you ascribe to Chinese medicine or yoga, these energy centers are alive in you. You have them, just like every other human being on the planet. The difference is how aware you are of them and what you do to properly manage them.

If we think of your body as a car, we know that certain systems need to be cleaned, tuned and repaired on a regular basis, or the car will break down. Your physical and energetic bodies are no different. They require attention and maintenance.

How Your Chakras Work

The chakras line up along your spinal column. The one at the bottom connects and grounds you to the Earth, and the one at the top of your head connects you to Heaven. Each of these chakras has a specific function. Each one contributes to your spiritual connection, sense of aliveness, spiritual awareness, emotional happiness and physical health. Pretty important things, don't you think? Aren't you glad you're aware of them now?

I didn't know a lot about them until the angels showed me how to walk into them and have a look around. That's where I see most of what is going on within someone.

When I am in a chakra, I perform a sort of diagnostic check of these energy centers. I use my special sight to do an initial inspection of the area. This will show me if it's open or closed, light or dark, empty or occupied. If the person has been traumatized or suppressed, I will see that too. Certain emotions and energies are stored in specific places within the chakra system. There are also colors and sounds associated with each of the chakras.

The chakras correspond to various aspects of our emotional lives. You need these energy centers to be working well and clear in order to have a happy and fulfilled life. It is fairly common for certain kinds of traumas and events to get lodged in these centers.

Most chakra systems work from the ground up, referring to the root chakra as the first chakra, but I work with them from the top down.

Gift To See What Is Hiding

I've been given a divine gift to see what is hidden. It's like a special pair of x-ray goggles that let me see what is invisible to many others. This gift helps me uncover things that have been secret or hiding your entire life. I can see all kinds of energies that may be stuck, feeding off of you, or refusing to release you from their influence.

When I enter into a chakra space, I see what is stored there live, just like real life. It's like walking into a movie. I see all the characters, see, hear and feel everything that's going on, usually with all my senses. I see scenes from the past or what is currently going on.

I am able to see you, your abusive mother or your frightened inner child in these chakra spaces. I will also be able to see video clips or still images of what has caused you to be hurt.

Checking the Cupboards

Some chakras always appear the same way. For example, the crown chakra is the "command center" within the brain. Accordingly, it is a very organized space with equipment related to computer processing and storage space, for memories. Many times it has cupboards, bookshelves, cabinets and a workspace.

The chakras change and shift as I work with them. One client had a very small workspace at the start our session. She huddled over the table, trying to figure things out, which represented her anxiety. Her mental space was cluttered with books and bookshelves.

Once I started releasing things from *other* chakras, this little library

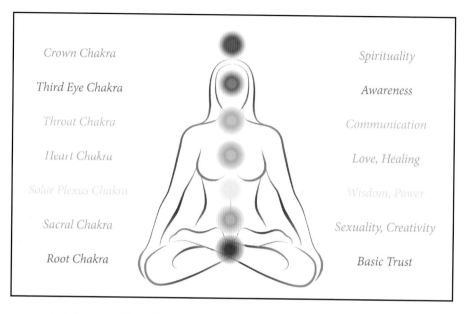

Crown Chakra	*Spirituality*
Third Eye Chakra	*Awareness*
Throat Chakra	*Communication*
Heart Chakra	*Love, Healing*
Solar Plexus Chakra	*Wisdom, Power*
Sacral Chakra	*Sexuality, Creativity*
Root Chakra	*Basic Trust*

opened right up. When I came back to check on it, it had tripled in size. The table she had been working on was much larger. The bookshelves had moved back. She was so relaxed and at peace that she sat back in her chair with her hands behind her head and now had her feet up on the desk!

Chakra Chart

The chakra chart above provides a little "cheat sheet" on chakras, the role each of these energy centers plays in your emotional and physical life, and how stuck energy can impact you.

How The Chakras Affect You

Crown

This is at the top of your head in the center. This includes your brain, thinking and connection to Spirit. If your crown is clear, you'll be able to think clearly, have organized thoughts and be able to achieve your goals. If there's a blockage, you'll have trouble thinking. You'll feel distracted and foggy. You may even not feel in control of your own mind or thoughts. You may feel anxious and unable to make progress. I want to see you, clear and directed, in the Command Center of your own mind, ready to take charge.

3rd Eye

This is in the middle of your forehead. It's the center of clairvoyance and ability to see into the future. If this is clear, you'll be able to easily visualize or imagine things. Everyone is clairvoyant; some people just have blocks. If this is congested you won't be able to do guided meditations very well or use your innate psychic abilities. I want to see this space as a lighthouse with huge, clear windows that are able to see out into eternity.

Throat

This is literally your throat and voice. If your throat chakra is open, you'll be able to clearly express yourself, set boundaries and speak your own truth. If it's blocked, you may have trouble standing up for yourself and telling people how you truly feel. You could also frequently have a high, weak or quiet voice, or have to clear your throat when you speak. I want you to be able to stand up to a microphone in this space and feel confident telling the world who you are.

Heart

Your heart chakra is in the center of your chest and expands into the middle of your back. This is why we ache and have pain there when our hearts are broken. When the heart energy is open, you'll feel full of love, forgiving, caring, warm and joyous. If it's blocked, you'll feel cold, empty and unloving. I want this to be a nurturing space with a wonderful place for you in its center. You must love yourself!

Solar Plexus or Naval

This is where your "gut feelings" come from. It's just below your rib cage in the center. It's a portal for Divine guidance. It holds your sense of identity and your willpower. This is one of the most frequently congested places in the body, attracting negative entities and spiritual parasites. It's common for people to "eat their feelings" and stuff fear, anxiety and trauma here, resulting in digestive problems. I want to see this chakra clear and open, so you'll feel safe and able to receive Divine guidance.

Sacral

This is located in your lower belly, where the sex organs are. This area is associated with sexuality, groundedness and creativity. I want to see this as a lush, sensual place for you and a mate, if you desire one. If it's blocked, it could be used to store rage, anger, revenge, guilt and could result in low back pain and reproductive system problems. This is where a lot of negative entities take up space.

Root

This is located at the base of your spine and is your connection to the Earth and to the physical world. This is where your money and security are located. I want to see this as a solid foundation of gold bricks. If you have problems here, you could lose money or your sense of safety may be eroded. You might also feel flighty and disconnected, like a kite in the wind.

I hope this helps you undertand the vital role that each of your energy centers plays in your physical and emotional life.

What You Need To Know

- Every human being has built-in senses that help us connect to ourselves, our Creator and other life forms. We use this "Extra-Sensory Perception" in many ways, often without realizing it.

- We all have the ability to receive Divine guidance at any time through these built-in senses.

- Using these innate senses is as normal and natural as breathing.

- The human body is made up of energy. This energy is in each of our molecules and even exists at the subatomic level. We instinctively use energy in everything we do.

- The human body has seven major energy centers, which are known as "chakras." These places correlate with specific emotions and functions. Understanding your own chakra system can help you identify emotional or physical problems.

- These abilities are tied to the chakra system. If an energy center is clogged or shut down, your ability to use the perception associated with it may be impaired.

- The body can be healed using only energy, because fundamentally, we are only energy.

- I see what is hidden within a person's chakras and help them by clearing out negative energy and replacing it with pure angelic energy.

What You Can Do

- Get to know your own energy system and how energy moves through you.

- Clear your chakras for greater health and happiness.

- Use your intuition and other sensory gifts more often. They will build in strength and accuracy the more you use them.

In the real-life accounts that follow, you'll see how emotions trapped within the chakras can affect your body and spirit. Our next story takes you into the life of a businessman who thought a car accident had severely impacted his eye. The real culprit, however, lay deep within his past.

HEALING EMOTIONAL ISSUES

4

DAVID'S CAR ACCIDENT TEACHES HIM TO "PUT ON THE BRAKES"

L et's look at the incredible case of David T, a successful businessman in his late '50s. David had a great career and established himself as a beloved leader in his community. But in 2013, David was rear-ended at a stoplight by a young man who slammed into David's SUV while driving 40 miles an hour and texting his girlfriend. The impact gave David severe whiplash and rammed his truck into a van in front of him, causing a multi-car pileup.

A few weeks later, David's left eye began to give him trouble. He had minor pain and blurred vision. His ophthalmologist determined that he had a vein occlusion at the back of the eye near the macula, and referred him to a retina specialist. The retina doctor discovered a blocked blood vessel near the optic vein in the back of his eye.

Needle Injection Every Three Weeks

The only solution was to insert a needle with special medication into David's eye to reduce the swelling in the blocked vein. David endured these eye injections every few weeks for the next 36 months. Nothing relieved the symptoms completely, and each time they did the retinal scan, David could clearly see the occluded vein on the digital screen, a bright round yellow and red area at the back of the eye.

David heard me during my first appearance on "Coast to Coast AM" in August of 2016 and called me the following month. He told me about his eye injury and asked if I could help him. At first, I was doubtful: how could a soul clearing possibly help his eye injury? I told him I would do my best, and we began the session.

Repressed Rage

David's energy centers held a strong, repressed rage that had lain dormant for many years. David had been dominated by an overbearing and controlling father who forced his will upon the family, even dictating what religion his children would adopt as adults. When David grew older and wanted to marry a woman of another religion, his father refused to attend the wedding, tried to legally cut him out of the family business, and then disowned him.

This was devastating to young David. He tried to reason with his father, but his attempts at reconciliation were met with more rejection and control. He struggled with wanting to have a loving father and having the life he wanted. Inside, he quietly resolved to be a better father than his Dad, and to let his children make their own choices.

Remnants Of A Bully

More than 30 years went by. David created a great life for himself. He became a very successful businessman and truly believed he had put his past behind him. David and I were both surprised when his father's energy appeared in several of his chakras. I didn't understand why David's father was there—until the angels showed me the accident and the moment of impact.

It felt just like being shoved from behind by an enormous bully. I asked David if he'd gotten angry at the driver who'd caused the accident. David thought for a moment, then realized that he didn't get angry then. He'd just told the young man he hoped he would learn a lesson from it.

I asked David if he had ever stood up to his dad, either. "Well, no, I guess not," he admitted. He said that they argued quite a bit, but he was always trying to get his dad to back down and be more reasonable, not really standing up for himself and his own worth.

Getting shoved from behind in that accident was "the last straw" for David. One more time he'd been pushed around by a bully, and one more time the bully got away with it. The driver didn't even end up with a citation. The bullies had won—one more time.

Shattering The Silence

All the anger that David suppressed his entire life welled up within him. The angels showed me that he needed to get really angry to release this from his system, even though his father had passed away many years ago. I encouraged David to tell his father everything he needed to; everything he'd held in for so long. David spoke up and told his father just how unfair, cruel and controlling he had been. He spoke up for himself and for his mother, who had also endured years of her husband's tyranny.

Suddenly, David's father appeared to him from the other side. "Forgive me," he said. But David felt that his father was saying it just to shut him up and get the matter over, not because he was truly sorry and repentant.

For the first time in more than 60 years, David stood up for himself. He didn't just accept his father's false apology. He told his father, "Wait a minute—you're going to have to listen to me first." David then told his father how much he'd hurt him. He told him all the things he'd always longed to say. Tears and anger and compassion for all the things he'd gone through as a younger man poured from him. He wept and wept, astonished at all he had kept hidden away within him all these years.

Pushing Back

When the emotion subsided, all that remained was for David to finally *push back*—against his Dad, against the driver, against all the injustices he'd endured. David stood up and physically pushed back as hard as he could, shoving his father and the driver away. He finally let his body and soul know that he was done taking it.

When it was over, a profound sense of relief washed over him. David then saw two hands cradle his head in a healing blessing, as tingling and warmth flooded his entire body. "Oh my God, this is amazing," he said as the healing gently surged through him.

A few minutes later, he saw four angels bring him a new body made of pure white light. "I just can't describe it," he stammered. "It's so beautiful!

Normal Retina Scan

Just then, David was shown his damaged retina. The big red area was gone. A voice within him announced, *"The pressure has been released. Healing will happen."* David had a regularly scheduled eye injection the next day. To the doctor's astonishment, *the clot had completely vanished.* There was absolutely nothing wrong with the optic blood vessel at all. His eye was healthy and normal in every way.

David's eye healed because he stood up for himself—thereby relieving his body of the need to *protest for him.*

"I'm The Brake"

David called about a month later and told me that his eye had begun acting up again. I immediately got a vision of a foot pressing down on the brake pedal of a car.

"I'm like the brake," the eye said, explaining that David was not "putting his foot down" enough. I thanked his eye for caring so much about him, and David and I spent the rest of his session peeling away more layers of guilt and shame. When it was over, David felt a renewed sense of self-love and compassion for himself. He vowed to keep putting himself first, so that his body would not have to intervene and force him to love himself completely.

Today, David is actually grateful for the accident that impacted his vision. "I'm so glad I met you," David told me. "You opened doors for me. I'm more joyful now. I don't take day-to-day life as seriously as I used to. I flow with life now. Thank you! That was life-changing for me."

David's story is a powerful reminder of the role that emotions play in our lives. Lisa unknowingly developed breast cancer as a way to avoid standing up for herself.

5

LISA USES BREAST CANCER AS A BOUNDARY

Our next case deals with a woman who developed breast cancer as a boundary to protect her from a toxic work environment. Lisa called me because she wanted to know more about the cancer she'd had for two years, and about her future career possibilities. Although on medical leave for the breast cancer, it seemed to be the least of her worries. She spoke about it almost happily.

"I don't have any symptoms. I don't have any pain. It doesn't bother me at all," she said. What concerned her was her longtime job for a governmental entity. She said she wanted to quit her job, but was afraid of losing her health insurance. She said her job was full of conflict and strife with her coworkers.

Cancer As A Boundary

Lisa's throat chakra was completely offline, which made it impossible for her to set and keep healthy boundaries. *She literally could not speak up for herself.* Meanwhile, the rage she'd suppressed by not being able to express her anger had turned into a a red-hot volcano in her sacral chakra, waiting to explode.

Lisa acknowledged that this had been a lifelong problem for her. I asked if she had tried speaking up for herself at work. "No," she admitted. "I try, but then I just lose my temper and walk away." At this point I began to understand that the cancer was actually Lisa's way of being able to set boundaries.

I invited in stronger guides for her, and replaced her throat chakra, now giving her the ability to speak up for herself without having to hold it in and then blow up once it got to be too much for her.

"Let Me Go!"

Next, I moved into Lisa's heart chakra, which includes the upper part of the chest. Not surprisingly, I saw a small black mass on the right side of her breast. This was the tumor. The first thing it said was, "I don't want to be here, but she won't let me go. She needs me." Instead of being menacing, the energy within this mass desperately wanted to leave and return to the Light.

As I discussed this with Lisa, she realized that she had been relying on the cancer to give her a way to avoid her workplace. It had given her a temporary solution to a problem in her life, but with the potential to become a permanent problem itself.

I sent more angels and guides to give Lisa the strength to face life on her own. By this time, Lisa was ready to release the tumor entirely. She thanked it for helping her, and realized that she had to let it go.

It happily flew into the Light, instantly.

Lisa wept as she realized the enormity of what she had done. She had created an illness with the potential to kill her, because she did not know how to speak up for herself.

Practicing Healthy Boundaries

She also realized that she now had within her all the strength and certainty she needed to set healthy boundaries for herself, now and in the future. Once she was able to tune into her own sense of power and use her newly recharged throat chakra, she was easily able to say "no" quietly and calmly, without losing her temper or feeling encroached upon. Lisa and I role-played several work scenarios to let her practice speaking up for herself and setting healthy boundaries.

Today, Lisa no longer needs the cancer to say "no" for her. She can do it herself. However, Lisa's predicament is very common.

Repressed anger is toxic for the body, as evidenced in these scientific studies as presented by the website Alternative Cancer Care.com (*http://www.alternative-cancer-care.com/cancer-anger-link.html*):

Breast Cancer Is Tied To Suppressed Anger

"Extreme suppression of anger was the most commonly identified characteristic of 160 breast cancer patients who were given a detailed psychological interview and self-administered questionnaire in a study conducted by the King's College Hospital in London, as reported by the Journal of Psychosomatic Research. Our principal finding was a significant association between the diagnosis of breast cancer and a behaviour pattern, persisting throughout adult life, of abnormal release of emotions. This abnormality was, in most cases, extreme suppression of anger and, in patients over 40, extreme suppression of other feelings." *(http://www.sciencedirect.com/science/article/pii/0022399975900628)*

The University of Rochester and Harvard School of Public Health followed 729 individuals over 12 years and found a 70% increase in cancer deaths for those who were scored at above the 75% level of suppressing emotions. Our analysis of a US nationally representative sample, followed for 12 years for mortality by cause of death, revealed significant associations between higher levels of emotion suppression and all-cause as well as cancer-related mortality."*(http://www.ncbi.nlm.nih.gov/pmc/articles/PMC3939772/)*

Cancer As An "Exit Plan"

I've seen this pattern many times. A dear friend's mother developed lung and colon cancer. The cancer told me it was her "exit plan" as a way to avoid setting strong boundaries between herself and difficult family members. Elka lost her sense of purpose after working for nearly 30 years caring for others in the healthcare field. Her career was abruptly ended when she develop severe pneumonia. The lung cancer was discovered during that chest x-ray.

Elka mistakenly thought of death as the end, which it never is. We are eternal beings and will always go on living and being conscious.

Death Is Never The End

The choices we make along our life journeys affect our karma, which is a Sanskrit word for the always-turning wheel of life. If we do not learn love for ourselves and for others, we will keep returning to Earth to have experiences until we master these skills.

Elka still had not learned to love and value herself, which is an essential part of the soul's curriculum. Elka's guides made it very clear that she would have to learn this lesson now, or come back and start all over again by being reborn in another lifetime. She reluctantly agreed to continue to work on herself now.

Elka had surgery for colon cancer a few weeks before this book was completed. Just before surgery, Elka told her daughter she was afraid she might not survive the procedure. Her daughter suspected her mother might try and "opt out" during the operation, and asked me to look in on her. I peeked in and saw that Elka's heart was weak. I asked an angel to come and strengthen it.

"God Wouldn't Let Me Go"

While I was in Elka's energy field, I reminded her of her agreement to stay and learn her lessons now. She argued with me. She said she was hoping to "just go" and be done with the struggles of this life. I told her it would not be fair to die and "just rip her daughter's heart out" like that, especially since her daughter had recently quit her medical practice and moved home to take care of her. I showed her a bright and happy future, and all the fun adventures they would have if she stayed.

A group of angels gathered around us as we talked. They gently but firmly shook their heads and told her no, it was not her time to go.

She rallied and made it through. The first thing Elka told her daughter after surgery was, *"God wouldn't let me go yet."*

I can't wait to see what amazing adventures life will bring her, now that she decided to give living a chance.

Like Elka, Vanessa never learned to put herself first. She prided herself on her ability to forgive the people who'd wronged her. However, she kept developing cancer. She was surprised when she heard what it had to say.

6

CANCER CALLS ON VANESSA FOR THE FOURTH TIME

Vanessa called me because she'd had cancer four times. Each time she had chemo, it went away for a little while, but always came back. Vanessa said cancer was in two places in her body, and now threatened her pancreas. "This one's got me a little worried," she admitted.

Like Lisa's tumor, Vanessa's cancer was eager to talk to me. Both tumors wanted to leave. They told me that she relied on them "as her exit plan" from having to deal with hateful family members. Vanessa told me repeatedly though, that she "had no bad feelings toward her family whatsoever," and had forgiven them completely.

Like most people in our society, she thought that forgiveness was a good thing. But I was not satisfied with that answer. I wanted to know where Vanessa's sense of outrage was. I wanted to know why she was not angry—at all. I believed her cancer was a result of her not standing up for herself, and believing there was no other way to escape the abusive people in her life.

Learning Her Own Worth

Over the course of an intense two-hour session, I helped Vanessa see how she had completely abdicated her sense of self throughout her entire life. She was almost 70 years old and had never really, truly been angry at anything done to her. Like David, she had expressed anger before, but it was always an anger rooted in victimization, coming from a place of, "Why are you doing this to me? Please stop!" as opposed to the sense of moral outrage and indignation that comes from realizing that she was a person of supreme worth who did not deserve to be treated badly.

Like David, I helped Vanessa stand up for herself. I took her back in time to her childhood. For the first time, she was able to see herself as she was—a beautiful, gentle, happy person who had always been ignored and pushed aside by people who were not as sensitive or artistic as she.

During this part of the session, she found herself saying things like, "I do not deserve this!" and "How dare you!" to the people who'd walked all over her throughout her life.

She realized how much she'd avoided standing up for herself, and understood that she had to be her own advocate, once and for all. She deserved protection and care and she vowed to give it to herself—so the cancer didn't have to.

Vanessa does not deserve to die—just because she doesn't know how to fully live.

What You Need To Know
Repressed emotions can affect you in the following ways:

- Stuck
- Empty
- Childlike
- Powerless
- Confused
- Limited ability to feel anything
- Frequently irritated
- Lashing out over small things
- Depressed
- Anxious
- Physical pains
- Stomach problems
- Throat problems
- Disease
- Cancer
- Bad relationships or no relationships at all

What You Can Do

If you think you may be suppressing your feelings, it's likely that you may have suffered from abuse, neglect or control in your past. A good way to look at your past is to ask yourself if you ever felt intensely uncomfortable, scared or alone. If so, then you may be suffering from trapped emotions.

Many people who have actually been abused do not recognize it because it seems normal to them. They deny or justify it, because facing the pain might be too overwhelming. Instead of being frustrated or angry with your pain (and not the people who really deserve it), try and see your pain as a stalwart soldier who loves you so much that it won't leave you until you learn to love yourself. Your pain may actually be your biggest advocate. It won't leave unless someone else takes its post. So, you must connect with it and see what lesson it may be trying to teach you.

Three Ways To Connect With Your Pain

a) Put your hand where it hurts and have an internal conversation
b) Write out the conversation
c) Visualize yourself in a safe, beautiful place. Ask the pain to take the form of a person or animal and then communicate with it.

How To Free Repressed Emotions

1. **Begin to recognize how you feel—or don't feel.** You may feel sadness or rage. Or, you may feel numb. Just notice and pay attention to what role emotions play in your life.

2. **Note the chakra that correlates to the emotions that you are over-expressing or under-expressing.** See how your body is affected.

3. **Put your hand on the chakra or close your eyes and place your attention where the pain or problem is.** Truly desire to see or receive whatever message it is trying to send you. Don't be

overwhelmed. It may scream, cry, speak to you, or be totally silent. Don't judge.

4. **Ask: What do you need?** Listen. Be open-minded. Be completely present. It will usually speak in short, one-word answers or short phrases. Just allow it to communicate with you.

5. **Ask: What would it take to clear you?** Talk with it. Have a conversation. Keep it brief and to the point.

6. **Do what it asks, if possible.** It may ask you to do something you can't do right now, or to make a big emotional change. Keep it realistic and break it down into baby steps. Keep going until you have an agreement.

7. **Make a promise to make those emotional shifts.** Negotiate until you have a workable plan. Keep your promise!

8. **Ask: What would you like to be replaced with?** If you agree with the choice, go ahead and allow it, as long as it feels safe and helpful. You have choices here, too.

9. **You can choose another guide, protector or angel to be with you instead of this pain.** When you invite that guide or angel, be very specific about how you invoke it. Make sure you specify, "*The one and only Divine Archangel Michael, who is of the highest possible frequency and who has only my highest and best interests at heart,*" and invite your guide in "*only for my absolute highest and best good.*" Unfortunately, there are many imposters in the spirit realm.

10. **Keep that promise to yourself.** This is key. Our emotions get stuck because we refuse to honor them. Many of them are actually hanging around because they care about you and want you to finally stick up for yourself. That energy has chosen to remain

stuck, in a very small space, all in the hopes that one day you will see your own value and realize you need to stand up for yourself. Speak up. Push back. Have real and true compassion for what has happened to you.

Symbiotic Relationship

You and your pain have a symbiotic relationship. It's holding trauma, anger, sorrow or fear for you. Try talking with it to see what it wants from you. You can write it out and just have a dialogue with it in your mind:

Sample dialogue with my jaw while finishing this book:

Me: Hi Jaw, why do you hurt?

Jaw: *I'm angry*

Me: Why are you angry?

Jaw: *I don't get enough support.*

Me: What kind of support do you need?

Jaw: *Love, money, appreciation, sunshine, laughter, nature, water, air, freedom, Spring*

Me: Wow- that's a cool list

Jaw: *Why don't you do them?*

Me: Kinda' hard right now, with the book.

Jaw: *I will be glad when it's over.*

Me: Me too. How about we do all these things when I'm done.

Jaw: *Ok.*

Me: Can you stop hurting between now and then?

Jaw: *Yes, but you better promise because I am sick of holding all this in.*

Me: I know, me too. I promise.

Jaw: *Ok.*

Me: I'll start with 15 minutes outside today ok?

Jaw: *Ok.*

I kept my promise and took my dog for a nice walk in the sunshine. My jaw was much looser.

Befriend Your Pain

Ironically, you must be a good friend to your pain so that it will be able to leave you. Keep your promises. If you slip up, own it. Apologize and keep trying. If you are not willing to do your part, things may get worse. You can expect the pain to come back, to get worse, or to migrate to more places in your body.

Sometimes, however, the pain may be too deep for you to handle alone. In that case, you may need Angelic Soul Clearing™ or another healing modality (see Resources).

Our next story is about how angels cleared a mugging victim of the paralyzing fear that held her captive for many years.

7

CRISTIN IS SAVED FROM SUICIDAL THOUGHTS

ristin suffered from depression and suicidal thoughts her entire life. She was just nine years old the first time she considered killing herself. "My mother found me with my father's revolver. I was contemplating suicide, wondering what it would be like for them when they found me: 'What would they say? How would they react? How would they feel?'"

This started Cristin on a path of therapists and medication. "For years, medicine and therapy were how I 'maintained.' However, these treatments didn't make the problem go away. I still felt misunderstood and unhappy."

More than anything, Cristin wanted to feel normal. She didn't want to have to battle the constant war going on within her. "I had recurring dreams of being in a kaleidoscope maze. It was very hard for me to think straight. I just wanted to be in as many activities as possible. I think it was a way for me to try and escape all the confusing thoughts going on in my head."

Despite these childhood difficulties, Cristin grew up to have a successful marketing career. She'd managed to keep her depression and anxiety at bay for many years, until she was brutally carjacked in 2005.

Two women and a man jumped her as she walked to her car on a sunny May morning in an upscale shopping district.

Cristin then endured a savage and prolonged attack that nearly killed her.

The Attack

She remembers every moment as if each were a lifetime. "Time slows down and it's like everything happens in slow motion. I remember everything in clear detail, with all my senses. I was a total stranger, but he looked at me as if he wanted to kill me. His eyes were just crazy and black and filled with this fuming hatred. I could even smell the evil in him."

Despite the trauma, Cristin gave such a detailed description of her attackers that they were captured and put in jail. It took several weeks to recover from her physical injuries, but the psychic scars of that life-threatening trauma threatened to overwhelm her for the rest of her life.

No Longer Felt Safe

"For more than 20 years, I worked to keep everything in check. I'd been in bad shape before, but now all I could think about was, 'Why did this happen? What did I do to deserve this? I was always so careful. I didn't go out alone at night, I watched where I parked, I always looked around me. Nothing prepared me for this attack out of nowhere, in public, in broad daylight."

Her depression and anxiety came back with a vengeance. She was constantly afraid. She no longer felt safe. She couldn't sleep. She couldn't trust people. The world no longer made sense. She had recurring nightmares of men breaking into her home and slaughtering her and her pets.

Cristin became convinced she would have to struggle with all of this for the rest of her life, using medication and therapy to try and keep any sense of stability.

Spiritual Intervention—Delivered From Suicidal Thoughts

Cristin called me during the summer of 2015. She was having panic attacks every morning and was consumed with suicidal thoughts.

"I just can't make the thoughts stop," she said. "They're in my head constantly. I just keep thinking that I want to die—but I know I don't. I don't know where this is coming from, or how to make it go away."

She sounded truly desperate. Archangel Michael and Archangel Raphael showed up for Cristin the moment I opened up sacred space for her. They were very compassionate and gave her a sincere outpouring of love. I worked delicately through Cristin's chakras, removing many layers of the toxic shame and guilt that had permeated her since the day of the attack.

I saw the panic in her mind, but I was first led to her lower chakras. Her solar plexus was filled with screaming darkness. The shock and terror of that day had lodged in there. This trapped energy created the panic attacks, keeping her in a constant state of fear.

Removing The Fear

The angels lovingly gathered all of the shock and released it to the Light. The parts were so glad to go, relieved that they no longer had to continue being afraid or hypervigilant in an effort to protect her.

We cleared the sacral area next. This was filled with black energetic eels and snakes and contained a large, dark monster. These represented her primary assailant, and other negative energies who had been drawn to her since that experience.

The angels removed all the energetic invaders and gave Cristin a lovely new space in which to feel safe and grounded.

"I just felt this heaviness being lifted right off my chest," she told me. "It's like when you go to the dentist and they put that heavy thing on you to protect you from the x-rays. Right now, it felt like somebody just lifted that heavy thing off my chest. Thank you!"

The angels then instructed me to re-wire Cristin's traumatized brain. The wiring was broken in places, leaving it unable to function properly.

I then looked into Cristin's "belief basket," a place that holds thought patterns and beliefs. It sits like a small built-in trash bin on a counter within the crown chakra. A normal-sized one is usually about nine inches long.

Cristin's was almost three feet deep. It was filled with self-hatred, recrimination, regret, self-blame, unworthiness and shame.

I asked the angels to take this out of her and to replace it with self-love and nurturing.

Suicidal Thoughts Removed

Right then, all suicidal thoughts left Cristin completely. "Oh my God!" she cried. "I literally just felt that lift right out of my energy field. They just reached in and took it away. The depression and suicidal thoughts are gone! I can feel it!" While Cristin marveled at her newfound peace, the angels replaced her negative thoughts with self-affirming and positive beliefs.

Her Life Today

Cristin has not had a single panic attack or suicidal thought since then. "It's been over a year and a half, and I have not had any suicidal thoughts," she told me in February of 2017.

"I struggled with depression my entire life. But now, depression is no bigger than disappointment. Anxiety is no bigger than a small-scale worry. My suicidal thoughts have transformed into reminding myself about how beautiful I am, inside and out. I am happy to say that I now live in a strong, safe and grounded place within myself."

Cristin is not the only person to battle these kinds of thoughts. We've all seen famous people succumb to suicide. Some of you may even have lost loved ones in this way. It's a terrible, tragic way to end life—for the person involved, and for those they leave behind.

What You Need To Know

Do not listen to suicidal thoughts!

1. **God never tells you that you are bad.**
2. **God never tells you there is no hope.**
3. **God never tells you no one cares about you.**
4. **God never tells you that you are worthless.**
5. **God never tells you that you should just give up.**

Whatever is causing these thoughts is not of the Light. Don't listen! It is not the truth about you—or your life. It is also a permanent solution to temporary feelings.

If I had given in to suicidal thoughts all the times I felt like my life was never going to get better, you would not be holding this book in your hands. *Don't give up. Your life is not over.* It is just beginning!

Get Help Immediately For Suicidal Thoughts!

If you are having suicidal thoughts, please get help right away. You are so much more precious and valuable than you realize! Don't continue to struggle on your own. The Light loves you. Seek medical, psychological and spiritual help. Please.

National Suicide Prevention Lifeline: 1-800-273-8255

http://www.youcannotbereplaced.com/

https://suicidepreventionlifeline.org/

Like Cristin, Jackie fought her whole life against a feeling she could not shake. Rage against a certain ethnic group had been her constant companion— and she had no idea why.

8

JACKIE IS RELIEVED OF RAGE

I'm so angry. I have this terrible rage. I hate Mexicans, Latinos, Hispanics—whatever you want to call them—I've hated them with a passion all my life. And I don't even know why."

Jackie pulled her big-rig off to the side of the road so she could concentrate on our session. "I don't know what's wrong with me," she confided. "I don't like being this way. I am not a hateful or angry person. I love everybody."

I asked if she'd ever been hurt by someone of that ethnicity. "No, never," she said. "They've never done anything to me. So why do I hate them so much? I don't understand what's wrong with me. I feel awful about it. I've tried to get rid of it so many ways, but it's still always there. I'm really hoping you can help me."

Back In Time

The angels instantly took me back in time as soon as I started Jackie's session. I was inside a plain stucco apartment complex, looking into a small kitchen. Behind me, a long row of windows looked out to a sea of concrete buildings that looked exactly the same. The style of the building and the inside décor looked like the early 1960's. I got the feeling that the apartment complex was in Los Angeles. When I described the scene, Jackie said, "Oh yes, that sounds like the Projects. We lived in the Projects in L.A. when I was a little kid." The Projects were a large housing development for low-income residents.

I placed my attention back inside the apartment. A young African-American woman stood alone by the kitchen counter. I assumed she was

Jackie's mother. Just then, three Latino men burst through the front door, yelling and screaming. They ran up to Jackie's mother and demanded something. In most cases, I experience everything that is going on with all my senses. But this time, there was no audio. I could not hear anything that was being said, I could only watch and read their body language.

It was as if something had been stolen from them and they wanted it back, or they were there to demand payment for something they had been promised. They were very angry and indignant.

A Near Kidnapping

Jackie's mother was terrified. She waved her hands around her face helplessly. She didn't know who they were. She didn't know what they wanted. She didn't have anything to do with it. She started crying. When their threats didn't seem to work, they pushed around her and searched for something valuable to take instead.

They found Jackie. They held her up in front of her mother, shouting threats and shaking her violently. Jackie's mother clawed and screamed at them, but they held her back and kept the baby out of reach. After a few more minutes of chaos and terror, they decided to let Jackie go and stormed out of the apartment.

Woah. Now I understood Jackie's lifelong hatred and fear. *She had been hurt.* She just hadn't remembered it, because she'd been a baby. But her body knew. Her spirit sensed the danger from so long ago, and kept reacting as if that moment was still happening. Trauma takes moments and freezes them inside us.

Angels Take Away The Fear

I asked the angels to please remove all the fear and terror from Jackie's mind and body and replace it with love. As I did this, Jackie inhaled deeply. "Oh, I can feel the peace starting. My heart feels differently already. I don't feel that anger. It was always so big inside my chest. But it's gone now. Thank you!"

I could feel the happiness in her voice. "I am smiling so big right now." she said. "It feels so good to have all that hatred gone!"

Miraculous Turnaround

Jackie checked in with me five months after her clearing. That lifelong hatred had completely disappeared. "I just can't even believe it," she said. "It's gone—and it was gone from that moment on."

"It was a hundred percent turnaround," she said. "I hated them for over fifty years, but I love them now. That one session changed everything. I've absolutely transformed.

"It's so miraculous! Thank you!"

Jackie sought help for getting rid of something she no longer wanted. Carlos hoped I could give him something he desperately needed. Thankfully, the angels knew just what to do to give him a fresh start.

9

CARLOS GETS A NEW BADGE

arlos Jackson called me because he was demoralized after leaving his job at a state law enforcement agency. No matter how hard he tried, he just couldn't regain his confidence.

Carlos dreamed about being a police officer all his life. All he wanted was to protect and serve. However, after three years on the force and many commendations, Carlos's job was suddenly threatened. His supervisors made it clear they wanted him to leave the department. He didn't know why. He asked for answers, but none were given. Carlos hoped that a session with me would give him some much-needed answers and lift the depression that had overtaken him.

As I looked into Carlos's soul, I saw what a truly noble person he was. It was clear that this had nothing to do with his performance. The angels showed me he had been pressured to leave because of internal corruption within the department. Senior management knew that they could not ensnare him in their web of lies and deceit. They knew that Carlos would do the right thing and report them if he ever found out what was going on. The issue was indeed with his character, but he had been fired *because* of his great nobility, not for lack of it. He had simply gotten too close, and they had fired him to protect themselves.

Dismissed For Doing The Right Thing

Carlos breathed a huge sigh of relief once he learned the truth. "I knew it!" he said. "I really felt something like that was going on, but I couldn't prove it. There was no reason for them to pressure me to quit. Yet I've carried this terrible sense of guilt and shame with me ever since."

When I looked in on Carlos's current career prospects, I clearly saw him involved in two different enterprises. Though he currently worked as a security consultant, Carlos said he felt like something was holding him back. The feeling of failure he still carried from being forced out more than a year ago still hung heavy within him, preventing him from being able to see himself as a successful businessman.

The angels were happy to remove the false sense of failure. However, this left a gaping hole within him. When I asked the angels how to fill it, they instantly produced a huge police badge for Carlos. The badge gleamed

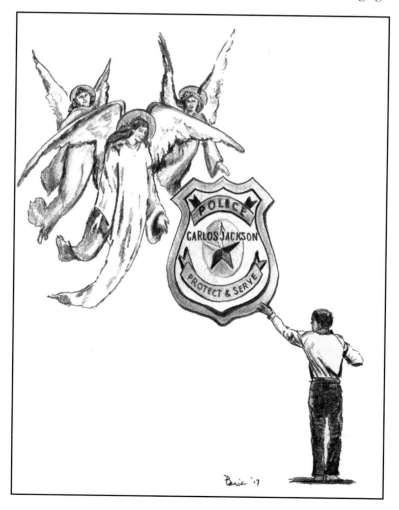

bright gold and blue, and had his name emblazoned above the crest. The badge itself was enormous—at least three feet wide and more than three feet tall. This was Heaven's way of letting Carlos know how just worthy he was and just how much being a police officer meant to him.

Angels Give Carlos A New Badge

Carlos told me he felt a huge expansion in his chest when the angels gave him the badge. "I can feel it!" he said. "I feel something very warm and solid coming into my heart right now." He was overwhelmed for a few minutes. I heard him saying "wow!" over and over again as the old, stuck energy lifted and new, positive energy flowed into him. "I can't explain it, but I can definitely feel it. That terrible feeling I had about being lost and unsure of myself is gone. I feel happy and strong now!"

I called him a couple of weeks later to check in on him. "Thank you again," he said. "I can't tell you how enormous that was. That changed everything. I feel like a new man with a new lease on life."

Carlos's business bloomed immediately after the session. New clients and large contracts came flooding in. He is now happy and fulfilled, doing what he was always meant to do: bringing his own special form of protection and security to the world.

Carlos was stuck because he couldn't let go of a disappointment in his past. Rhonda couldn't let go of a current obsession, even though it was robbing her of everything close to her.

10

RHONDA RESCUES HERSELF

Rhonda bounded up to my table at the Temple of Light holistic fair in 2014 with a big smile on her face. She'd heard about me from some friends, and was curious about what I might see for her.

An avid animal lover, Rhonda worked tirelessly in animal rescue for many years and immediately bonded with my Pomeranian, Max, who was seated next to me. She picked up a flyer for my Life Plan Action Class (LPAC) and signed up right then and there.

Rhonda became one of several students who met with me regularly in class over the next year. A true Scorpio, she is passionate, emotional and strong-willed. However, in those first classes, Rhonda often cried from depression and an unnamed sadness. She talked about how burned out she felt by the animal rescue work, especially since she fielded calls all night long while still maintaining a full-time job as a legal secretary. She wrestled with it week after week, aware that she was neglecting her own animals and husband. Still, she could not let it go. Some powerful, subconscious reason compelled her to keep giving too much of herself away.

Every LPAC student gets a free Angelic Soul Clearing.™ Just before her session, Rhonda said, "I wonder if I am under a curse. I always feel like something is working against me. Some people think that my mother may have something to do with it." Rhonda also said that she and her husband were distant, and she longed to have more closeness between them.

Mother With The Pitchfork

I told Rhonda I would have a look into her energy and let her know what I found. The angels showed me scenes from her childhood in which she'd been abused and alienated. I saw how her mother trained her to be very codependent and fearful, always calling Rhonda away from play to help her in the house. It wasn't that her mother really needed help; she really just wanted constant control of Rhonda, and was afraid that too much time with others would break that hold.

In fact, her mother even tried to maintain control of Rhonda during her soul clearing session. When she saw I was there to try and help her daughter, she screamed, "Stay away—she's mine!" and then snarled and charged at me with a pitchfork. The angels had to hold her back so I could finish breaking the curse.

When I told Rhonda what her mother had done, she said, "Wow—I knew my Mom was evil, but not that evil!" Like all abused children, Rhonda always wondered why her mother hated her. I was able to tell her that her mother's abuse was rooted in a deep jealousy, not only because of Rhonda's beauty, but because she had an innate sense of freedom and joy that her mother lacked completely.

Rhonda Gets Rescued

I was also able to get to the root of Rhonda's tremendous love and compassion for animals. Rhonda learned that her only role in life was to help save others in crisis, while pushing aside her own very real needs for nurturing and protection. All this created an overwhelming, compulsive desire within her to save other defenseless beings, since no one had rescued her. With no children of her own, animals became Rhonda's children. Every day she was faced with an entire world of them—suffering, hurting and scared—just the way she still felt deep inside.

The angels released that scared and helpless part of her to the Light, eliminating all the feelings of hurt, shame and terror. Rhonda wept as she felt the feelings of unworthiness literally lift from her heart. The angels also removed Rhonda's mother from her energy field completely and sealed it so that she could never bother her again.

Retiring From Rescue

Just three days after the Angelic Soul Clearing,™ Rhonda called me with some startling news. "It's the weirdest thing," she said. "I no longer feel compelled to devote all my time to rescue! Before, I felt like I had to save them all. But now, I just don't feel it anymore. I can't even tell you how HUGE this shift is for me. I am just blown away."

Rhonda had been rescued, she no longer had to try and kill herself to save animals. She realized that all these years, she had been desperately trying to save herself. The problem was not in her desire to help animals, but in how much of herself she gave away doing it. She could now see that her unrelenting drive to help had taken a severe toll on her health, marriage and finances. She spent many thousands of dollars paying for animal surgeries, gas money to and from the shelter, and providing pet portraits for the animals she'd rescued over the years. This strained her marriage, as her husband tried to get her to spend more time at home and curtail her spending.

Suddenly, Rhonda saw that although she did truly love animals, her caring had turned into an unhealthy obsession and compulsion. Once we addressed the inner turmoil that lead to her seeing her own abandoned and neglected self in each of the orphaned animals, the obsession left her completely.

Free of the Obsession

"It's unbelievable how much lighter and free I feel," she told her classmates the following week. "I was giving too much of myself, but I just couldn't stop it. Now, I realize that I've been neglecting my husband and my own animals for so long! They need my love and attention. It feels so good to finally be able to say 'no' and not feel guilty."

Her classmates were astounded at how far Rhonda had come in such a short time. It was truly miraculous. Two weeks later, they were even more surprised when she announced she was actually retiring from rescue completely. We held a special retirement party for her. The angels told her to get herself a tiara and a trophy for all her years of devoted service, which gave her a great sense of self-appreciation and closure.

More Love At Home

The renewed devotion to her own home restored her marriage. She happily reported that she and her husband had never been closer throughout their 30-plus years of marriage.

Rhonda and I did a few more sessions on her guilt and work issues. While she experienced waves of occasional grief over all she had given away, she was able to forgive herself. If the angels had not intervened, she probably would have continued on that self-destructive course for the rest of her life. But, thankfully, once Rhonda knew she deserved happiness, she returned to her ebullient self once more. She even noticed that she became more even-tempered in every aspect of her life. Balance had truly been restored.

Rhonda's obsession blinded her to the fact that her love and care were needed at home. Camron's refusal to let go of a past love kept her from finding the love she truly wanted, even though it was right in front of her.

11

CAMRON PUTS AWAY THE
PROJECTOR IN HER MIND

Have you ever been unable to move on after a relationship because you truly believed that person was "the one" and somehow you'd end up back together again?

Camron is a hard working entrepreneur who came to me for Angelic Soul Clearing™ in 2014 because she felt stuck with her love life. She'd been single for three years following a breakup. No matter what anyone said, she was certain that he was "the one" and that they were going to end up back together—even though he was now in a committed relationship with someone else.

The Projector In Her Brain

I removed old pains and patterns in Camron's lower chakras, but didn't locate the source of her overwhelming attachment until I got into the command center in her brain. I saw a huge, old-fashioned white screen about 15 feet across and a small metal overhead projector, much like the kind they used to use in schools. This screen was blocking an entire row of windows.

I chuckled. It made perfect sense. How could she possibly see reality when this projector had taking over her inner vision?

Projecting Fantasy

As I explained this to Camron, she realized that she had been using fantasy as a way to cope with life's disappointments from a very early age. She often daydreamed as a child, pretending she was someone else. This helped her to escape a painful childhood, but was now making it impossible for her to see the very real possibilities for love that were waiting for her in the here and now.

With her permission, I removed the projector and screen and replaced it with a huge window so she could see her life exactly as it was. She felt the old obsession leave her instantly. In its place, she felt a new excitement about dating and the future. Several wonderful men had expressed interest in her, but she had refused to go out with them, believing that her ex was going to come back to her.

"I was SO convinced that my ex was 'the one' and I just could not let him go. I never would have dreamed there was a real, old-fashioned projector in my mind, keeping this fantasy going," she said.

New Love in Just Three Weeks

Only three weeks after our session, Camron called to tell me that she'd met a great guy. He had been there all along, but she had never "seen" him. They hit it off and started dating right away.

A few months later, I told Camron I felt she was going to get pregnant. She thought that was absurd: they used birth control and she certainly wasn't ready to be a mother. Nonetheless, I kept seeing it, and the Parent card of my Career Cards deck kept popping up whenever we talked.

Sure enough, about six months into their relationship, Camron discovered she was pregnant.

The man she once couldn't see is now the father of her child—and they have a beautiful life together. However, she may never have noticed him if we hadn't stopped her from projecting a future that was never meant to be.

Like all of us, Camron longed for a lost love. The people in this next section longed to reunite with their loved ones who had passed away. Thanks to the angels, they all found a way to reconnect, reminding us that love never dies.

SIGNS
FROM THE
OTHER SIDE

Love This Book?

Then please REVIEW it on:

- **Amazon**
- **Barnes & Noble**
- **Goodreads**
- **Facebook**

And SHARE on
Your Social Media!

- Take a selfie with the book
- Post a snapshot
- Write a meaningful post

Post to your friends with the link to order:
www.freedbythelight.com

It's the only book of its kind,
So let the world know!

www.freedbythelight.com

12

PENNIES FROM HEAVEN

What do a 1983 penny and a ray of light have in common? They are demonstrations of love from the Other Side. In this chapter, you'll see pennies, quarters, rainbows and other signs sent from those on the Other Side to their loved ones here on Earth.

The first story is mine. It took place almost ten years ago, and it is still one of most amazing things that ever happened to me.

Celebrating Sobriety

In 2008, I celebrated 25 years of sobriety in Palm Springs, where I began my recovery. On my trip back home, I suddenly had the urge to sit down while making my way through the Palm Springs airport. I wasn't tired or out of breath, but my inner voice told me to sit down anyway.

Now, almost 10 years later, I know that "inner voice" is the voice of my angels. But then, I just thought of it as a hunch. I found a row of chairs in the empty airport and sat down with my briefcase resting in front of me. I took the moment to reflect on how far I'd come, and gave thanks to my Higher Power for helping me through so many tough times without relapsing.

When I went to stand up, I saw something shiny just to the left of my briefcase. It definitely had not been there when I sat down. I looked closer and saw that it was a bright penny. I looked around to see if anyone had dropped it, or if there was other change on the floor, but there was no one else around and no other change anywhere on the floor.

I reached down and picked it up.

A 1983 Penny Just For Me

It was a 1983 penny: *the very year I got sober. What are the odds of finding a penny from the exact year I got sober—at the conclusion of my trip to celebrate my sobriety?*

I picked that penny up and wept. How could I not feel loved, knowing that an angel had placed that special penny there, just for me? It still remains a highlight of my life.

That penny is safely in storage in Oklahoma right now, along with other belongings that remained after an EF-5 tornado wiped out my home there in 2013. My partner Tiffany and I met Kathy G. during that tornado. She was the Federal Emergency Management Agency (FEMA) representative assigned to help us. Little did I know then that Kathy had recently sustained a major loss of her own, or that she would become an integral part of this book. Her story follows.

My partner Tiffany lost her mother in 2015. They were very close. Her mother came to her in a dream immediately after dying, just as Tiffany fell asleep from exhaustion in the hospital chapel. Her mom appeared and made eye contact with her, before dancing a happy jig off to Heaven. Since then, she's shown her presence in many ways, including changing her own photo in Tiffany's phone, projecting mystical rainbows onto the bedroom ceiling, filling a room with her perfume, moving objects around the house and sending butterflies to show her love—including a beautiful yellow one that danced outside my window as I finished this book.

We've all seen rainbows, but aren't they usually outside? Kathy gets rainbows everywhere—even on lampshades, skillets and ceilings.

13

RICK'S RAINBOWS

Kathy began getting pennies and rainbows from Heaven the day after her son, Rick, passed away in 2013. Rick loved pennies and always told his kids that pennies were good luck. The morning after his death, his children woke up to find dozens of pennies strewn all over their apartment. "They found pennies everywhere, in every room, all over the place," Kathy remembers. "They showed up out of nowhere."

Rick sent Kathy the first rainbow just five days after he died. "I was sitting in my living room, and all of a sudden there's this huge white light up on the ceiling. I looked at my granddaughter and asked, 'Are you seeing this too? What do you see?' She said, 'A rainbow.' I looked around to see where the light was coming from. Rick's CD's were on the table and the sun was setting. Light hit the CD's at just the right time, which projected this beautiful rainbow onto the ceiling. That was the start of many beautiful rainbows to come."

A Rainbow In The Pan

A few weeks later, Kathy decided to cook Rick's favorite meal. While she stirred the peas and rice, trying to keep her tears from getting in the food, *a tiny rainbow miraculously appeared on the side of the pan.*

Kathy was even more amazed by the light because "there's no way that light could have happened without supernatural intervention. It was late afternoon, and my house has huge trees all around it, so the kitchen is dark that time of day. Plus, there's a patio on that side of the house, which means that it doesn't get direct sunlight most of the time. I have no idea where that light would have come from."

On the first year anniversary of Rick's death, Kathy drove to her mother's house for comfort. Suddenly, a rainbow appeared on the wall. "I

couldn't believe it, so I ran and got my Mom. She walked over and put her hand on it. We just couldn't believe there was a rainbow right there, on the wall inside her house!"

In January of 2017, Kathy was shopping inside a tile store and feeling overwhelmed with remodeling her house and raising her three grandchildren on her own. Just then, a rainbow (at left) appeared on the counter, ten feet *inside* the store. "Rick always knows when I need uplifting," Kathy said.

A few weeks later, she took her granddaughter out to get a hot dog and felt Rick's presence. 'I turned my head, and saw a man that looked just like Rick. I had to take a double look, because he had a gray hat and shaved head just like Rick." Rick always sends Kathy coins from 1978, the year he was born, so Kathy searched through the change she'd received from the hot dog purchase. Sure enough, there was a 1978 dime, right there in the palm of her hand. You'll see a 1978 quarter he sent—along with other amazing rainbows and a foil heart she was led to find on the beach—on pages 78 and 79.

I gave "Rick The Rainbow Maker" a bit of a dare while working on his chapter. I walked out to the mailbox and asked if he would give me a rainbow. I looked all around, but didn't see anything. I'd almost given up and started to head back, but then heard I Rick say, "Hey! You gotta give me a minute, this takes some time!" I laughed out loud and told him I'd wait. Just a few seconds later, I turned to come back in the house and and there was an orb of light above my door! I immediately posted it to Facebook.

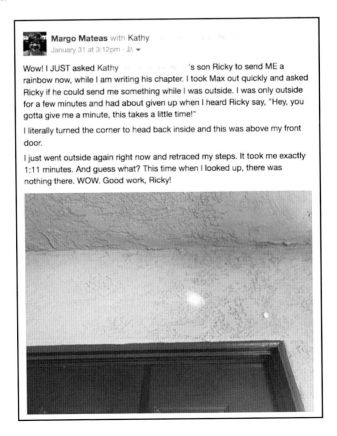

Margo Mateas with Kathy
January 31 at 3:12pm ·

Wow! I JUST asked Kathy   's son Ricky to send ME a rainbow now, while I am writing his chapter. I took Max out quickly and asked Ricky if he could send me something while I was outside. I was only outside for a few minutes and had about given up when I heard Ricky say, "Hey, you gotta give me a minute, this takes a little time!"
I literally turned the corner to head back inside and this was above my front door.
I just went outside again right now and retraced my steps. It took me exactly 1:11 minutes. And guess what? This time when I looked up, there was nothing there. WOW. Good work, Ricky!

That night, Kathy sent me this photo of Rick with rainbows streaming from his face (right). Note that the sun is actually *behind* him, and the rainbow extends to the chain link fence behind and to the side, too.

Just as I sat down to finish this chapter on March 22, 2017, Kathy tagged me in a Facebook post. (below, left). I was amazed at the synchronicity.

Kathy messaged me again ten minutes later, to ask how many chapters were in the book because she'd just heard the number "13." The last time I sent her a picture of Rick's chapter, his was 14. I checked, and it was now 13. **Rick let us know that HE knew his new chapter number!**

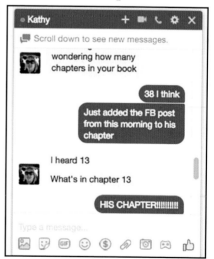

Note Rick's face in the sky, at the top right. See how his widow's peak is the same as in the photo across. Kathy wasn't sure what the big white blob beneath him was at first. Then, she realized it was a surfboard.

Kathy tells the story of how she saw Rick's face in a cloud (opposite page). "Everyone kept telling me that Ricky was appearing to them in dreams, in a cloud. One day, as I was driving to the bank, I suddenly had the thought that maybe I should start looking at clouds. So, I stopped at the light right by his former high school, and snapped a picture of the sky. At the time, I didn't see anything, I just knew I had to take the photo. Later that night, I looked at the photo on my cell phone, and that's when I saw his face in the clouds."

Rick's amazing ability to remain so close to this dimension is unusual. Most people who cross over are not able to give so many signs, because they are busy doing their own soul work. I asked Rick why he was able to stay so connected here. He told me, *"I made a special deal with Heaven so I can watch out for my kids."* He said he would be allowed to stay close to Earth for the next 15 years.

It was no surprise when Kathy told me that Rick's youngest son will be 18 years old when Rick returns to Heaven. Until then, I am sure that Rick will be looking out for all of them, sending rainbows to guide the way.

14

JIMMY FINALLY COMES TO VISIT

Tami K. struggled for years to overcome the loss of her son Jimmy to an accidental overdose in 2010. "It was the worst day of my life. I crawled around in a fog for the next two years. It was so painful and debilitating. Some days it felt like I couldn't breathe."

I met Tami via a metaphysical Facebook group in early 2014. During that time, I tried to comfort her and answer some of her questions about the afterlife. In April that year, I met Tami and several of her friends in person while visiting my sister and family in Chicago. Tami invited me to do an evening of readings at her home. She was warm and kind, and we connected immediately. When the evening was over, I had a chance to talk with her at more length. My heart hurt as I felt the depth of her pain and guilt.

Tami remembers those days. "I was still buried deep inside my grief, going through the motions, but just not finding my way back from my son's passing. When Margo walked in that night, I could just feel her spiritual energy. She told me that I had to start loving myself again and let go of the guilt I felt deep inside. I kept asking myself, 'Did I cause my son to become an addict? Had I loved him enough? Was it my fault?' These questions tormented me. But that night, Margo kept telling me that I had to forgive myself. She said it wasn't my fault, and that Jimmy wanted me to be happy again."

Over the next year, Tami and I stayed in touch through Facebook. One night in April of 2015, Tami posted a photo of herself and her family taken five years prior. The difference in her between then and now shocked me. I could see that she had been a whole person before Jimmy died.

Now, she was fragmented and empty.

Just then, the angels showed me what really happened to Tami when Jimmy passed away. A part of her spirit literally jumped in that grave with him, and said, "*If he can't live, I won't live, either.*" She was unable to move on, because she felt her was honoring Jimmy by staying miserable, but also because part of her soul was literally trapped in that coffin.

Tami's Soul Is Trapped Too

I wrote Tami and told her what I'd just seen. "Yes," she affirmed. "That Tami is gone. She left when Jimmy passed away. I'm a different person now."

The angels pushed me to try and help Tami let her son go. She had suffered enough. I broached the subject, but it was like he was being ripped from her arms all over again. "How can I let him go?" Tami cried. "I can't stop loving my son and wanting him to be with me! It's like we're one now, we've become one person." She said she talked to him every day and asked him to visit her. She was heartbroken that he had never come.

I could see that Jimmy was still stuck. He didn't understand his addiction yet, and wasn't evolving as a soul. Tami's intense emotions and her strong desire to see him again were actually preventing both of them from moving on.

Work To Do On The Other Side

I explained to Tami that each soul has a job to do while they are here, and also while on the Other Side. Life is always moving ahead. Sometimes we mistakenly think that once a person dies, they have nothing to do but fly around and have fun. We think that their purpose ends with this life. That could not be further from the truth. There is always something for the soul to do. Just like us, spirits who have crossed over can't be focused on too many things at once. They either have to commit to their own spiritual evolution, or remain here on this plane. If they do that, their own soul growth will be delayed.

Tami came around once she realized she was holding Jimmy back.

Finally Time To Let Go

"It was finally time," Tami realized. "I needed to let go of my son so that I could heal, and he could be free to let go of his addictions and learn all that he needed to up in Heaven." Tami then put her son's needs ahead of her own. "That night, after talking to Jimmy for a long time, I laid my head down on the pillow and gently and lovingly told my beautiful, oldest son that it was time for him to go. I wouldn't hold him back any more. I cried and I was happy all at the same time. I told him, 'Time to fly, son. Time to learn all that you need to learn to be the happiest angel that you can be.' I also told him that any time he wants to come visit me, I will be here."

I told Tami that I believed Jimmy would come and visit her, now that she had released him.

"I feel deep down inside that he is more at peace now," Tami wrote the next day. "I didn't want to let him go, but now I know that it's best for both of us and he's free now. And so am I. I feel so much lighter in my heart. I'm crying, but they're happy tears!"

Finally At Peace at 11:11

Just then, Tami noticed that it was April 11th, and the time was 11:11. "I always see these numbers," Tami told me. "I know that it's a sign from the angels!" I explained that 11:11 is a master number and indicates that everything is happening in perfect and Divine order.

"I feel so much better," Tami wrote. "Of course I still miss him, but that weight has been lifted from my chest. I know he's where he's supposed to be, doing what he's supposed to be doing. The loss was horrible enough, but then not to be able to leave it behind… that is hell.

"I'm at peace with it. I know that he can't be here, and I miss him, but I'm no longer begging him to visit me any more. That's over. I honestly feel like it would have gone on like that forever if you hadn't intervened. I didn't know any other way. But Jimmy's free now, and so am I. Thank you again!"

I asked Tami to please take a selfie and send it to me. The photo on the left is from that day. The one on the right was taken two months before.

Her hair, makeup and jacket are all the same. Only Tami is different. You can see the new radiance in her soul shining through.

But Tami and Jimmy's story doesn't end there. *Tami soon discovered that letting him go was the key to actually seeing him again.*

Tami and her children gathered on January 10, 2016, to celebrate Jimmy's 30th birthday. Tami bought him a birthday cake, cooked his favorite meal and wore his Chicago Bears jersey. She put his photo on the table next to his cake, snapped a picture and posted it to Facebook, where I happened to see it.

"While waiting for my other kids and boyfriend to arrive, I got a message from Margo. She always seems to know when I need any kind of message at all about my son. She told me that Jim was watching me cook his favorite meal, and that I should acknowledge him and talk to him. So, I did just that. I sat down and verbally spoke to him. I told him how I missed him, and that I never see any visions of him, nor do I feel him around. I asked him if he could please come and visit us on his birthday.

"After dinner, we sang Happy Birthday to him, and ate his cake. I got up from the table to do the dishes. My girls were being silly and laughing. My oldest daughter playfully told her sister that she should mind her language, because Jim was listening, and wouldn't like it. All of a sudden, my boyfriend and my oldest daughter both started yelling and covering their mouths. I ran back into the dining area. They told me they both saw a throw pillow on the couch suddenly stand up on edge and rock back and forth!"

Tami took a photo of where the pillow had moved and then sent me the picture above. You can see the white streak of light on the blinds.

"Margo, it was laying on the couch," she wrote me excitedly. "It stood up and started wobbling!!! Right after, I asked Dani to take a picture and this orb on the blinds was there!!! I could not thank him enough!!! I love my boy. I can't get rid of the goosebumps now, and Dani keeps getting chills also! Jim came to his party!!!! No way was he going to miss his 30th birthday!"

I looked into Tami's house, and saw that Jimmy was indeed there, grinning from ear to ear. He was so pleased with himself! Jimmy told me that his energy was waning, though, and that he would have to leave. He promised he would come back soon. I didn't say anything to Tami because I didn't want to get her hopes up. But Jimmy kept his word.

Jan 11th, 2015 7:06pm

Tami messaged me the next evening: "Hi, help me out here please... Danielle's Ipad was laying on the couch next to her and it was face up for watching TV, and all of a sudden the light went out on her iPad, and the volume suddenly went up. Then it shut off....

"Then we saw that oval-ish mark on the blinds. What do u think?

"The iPad was in the same spot that the pillow was in last night that was moved, and later on in the night I was upset that I wasn't able to see this pillow move, and I cried. I don't know, Margo, would he have come back to show me this??"

Jimmy grinned proudly as we wrote back and forth. Tami wrote that she and her daughter were so happy they were laughing and giggling.

Then, I saw Jimmy dancing barefoot with his mom and sister.

Dancing Barefoot In Winter

I thought this was a little odd, since it was the middle of winter in Chicago, *but Tami confirmed that she and her daughter were indeed both barefoot and dancing in her living room*—even though the temperature was zero outside.

Tami was so thrilled to hear that Jimmy was dancing with them! She thanked him so much for coming and giving her a direct sign. "I'm so happy I could burst!" she wrote giddily.

Jimmy Hides The Remote

Jimmy still visits his mom from time to time. He even playfully hid the remote from her one day. "I was watching TV and the remote just disappeared. I live alone, so it's always on the couch with me. But

one minute it was there, and the next it was gone. I asked Jimmy if he had hidden it, and right then I found it on the floor beneath the coffee table, tucked in between two eight-pound weights.

"It was obvious that it didn't fall there. Jimmy hid it there, and even rolled the weights over the top of it!"

"I smile every time I think of our visits from my loving son, with his funny grin and

Tami and I at the psychic party in April of 2014.

silly smile. He was full of love in his life here on Earth, and he's still full of love now. He's just in a different place."

Happy And Free Now

Once Tami let him go, Jimmy was free to do his own soul work and to even come and visit her. She held on to him so tightly that he couldn't get out. Once she set him free, he was able to move around in both the spirit world and the physical dimension.

Today, Tami is free, happy and back in life. "I know that Jimmy is happy, too. His Spirit lives on in all of us and he will never, ever be forgotten."

Karl longed to know his father loved him. He received a sign from his father in the most unexpected and delightful way, during a session that was not even supposed to be his own.

90

15

KARL'S DAD SENDS HIM
A WINDOW OF LIGHT

Most of us long to be reunited with our loved ones on the Other Side. It can be frustrating to wait for a sign that never comes. Like Tami, we wonder what we are doing wrong. We wonder if our loved ones are mad at us, or if perhaps they never really loved us at all. It can be heartbreaking.

Karl had an uneasy relationship with his dad. He tried to get his father's approval all his life. He worked hard, became successful, all the things he knew would make his dad proud. But no matter how much he asked, he never got a sign from his father—until Karl booked a session for his unruly teenage daughter, and ended up meeting with me instead.

Karl and the Window

In November of 2016, I called Karl for the session for his daughter. When she refused to come to the phone, Karl decided to hang out with me for the hour. At first, he didn't know what to talk about. But then, he thought about his father who had passed on six years earlier.

Karl was very sad and confused about why he had never received a message or a visitation from his father since he died. He spoke of his father lovingly, but admitted the relationship had been rough. "No matter what I did, I never felt like I really ever got his approval. It hurts. I try to be the best Dad I can be, so that my kids never wonder if I love them."

As he talked about his dad, I kept getting the image of a window suddenly illuminated by a ray of light. I saw the windowsill very clearly and the entire window being completely filled with sunlight. I asked Karl if he recalled any scene from his past that may have included this special light.

He said no.

His father then showed me baseballs. Karl said his office was full of them and that he was looking at one right then. We thought perhaps that was how his Dad was reminding him he was around. However, I kept being shown this image of a window suddenly being filled with light. I felt compelled to mention it, even though it wasn't resonating with him. I felt somewhat confused. Why would I keep seeing this very specific, East Coast type of window filled with light, if it had no meaning to Karl?

Window of Light

However, just when I was thinking about giving up, Karl suddenly exclaimed, "Oh my God! It's happening right now! This whole window just filled up with light, and now my whole room is full of sun!"

He told me that it had been cloudy all day, and just then everything happened the way I saw it: the window completely filled with sunlight and that light spilled out into the room. The window was even as I saw it.

"Now the sun is out all the way and it's staying that way. I can't believe it!" To say he was stunned is an understatement. Now Karl knows for certain that his father loves him.

What You Need To Know

- Life never stops. It is eternal.

- Our loved ones must continue their own evolution and growth once they leave this plane of existence.

- If a loved ones do not come to visit, it may be because they are unable to make the connection on their own.

- It is possible for you to use your own innate supernatural gifts (clairvoyance, clairaudience, claircognition, clairsentience and clairalience) to see, hear, know smell and feel your loved one's presence. Many people report smelling their loved one's cologne, perfume, or even cigarettes and cigars when they are around.

- Your loved ones do not automatically become your "guardian angel." They may have their own soul work to do, or have another soul purpose.

- People do not suddenly change their habits, beliefs or become perfect after death. They are the same people you knew before. The longer they are on the Other Side, the more loving, understanding and peaceful they may become.

- All souls do not automatically go to what we know of as "Heaven." Some go to an inbetween place known as Purgatory, where they learn lessons and improve their soul's development before ascending to higher planes of consciousness.

What You Can Do

If you long for these kinds of experiences, try looking for feathers, pennies or other things that remind you of your loved ones. It may be birds or butterflies or something else entirely. They may come to you in dreams, too. Dreams are a portal between worlds, a place where you can actually commune with loved ones who have crossed over.

The biggest step you can take toward receiving messages is to start looking and listening for signs. Kathy would never have known that Rick was reaching out to her unless she stopped to look at shiny coins, or sort through change. She could easily have missed the signs by not seeing what was placed right in front of her.

Ways To Communicate With Those On The Other Side

Spirits like to be honored with their favorite things. The night Jimmy visited, his Mom wore his favorite jersey, made his favorite foods and put his picture on the dining table next to his cake. Rick also came back when his mother cooked his favorite meal. Both mothers intensely thought about their sons while preparing their favorite things.

Tami even specifically asked Jimmy to visit her that evening. Talk with your loved ones, but give space for them to answer. Don't overburden them with your grief.

Find a balance between letting them know how much you miss them and realizing that they have a new life now, too, and must attend to their own business. It isn't just their job to take care of you: they must continue to grow and move on, too.

Set Boundaries That Make You Feel Safe

Kathy and Tami are both frightened of apparitions, and didn't want to have this type of relationship with their deceased loved ones. If you feel like this, too, it's perfectly fine to just tell them how to contact you.

Understand that people don't change instantly once they cross over. They are still the exact same people as they were before: so if they teased and rebelled against you in life, you can expect them to bend the rules in death, too. They may push the boundaries from time to time. Rick sometimes throws things around the room to get his mother's attention, and he knocked a tissue box around on my desk while I was talking to her.

The day after our phone call, I noticed that my wedding photo had fallen from the top shelf of my entertainment center onto the floor. Nothing else was touched, including the delicate wedding glasses perched on both sides of it. Perhaps this was Rick's way of letting me know that he had indeed been in my home.

Seek Out A Qualified Medium or Spirit Circle

People who are able to connect with spirits can provide a great deal of comfort and closure to those grieving the loss of a loved one. A psychic can usually tune into energies of all kinds, but not all are attuned to communicating with those who have crossed over.

A person who is comfortable with and able to talk with the dead is called a "medium" because they act as a conduit between you and the other person.

Some mediums use photos or personal items from the deceased to tune into their vibration, so be prepared if they ask for that. Some "evidentiary" mediums will ask the person on the Other Side to describe something in your environment or reference something special between you as evidence that the medium has indeed connected with them.

Some mediums draw portraits of the people who come through, which can leave you with a cherished item after the session is over.

Although I have definitely talked to those who have crossed over and helped them convey important meanings and messages to the living, I don't get details such as names and things, so I often refer people who are looking for that kind of experience to qualified mediums (see Resources section).

Don't Take It Personally

However, even if you do all these things, your loved ones may not appear. Please don't take it personally or think that they don't love you or are angry with you.

Sometimes they are working on their own karma or lessons, or need to leave you alone to achieve closure and complete your grieving process. Sometimes they are literally so busy with their work that they cannot lower their vibration enough to make a connection with you. Sometimes they are actually prohibited from contacting you, especially if they were abusive or cruel to you in some way.

If your loved ones don't come to you, please do not assume that they don't love you. They are still living souls with work and a mission and a purpose.

Just remember that Life never stops. Life needs to go on—for you and for those who have crossed over.

Have you ever felt like you've been somewhere before, or already knew someone the first time you met? Do you ever feel drawn to certain time periods, cultures or places?

This next section takes you back in time through the experiences of Sharon, Beth and Diane, who were plagued by issues that turned out to be connected to lives they didn't even know they'd lived before.

PAST LIVES

16

DIANE REVISITS THE BLACK PLAGUE IN A PAST LIFE

You May Have Lived Before

If you've ever met someone and instantly loved them or felt an affinity for a place or civilization, those feelings could be from a past life. Many people feel drawn to certain places or time periods, such as the Civil War or the Renaissance. I believe that people who go to these type of re-enactments are trying to relive those lifetimes. Several well-known psychiatrists and hypnotherapists such as Bryan Weiss, M.D. ("Many Lives, Many Masters,") and Dick Sutphen have written numerous books about the reality of past lives and have even traced the information that surfaced in the past life recall to actual people and historical events.

Uncovered Past Life In Ireland

"I experienced a past life regression with Margo Mateas more than twenty years ago that permanently changed the way I view myself and my life," Diane H. wrote. "The details of the past life regression are clearer, more lasting, and more vivid, than any other memory I can recall. It is as though the experience is tattooed in my memory."

Diane came to visit me in 1996, along with a mutual friend. Diane approached me one morning after breakfast and asked if she could discuss something with me. She told me that she had a deep connection to all things Irish, including traditional Irish music and culture, Celtic symbols, Irish history and the Irish people. Since her family was not Irish, she couldn't understand the allure.

I agreed to do a regression for her. I gave the instruction that she be taken to the lifetime that created these feelings in her.

Pieter Brueghel the Elder, *The Triumph of Death* **(c. 1562)**

"In the regression, I learned about a past life in which I had lived in Ireland, and was a physician or healer. I experienced sights and smells that I didn't understand, with people dying in droves, from an unknown cause. It seemed to be medieval times."

The experience answered many of her questions. "It all makes sense now," she told me, looking relieved. "I did live there! I can see and feel everything. I was really there." Though she had become a lawyer in this life, Diane began her career as a nurse, and was still drawn to healing and the medical field.

A few years later, Diane made a point to go see Ireland. While in in Dublin, she took a self-guided historical tour, set up much like a museum.

"One exhibit had a scene that was virtually identical to the one I'd seen in my past life regression. The exhibit stated that it was depicting the Black Plague, which had devastated Europe and occurred in the early 1300's in Ireland. It made me stop short, as the understanding flooded me.

I never studied European history, so this affirmation and explanation of what I had experienced gave me so many answers. It really confirmed the reality of the past life memory," she told me.

"It just changed everything. To know that I lived before, and tried to help people, makes me even more determined to continue doing so in this lifetime."

_____

At least Diane had an inkling of her past. When Sharon experienced a strange problem with someone from a past life, neither of them had any clue what they had once been to each other—or the gruesome sacrifice that threatened to bind them for eternity.

17

SHARON RECOVERS FROM A FORGOTTEN INCAN SACRIFICE

An Inexplicable Conflict

Sometimes, a seemingly insurmountable obstacle or challenge in this life can be traced to a past one. One of my friends from high school called me for help because she had suddenly developed a problem with her hula dance teacher. Sharon explained that up until now, they had had a close and supportive relationship, but that recently he had begun to pick on her.

She was to be a soloist at a large competition, but he kept finding fault, instead of being pleased with her practice performances. He criticized every move and acted as if he was angry with her. She was very surprised and hurt. She wracked her brain for weeks, trying to figure out what she had done to upset him. Try as she could, she couldn't come up with anything that explained his sudden and drastic change in demeanor. "I've exhausted everything I can think of," she told me. "Perhaps you can figure out what's going on."

A Past Life Peril

When I looked into the situation, a past life appeared to be the culprit. I was taken to the center of a lush tropical jungle. Up ahead was a dirt path that led to a small enclave of huts. To the left was a large, looming Incan pyramid. I heard a woman screaming. As I looked up the path, I saw a young woman on her knees, sobbing with grief. As I got closer, I saw it was my friend Sharon, dressed in the garb of the time, but with the same face. She was absolutely devastated. "My baby!" She screamed. "He's taken my baby!"

I turned back toward the temple. Atop the structure, I saw an Incan priest raising a blade to the sky and preparing to sacrifice her child. Since I was at the bottom at the pyramid, there wasn't time for me to intervene and save her baby. Desperate to help, I went back and tried to console her, but her grief and rage were boundless.

I asked the angels what I should do next. They told me to confront the priest. I stayed by Sharon and called the Incan priest to appear before us. He was surprised and outraged. "Who are you?" he demanded to know. I explained that I came from the present day as an advocate for my friend, whose child he had kidnapped and murdered.

Confronting The Sins of The Past

Sharon vented her terrible grief on him. "How could you?" She screamed. "You took my baby without my consent!" Something about her raw, inconsolable grief moved his soul. He seemed to come out of his role as the priest, who was required to make such heinous sacrifices, and return to the noble, good man he was. In that moment he was just a man, a man who realized the true horror of his actions. He fell to his knees. He knelt at her feet and said he was sorry. "I should have told you," he admitted. "I should have asked you. I should have asked for your consent, but I knew that you would never give it." He told her that he chose her child because she was the purest in the village, and would be the best to appease the gods. Sharon remained adamant. "You had no right to take my baby without my permission."

Balancing The Karma

"You're right," he said quietly. Then, he withdrew his sword and held it above his bowed head for her to take. "Please accept my sacrifice as atonement for yours," he said, waiting for her to cut off his head. Sharon was reluctant, because violence was foreign to her. "Please," he insisted. "Allow my soul to make amends to you to balance our karma, so we can move forward in peace."

With that, Sharon raised the sword and did the deed. "I did it," she told me through tears. "But I'm glad I did. I can't explain it, but it feels better, like a huge weight has been lifted from me."

The Incan priest appeared before us again, this time as an apparition. He touched Sharon's arm and said softly, "Let me give you something else to heal the hole in your heart."

Restoring What Was Taken

Suddenly, we heard a newborn baby crying from across the jungle. We all looked over to see a beautiful band of light streaming down from the heavens. An angel appeared, holding a perfect new baby. Sharon ran joyously to her infant, and the angels gently placed her in her waiting arms. As Sharon wept with gratitude, the Incan priest smiled and said, "Thank you. Thank you for coming to make this right. Our karma is now complete."

With that, Sharon and I felt ready to return to the present day. Sharon definitely felt a major shift inside. She was shocked at the intensity of emotions she'd experienced during the recall. "Everything felt absolutely real," she said with wonder. "I actually felt that terrible grief and overwhelming rage at him for stealing my child."

Real Feelings of Grief

As she collected herself, she said, "I had no idea that past lives were real, or that they could affect us in such profound ways! I'm curious to see what his reaction will be the next time I see him."

Sharon called me a few days later. "Oh my God," she said, "I can't believe it! This time, he was totally different. I came in the door for class, and instead of being aloof and cold, he hugged me and kissed me on both cheeks. Everything just went back to being normal and loving and comfortable between us—just like that."

Present Day Peace

It's important to note that Sharon and her teacher did not talk about what had happened at all. She never mentioned it. He had no knowledge of our session, or what had transpired. Simply removing the karma that existed between them instantly restored harmony to the relationship.

What You Need To Know

Changing dynamics in the spirit world changes things here. I've seen this happen many, many times.

One woman told me that her mother criticized her endlessly. She could not even recall a time when her mother had ever told her she loved her. We worked on this in a session and I helped my client take back her power.

The next time she and her mother spoke on the phone, her mother said, "I love you." My client was stunned.

Another client's father berated him so much for getting a kitten many years ago that he was now reluctant to tell him he had recently adopted a dog. After we dealt with these dynamics in the spirit realm, what had previously been a two hour guilt-fest turned into a simple happy, congratulatory text. My client was dumbfounded. His relationship with his father completely changed from that moment forward.

Other clients have been ready to leave jobs because of issues with their bosses or co-workers, and been surprised to see that their feelings—and the behavior of the other people—suddenly and mysteriously change after their sessions with me.

———————————

Beth needed help leaving a bad work situation. She wanted to leave, but found herself unable to quit, even when she received new offers. She never suspected the cause might be sequestered away in a past life.

18

BETH GETS HER DREAM JOB AFTER BREAKING PAST LIFE BONDS

When I met Beth in 2014, she was working at a job she hated, for a man she detested. She had been trying to leave her job for the past nine years. "I feel trapped, like a slave. He doesn't respect or listen to me, but for some reason I can't leave. I've even had other offers, but I just can't seem to take them." Her desired outcome for the session was to be free to be herself, and to be valued by an employer.

As I looked into the situation, Spirit showed that Beth and her employer shared numerous past lives. I asked to be shown the lifetime that was contributing to her feelings of oppression in her current job. I was immediately shown a fast-moving collage of images from several lifetimes, including China, Egypt and the Wild West. It was no surprise that Beth felt like a slave to her boss, as she had indeed been a slave to him in many other lifetimes.

Many Lives, One Master

"She's mine," he said, when I came to advocate for her release. He still held many pieces of her soul, which is why he had such a hold over her and why she had been unable to leave her job. The angels showed me a lifetime in China where she had been sold to him as a child. He bound her feet to keep her close.

They showed me other lifetimes in Egypt, when she had been a beautiful maiden and he a cruel overlord.

Even though Beth was a powerful, strong and confident woman in this lifetime, in each of their previous lifetimes he had enslaved her completely.

Beth Reclaims Her Power

While still in the angelic dimension, Beth stood up to him and made it clear that she would no longer tolerate his tyranny. At this point, he realized what he had done, and apologized for the many lifetimes in which he controlled and abused her. He admitted that he found her power intimidating. It was easier to contain her, than to contend with her.

Job Of Her Dreams

Beth called me less than a week later to tell me that she had gotten a wonderful job working with one of her best friends, doing exactly what she loved! Her new employer now listens to her, respects her and encourages her to make decisions. More than two years later, Beth still loves her job as the "Imaginations and Ideas Manager" for this wonderful family-run business.

It was beautiful to see the transformation in Beth. The anger and frustration she had been feeling for so long melted away and she became happy and joyful in all aspects of her life.

What You Need To Know

- Many cultures and religions around the world believe in the concept of reincarnation. They believe that the soul requires more than one life to achieve Oneness with God, and to perfect itself.

- Feeling drawn to certain times, places and cultures in the past could mean that you actually lived there.

- Mysterious fears and phobias could be tied to a past life experience, such as drowning, being shot, hung, imprisoned, etc.

- We travel through time with the same people. Your friends and loved ones now have probably been with you in other lifetimes.

- Certain birthmarks or trauma marks on the body that cannot be explained in this life may be attributed to trauma you experienced in another life, for example, a mark on the neck could mean that you were once strangled.

- Strong feelings of attraction or repulsion toward a person or a place that have no rational reason could be the result of a past life experience.

- If you feel unable to let go of a person, the reason could be that you have unfinished business from a past life.

- Talents and skills may be mastered in another life and brought forward in this one. Child prodigies are good examples of this.

What You Can Do

- Seek out a qualified hypnotherapist or past life regressionist to help you revisit your past lives.

- Understand that you may have actually lived before, and that those experiences and memories may still affect you.

- Explore places and cultures you have strong feelings about and see if it triggers a past life memory.

Sometimes the past comes back to haunt us in different ways. Family curses can uproot lives, throw everything in chaos and leave nothing but turmoil in their wake. The people in this next section battled mysterious curses that were placed on their families.

CURSES

19

A CURSE TURNS LILY'S CHARMED LIFE TO ASHES

Are curses real? Can your life really be sabotaged by someone wishing you bad luck? Can family curses last for generations?

Charmed Life

Lily K. wanted to know if a curse might be plaguing her. "I lived a charmed life," she explained. "I was a jet-setter. I traveled the world. I had plenty of money. I was beautiful, I wore the latest designer clothes. I had lots of friends. I was healthy, and had tons of energy. I had the Midas touch—until my mother died."

"My mother and I were the best of friends, and I took care of her for six years until she passed away. She was very ill, so I had to quit my job to take care of her. I used all my savings and even had to take some loans just to survive and pay for her funeral costs. It left me in a very vulnerable position."

Once it was all over, Lily began to look ahead. She hoped things would improve. But instead of getting better, Lily's life mysteriously started to unravel. One thing collapsed after another, until there was nearly nothing left of the glamorous life she'd had before.

Life Begins To Lose Its Luster

First, Lily lost her beauty. "Before, people told me I was pretty all the time. I did not get that compliment at all after she died. I looked different. It wasn't just stress. My eyes were sunken and dark. I looked thirty years older than I was. I looked drawn, like something was sucking the life out of me. I looked like a hag."

Then, she lost her friends. "I was always popular and had so many friends. Suddenly, I lost friends. I was not invited to places or parties like before. People were very mean to me. People yelled at me for no reason. The friends I did end up making really didn't care about me at all."

Lily also began having severe money issues. "I lost four jobs in a row. Prior to this, I had never lost a job. I was very respected in my profession and made more than the average physical therapist. But suddenly, I could not make money or keep a job." Lily also began to have problems with her tenants, who had never before given her problems. "All of a sudden, I had all these problems with renters: they destroyed the home; they didn't pay; I couldn't get the places rented; people left after one year. It was a disaster."

Her car also broke down all the time, frequently leaving her stranded. "It was one thing after another. I'd fix one thing, but then something else would break down, too. It was very stressful."

Diagnosed With Cancer

Lily's health was the next to go. "I sustained a lot of injuries. I sprained my ankle very badly. Then I hurt my knee and tore a tendon, which required me to have knee surgery and rehabilitation." Just when she thought she was in the clear, Lily was dealt the worst blow of all: she was diagnosed with an aggressive form of sarcoma. "I really struggled with the cancer. That almost killed me. Thank God I had early intervention, or I would have died!"

Lily noticed that things were amiss at home, too. "Sometimes I felt scared. The house felt heavy and oppressive. My black cat would not cuddle or sleep with me. He also pooped outside the litter box. I tried everything to get him to stop, but nothing worked. The vet said it was because of stress."

As you can see, Lily really was at the end of her rope. Everything was going wrong.

A Familial Curse

As I looked into Lily's situation, I did see a familial curse going back to the Wild West times. I saw a man and a woman standing in the dust, outside a saloon. They held a tiny baby in their arms and spoke urgently with a small, wizened-looking woman, whose face was hidden by rags. I gathered from their body language that the baby was sick. The woman seemed to be a healer or witch of some sort. I got the feeling that the baby was going to die unless she did something to intervene. I wasn't shown the full details of the transaction that day, except that the couple was desperate to save their baby.

The healer woman's price was not revealed to me, but whatever she asked they would have gladly given, had it meant saving their precious child. I felt that their intentions were good, but the woman was dishonest.

Regardless of what created the curse, I was now free to break it. The angels and I intervened for Lily and cleared all ramifications of this curse through time, going back to that hot, dry day in the Wild West, all the way up until the present moment.

From Mother To Daughter

Lily had a realization: "I think my mother was cursed and it passed to me once she died. My mother had a very, very hard life. She struggled all the time. I began having trouble the minute she died."

No doubt the family curse was to blame, but I also removed a number of dark entities from Lily's energy field. I felt that the hag-type look was from the curse, but people had also been recoiling from this darkness. "I was always a happy, loving, fun person. But people just started avoiding me. I didn't know what was wrong. Inside, I was still the same person, but for some reason, people started treating me differently; like I wasn't me anymore. It was the strangest thing."

Lily Gets A New Light Body

The angels and I completely cleared Lily and she received a new Light Body. Lily felt completely renewed from the inside out. Lily slept twelve hours that night. "I wasn't afraid at all," she said. "I felt safe and protected."

That night, for the first time, her black cat came and cuddled in her lap. It also pooped *inside* the litter box for the first time.

Everything seemed to be headed in the right direction—until the next day. "I was in the kitchen, when something started to choke me," Lily told me. "It was really intense. I was very scared. The house felt heavy and scary again, like there was something really bad in it."

I scanned the home, but didn't see any entities. It felt like a cursed object was somewhere in the home; something attached to her mother or grandmother.

The Cursed Doll

Lily suddenly remembered an old porcelain doll her mother had given her, from the 1930s.

"It was in a black garbage bag downstairs," Lily recalls. "My friend Bill and I found it when we were clearing out my parents' attic a few years ago. It definitely gave us the creeps, so we just put it in a bag and stored it out of sight." Lily shuddered at the memory. "Bill died of cancer about five months after finding that doll. He just went downhill so quickly." Her voice filled with sadness. "He was a really, really good friend."

The angels told Lisa how to properly destroy and dispose of the doll. Every type of "magic" or curse has its own unique energy imprint, so a one-size-fits-all approach won't work for curses. Thankfully, the angels knew exactly what to do, and suggested protocols that neutralized the curse completely. Lily was also told to clean and sweep her house, especially in closets and dark places, to burn sage, and to place salt around the entrances and exits to purify and protect her home.

"Not only does the house feel lighter, but everything got more sparkly. It was like the house had been living under a layer of dust or something, too, and it came back to life when that final curse was removed. I can't believe how pretty and bright my house is now.

"It's like I suddenly have a lot more windows!"

Employment Just Days Later

After being unemployed for over a year, Lily got a job just four days after the curse was lifted. She got another one just a few days later.

The compliments started up again, too. "People started telling me I look pretty, and that I'm beautiful again." That hag look is gone from Lily's face. Her youthful beauty is coming back. Her eyes are light and filled with life.

"I have more hope now," Lily said. "Things are finally going my way, and I'm putting the pieces of my life together again. I'm so grateful I found Margo and that she knew how to help me. I used to joke with myself that maybe I was cursed, but I never really dreamed that would actually be the case. And a haunted doll, too? I never would have believed it, if it hadn't happened to me!"

———————————

I was just as surprised by Lily's curse as she was. I thought curses were just something made up by Hollywood. But shortly after helping her, another case came my way—and this one was straight out of a Stephen King novel.

20

"THINNER..."
A CURSE CAUSES ANOREXIA

You may remember the Stephen King novel and movie, "Thinner," in which a man is cursed and uncontrollably loses weight. I thought that was fiction, until I came across Alice and her curse-caused eating disorder.

In a matter of two weeks, Alice had gone from being a normal, happy girl to eating less than 500 calories a day. Her mother, Marie, is a friend and reached out to me on Facebook one evening to ask me if I could help her understand this sudden change in her daughter's eating habits.

When I looked in on Alice, an older woman with hag-like features appeared in her energy field. She almost looked right out of Central Casting: old, sharp peaked nose, deep-set squinty eyes, scraggly dark hair. I got the sense that the woman was not within the immediate family, so I wondered how she would have access to Alice. I asked the angels. They showed the woman handing Alice a gift—a gift that carried a curse.

A Gift That Bore A Curse

I asked Marie if anyone had recently given Alice a present. "At first, I couldn't think of anyone, but then I realized that Alice was wearing this shirt from one of our favorite teams," Marie wrote. "She'd worn it practically every day for the last week or so. That's weird, since Alice is pretty picky about her wardrobe. Then, I realized that we'd all been given these shirts by an older woman involved with the team."

I felt a chill go up my back.

Marie did, too.

"Oh, she hates us," Marie wrote quickly. "We confronted her about some unethical things she did, and she hates all of us now." We both realized that the woman had probably put a curse on the entire family. "Come to think of it, we've had nothing but bad luck since then. That was about seven months ago, and we've just had all kinds of problems."

Alice Suddenly Begins Eating

Just then, Marie noticed something else: *Alice was eating.*

"She's eating pumpkin seeds and an apple," Marie wrote in astonishment. "She started eating the minute we began writing. But she doesn't even know I'm talking to you!" Marie was so grateful. "She hasn't eaten a single thing all day, until now." It was 6:30 in the evening.

I was relieved Alice had started eating again, but still needed to get to the bottom of the curse. I headed back inside Alice's energy field to see how to neutralize the curse.

The hag turned out to be a very powerful and dark witch. She was not happy that she had been discovered, and she hissed and clawed at me. She was no match for the Light, though, and my angels and guides quickly sent her packing.

Resisted While Destroying The Curse

Now that the hag was gone, the objects carrying the curse had to be dealt with, too. Marie and her husband had to destroy not only the shirt Alice wore, but *all* of their shirts. The angels gave extremely detailed instructions as to how to properly neutralize the spell. As the curse was placed with black magic, it was not appropriate to burn it in a fire, as this would only increase the spell's power. Instead, they had to use the power of water. It was raining that night, so the angels guided them to do a ceremony in the backyard.

However, they immediately felt resistance. "We could feel something actually clutching at our feet as we walked outside," Marie wrote. "Everything felt really heavy and oppressive. We had to do everything three and four times, because something was always getting in the way." One part of the spell-breaking required lighting a piece of paper on fire. The rain was coming down hard, so they tried to light the match under an umbrella. But the wind came up and kept blowing it out. Then the umbrella slipped out of their hands. Her husband even fell in the mud and landed in dog poop.

"It was really a nightmare out there," Maria wrote. "We could really feel her working against us."

The Family Prevails

However, they continued to follow the angels' instructions exactly. They saged the home and put some special cleansing crystals beneath Alice's bed for extra protection. The final step involved taking the entire family to the ocean, even though it was 90 minutes from their home.

Once they finished everything, the family stopped at their favorite ice cream place for a treat.

Marie wrote me a few minutes later. "OMG. *She's eating ice cream! I can't believe it!*" The next day, Alice more than tripled her food intake to a healthy 1700 calories.

When Marie's husband came home from work the next night, he noticed that the house felt lighter and happier, as if a heavy weight had been lifted from it. The family started laughing together again, too. They hadn't realized how grouchy they'd all become until they relaxed and went back to normal.

Signs of Being Under A Curse

- Bad luck, all the time, in almost every area of your life
- You can't move ahead, something always blocks you
- Money, health and relationship problems
- You take one step forward, but get knocked back
- Strange maladies that defy explanation
- String of successive losses for a period of time
- Feel heavy, oppressed, targeted
- Family members may have similar problems
- The entire family seems like it's "under a black cloud"
- You suspect you may be under a curse

What You Can Do

You can petition the angels and God to help you break the curse. Create a quiet, sacred space so that you can focus. Light a candle. This helps to create an opening and closing of the space for the process, and allows you to "blow the curse out" when you're done. Ask that you be surrounded and protected by the Light, and that everything you do be for your highest and best good, and the good of all those around you.

Breaking The Curse

Whenever you see words given in this book, you should say them exactly the way they are presented. The angels choose them carefully so that they will have the most impact. Say this with authority:

"I now ask that if there is a curse placed against me or anyone in my family or my bloodline, that it be lifted, now and forever. I ask that any deed or action done by me or anyone in my family or lineage, known or unknown, consciously or unconsciously, that may have caused or contributed to this curse, be now neutralized and cancelled by the Light forever.

"I ask that any remaining karmic debt be fully paid by the Light on my behalf, with no negative consequences for me or anyone in my family, now and forever.

"I give thanks for the lifting of this curse for me and all generations of my bloodline, ancestry and lineage, past, present and future. I am sorry for anything myself or my family did, now or in the past, to hurt anyone. I ask that these bonds be broken and severed, immediately and for all time, now and forever.

"I give great thanks to the Light for paying this debt for me, and for releasing me and my family from any evil intentions, warranted or unwarranted. I give thanks for this blessing, now and forever, and so it is, amen."

Now, blow out the candle. This represents the curse being broken. Clap your hands together hard three times to break up the energy of the

curse. Go wash your hands, and drink some water. *Do not skip this part.*
This is to purify the energy and send the negativity of the curse down the
drain.

Be reverent and grateful for the Light being willing to break the curse
and pay the debt for you, if the curse was warranted. Act accordingly, and
go forward in kindness and love.

Wait a week or so and see how things change. Some people notice
shifts immediately. If nothing seems to change, it could be because the
situation may be complicated or is not due to a curse.

---

*Regina lived her entire life under a powerful bondage that felt like
a curse. She always felt held back by forces she did not understand. Her
astounding story of liberation brings us to a whole new understanding of
God, the angels, and the ongoing battle between good and evil.*

GODS
AND
GHOULS

Ghoul

One who delights in the revolting, morbid, or loathsome.

—The Free Dictionary

21

REGINA IS FREED FROM A LIFE LIVED IN CHAINS

don't know what's wrong with me," Regina said as she approached my table at the holistic fair. "I've tried everything, but nothing works. I'm so miserable, and I don't know why."

Regina had the look and feel of a caged animal. I saw heavy silver chains wrapped all around her as I scanned her. Her hands and feet were bound by energetic shackles, too.

"You are in chains," I whispered in her ear.

"I know I am!" she cried. "But why?" She looked utterly and completely tormented.

I didn't know who or what was holding her in bondage, I only knew that I had to pray for her, right then. We bowed our heads in prayer, ignoring everything around us. The words, "You are sanctified by the Light, you are purified by the Light," came pouring from my lips, over and over. She wept as energy began to surge from my hand through the crown of her head.

"Thank you," she sobbed. "Thank you for praying for me. I feel like I can finally breathe! I've been like this for so long, and I don't know why. Thank you so much!"

Regina's case is astounding on so many levels. It was the first time I began to understand the true nature of spiritual enslavement, as well as the underlying hierarchies of the Universe. It was also the first time I got to see the abrupt physical changes in my clients, because when Regina walked into my house one month after her clearing, I did not recognize her at all.

Spiritual Enslavement From A Life Lived Long Ago

The first thing I noticed during Regina's soul clearing was that her crown chakra was in disarray. It looked like someone had just come in and smashed everything to bits. Something had damaged her brain.

Regina told me she had indeed suffered a traumatic brain injury when she was three years old. She'd fallen onto a concrete floor while jumping on a bed with her siblings. Her mom rushed in to find blood seeping from her ear.

This led to a lifelong struggle with cognitive problems, and learning disabilities. Her home life was chaotic and scary. Her father was often drunk and violent. Her parents fought.

Love of God

Religion was Regina's only outlet. She threw herself into gospel songs, Christian music and scripture. "I now had someone to save me from all the troubles in my life. I clung to every word in the Bible, because my life was a living hell. It was like a demon was inside my Dad. I often thought that he must be the devil, but if I just prayed hard enough to God, maybe he would change."

This would be the first time Regina looked to God to help her. She felt safe and happy at church. Like so many people, she found comfort in the 23rd Psalm. It was the first scripture she ever memorized. As a young girl, she proudly recited it before the entire congregation.

The Lord's Prayer ~ A psalm of David
The Lord is my shepherd, I shall not want.
He makes me lie down in green pastures,
He leads me beside still waters, He restores my soul.
He guides me in paths of righteousness for His name's sake.
Even though I walk through the valley of the shadow of death,
I will fear no evil, for You are with me;
Your rod and your staff, they comfort me.
You prepare a table before me in the presence of my enemies.
You anoint my head with oil; my cup overflows.
Surely goodness and love will follow me all the days of my life, and
I will dwell in the house of the Lord forever.

A few years later, Regina taught herself to play piano. She spent hours playing and singing old-time hymns. Later, she joined a church choir. When she turned 12, she joined a religious service organization for girls. "Even though I had low self-esteem, and despite all the things that were happening, I tried to be a positive person. Eventually, I was called, "Bubbly Reg." I exuded happiness, because everything was focused around being a good person and being of service. It taught us about God's light. I prayed every day to be part of God's Light."

"I Don't Feel Alive"

Every day was still a struggle at home, though. Inside, Regina felt strangely oppressed. One day she came home from school and told her mother that she didn't feel alive. Her mother took her to a psychologist. Regina became more convinced that she was worthless and that there was something irrevocably wrong with her. She spent the rest of her teenage years trying to escape her father's rages and gather some self-esteem.

Shortly after high school, she got married and started a family. It was supposed to be the American Dream, but it was still a nightmare. Like so many others, Regina tried to flee her childhood, but ended up repeating it. She felt more trapped and miserable than ever. She prayed to God to help her, to make life easier.

But nothing changed. Whoever God was, He didn't seem to care about Regina. In 2001, she joined a growing mega-church in Orange County, California, hoping it would help. Instead, she just felt more isolated and confused.

No Help From Religion

"Week after week, I sat in the pews and listened to sermons, but nothing seemed to change. I really started to believe that religion had failed me," Regina told me. "No matter how positive I tried to be and how much I prayed, nothing changed. My husband constantly told me I was negative, so I started to believe it. It felt like something had dominion over me.

I screamed at God in the car and in the house: '*If there is a God, why don't you help me?*'"

Regina's soul earnestly cried out to God, over and over, throughout her life. But like so many of us, God did not help her.

Why? Why doesn't God come? Why are we allowed to suffer at the hands of evil?

Regina's Angelic Soul Clearing™ held the answers not just for her, but for ALL humanity. What I learned changed me forever and brought peace to many clients since. Perhaps it will help you, too.

First, the angels repaired the broken circuitry in Regina's brain. This helped her think more clearly. Then they moved on to her throat chakra. Regina's voice was completely gone. In its place, I saw only a division of light and dark. When I asked why the darkness was there, it said, "She's ours."

This was unexpected, because Regina is a wonderful, loving person. There is no way she would ever knowingly sign her soul over to anything but the Light. I didn't know what to do, so I asked the angels. To my surprise, they said, *"Ask to see the paperwork!"*

Show The Deed To Her Soul

Paperwork? What were they talking about?

I did what they said. I asked the Dark for proof of its claim to her soul. Instantly a long, off-white scroll appeared, with the date "1400" etched in black ink at the top. It looked like a contract of some sort. I was still confused, so I asked to be shown where this contract originated.

I saw Regina tied to a stake. She looked like she was in her late twenties. Her hair was darker and a little more reddish. She wore a white peasant dress laced at the bodice. I sensed that she was an independent woman and an herbalist, which made her a "witch" to the provincial rulers of that time.

I knew Regina did not deserve to have her soul handed over to the devil. So why did he have it? I fast-forwarded through time. She was literally squirming and screaming from the flames, about to be burned alive. As they often did in those terrible times, the townspeople tortured the women until they proclaimed their allegiance to Satan, even when no such allegiance ever existed. However, in that awful moment, as the false proclamation flew from her lips, the Dark literally said, "We'll take that!" and snatched her soul.

Dirty Pool

Soul-snatching? Scrolls and contracts? My mind was reeling. How could they trick her like that? I was also angry. It wasn't fair. With the

angels behind me, I announced in no uncertain terms that that was "dirty pool" and the Dark did not have a right to her soul. I demanded they give it back.

The Dark was not eager to give up its prize. However, the angels showed up with a small, white rectangular piece of paper with tiny writing on it—the rightful deed to Regina's soul. They held it high for the Dark to see. After a few moments of arguing back and forth, the Dark relented. The angels ripped up the contract. Then they rushed in and turned all the shredded pieces to Light, making sure that everything associated with this unfair deal was neutralized forever.

Regina Feels Free For The First Time

"Oh my God!" Regina cried. "I can feel it. I am free! Ever since I was a little girl, all I ever wanted was to be free. I used to pray, 'God, please, please, please free me.' At the time, I didn't know why I needed that so desperately, but it was all my soul craved. Even in my college psychology class I wrote that I literally felt like a prisoner, bound in chains."

Regina thanked me profusely. She wanted to do another session for her lower chakras, but had to go out of town for about a month to help a family member. During that time, I held a psychic party and invited about 25 people for mini-readings (you can see the video by searching You Tube for "Margo Mateas giving readings" or at *https://www.youtube.com/watch?v=jxkb_PdyzPA*).

Just as I was about to get started, a woman showed up at the front door. I didn't recognize her, yet the minute she saw me she lit up into a huge smile and said, "Hi, Margo! I can't believe I made it!" When I still looked confused, she laughed heartily and told me, "It's Regina!"

Changed So Much I Did Not Recognize Her

I could not believe it. She was so radiantly happy and healthy that I did not even recognize her as the same haunted, desperate woman I'd met just a month ago.

Regina traveled over nine hours that day to reach my party in time, so I offered to let her stay the night. Over breakfast the next morning, she told me about a special part of her trip.

"I went to my cousin's house, way out in the wilderness. On my first day there, we went to a beautiful waterfall hidden in the canyons. All I could do was stand there and let the sound fill me up. I have been around many sounds of water, but nothing like this. My soul was taking in every ounce of the sound of that water. For the very first time in my life, I was actually connected to my own soul. I thought, 'This is what I have been searching for all of my life. Could it be that I finally found what I was looking for?' What I realized at that moment was that Margo and the Angels really must have freed me from my chains."

We finished the rest of her chakra work the next morning after breakfast. The angels told Regina they wanted her to write affirmations to bolster her sagging self-esteem.

Regina chose these particular affirmations because she wanted them

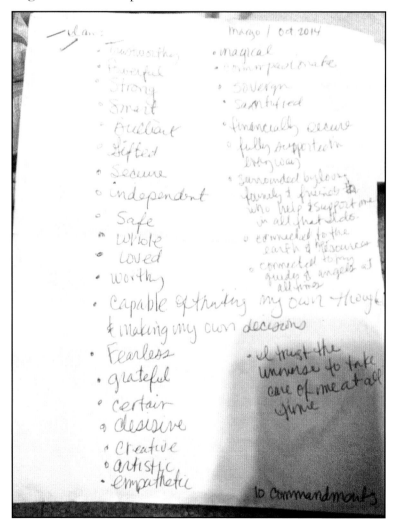

desperately. As she wrote them on my kitchen table, they seemed like lofty, unattainable goals, things she could only dream about; not things she ever thought would come true. However, they started to happen immediately.

Job Of Her Dreams Two Days Later

Just two days after her session, Regina got a phone call from Saddleback College asking her to start work part-time. She'd applied for that job before, but didn't get it. Now, out of the blue, they said they wanted her to start right away. That quickly morphed into a permanent part-time job, helping special needs students like her succeed at the very same college she graduated from. Regina graduated magna cum laude from Saddleback

College in 2013. Her story is so inspiring that she was selected to be the Student Speaker at the 2013 graduation. You can see her speech online by searching for "*Saddleback College Student Speaker 2013.*"

"I feel like a totally different person now. Everything about me has changed—everything." Regina told me.

"Today, I love myself. I accept myself. Most importantly, I am proud of myself and all I've done to overcome everything against me.

"I believe each and every one of those affirmations, and they seemed so foreign the first time I said them. But now, they live inside me.

"I have the job of my dreams—it seems truly custom-made for me. I am so very grateful, grateful beyond words, for what you and the angels did for me. I only wish I had found you sooner."

The Most Important Truth Of All

Regina's transformation was a turning point in both of our lives. She helped me learn the most profound truth of all. She opened my eyes to the spiritual world of laws and contracts—and who is *really* running things here on Earth.

The instant Regina's soul contract was severed, the angels rushed in and immersed her in love. They told her over and over again how much they loved her, how much they'd wanted to help her, how terribly sorry that they had not been able to help her before. They were genuinely apologetic, and so full of compassion. I actually wept their tears for Regina.

The angels quickly explained that they had desperately wanted to help Regina all her life, but *couldn't*. They said they had been *locked out of her energy field,* because *someone else* had laid claim to her.

What? How could this be? Isn't God all-powerful? Aren't angels supposed to come to us, whenever we ask for them? Aren't we always under God's Divine protection and care?

Angels Prevented From Helping Regina

The angels explained that the Earth is not really God's. They said that it is currently "owned" by the Dark—and that evil forces often prevent them from helping us. They showed me a verse in the Bible that illustrated this point. Daniel was waiting for angels to answer his prayers, but no one came. Finally, an angel appeared before him and explained why:

"Do not fear, Daniel, for from the first day that you set your heart to understand, and to humble yourself before your God, your words were heard; and I have come because of your words. **But the prince of the kingdom of Persia withstood me twenty-one days; and behold, Michael, one of the chief princes, came to help me, for I had been left alone there with the kings of Persia."** *(Daniel 10:12-13).*

We know that Archangel Michael is a warrior angel. In this passage, the angel explains that he was held at bay by opposing forces who fought him for 21 days, and that the only way he was able to get free was by the aid of another angel. This suggests that a war was going on—a war that kept the forces of Light from being able to assist people when they needed them. Are we at war? Is there a battle between good and evil, after all? The Apostle Paul answers this in Ephesians 6:12:

We Are Involved In a Cosmic War

"For our struggle is not against human opponents, but against rulers, authorities, cosmic powers in the darkness around us, and evil spiritual forces in the heavenly realm."

This passage explains so much about what's really going on in our world, don't you think? This really speaks to the reality that everyone in this book experienced, and the suffering that so many continue to endure at the hands of these "rulers, authorities and evil spiritual forces." This passage reveals so many hidden truths about life here on Earth:

a) There is a cosmic war between good and evil
b) People are not at war with other humans
c) God is not the only power in the cosmos
d) The Universe is governed by rules and authorities
e) There are "cosmic powers" who operate in the darkness
f) Darkness surrounds us here on Earth
g) There are "evil spiritual forces" in the heavenly realm

God Is NOT All-Powerful On Earth

Let's take a minute and let this sink in. So what does this really mean for us? We have all wondered: if God is truly in charge here, why is there such suffering, war and disease? How can people be so corrupt and heartless, if a loving God is in absolute control of our world?

Jesus explains the truth about Earth to his disciples. In John 14:30, Jesus tells His disciples that He has to leave them because a new ruler of Earth is coming.

"I will not speak with you much longer, for the ruler of the world (Satan) is coming..."

Darkness Rules The Earth And Its People

So, the answer to that age-old question is: No. God is not all-powerful on the Earth.

God is not in charge here. Darkness does rule this world: "We know that we originate with God, but the whole world is lying in the power of the wicked one." *(1 John 5:19).*

According to Biblical scholars, this happened during the "fall from Heaven," when Lucifer, originally an angel of God, became jealous of God and wanted to usurp his authority and got Adam and Eve to believe him and not God in the Garden of Eden. Hence, the torment of humans began.

Satan is further mentioned throughout the Bible as "the tempter," "the great Deceiver," and the "Prince of the Air" (you'll read more about this in the Galactic section).

The Bible Confirms That Satan Causes Suffering

Peter lets us know that people all over the world are being tormented and oppressed by this dark force: "Be sober and alert. Your adversary the devil prowls around like a roaring lion, seeking someone to devour.

Resist him, standing firm in your faith and in the knowledge that your brothers throughout the world are undergoing the same kinds of suffering.... (1 Peter 5:8)

Darkness IS trying to oppress you. People everywhere have been undergoing this same kind of torment and oppression for more than 2,000 years. The Bible calls this "spiritual warfare" and acknowledges that we are under spiritual attack. This is such a relief for so many of my clients, who mistakenly blamed themselves for their suffering or thought they must be imagining it all.

Somehow, everything just clicks into place once you realize that God is not in charge on the Earth. This explains war and hatred and violence. This explains corruption and fear and the worship of money. This explains why sometimes we feel the presence and power of God, and sometimes we don't.

Regina Was A Prisoner Of War

Regina was essentially taken as a prisoner of war. Her soul was stolen and kept by the enemy for hundreds of years. This is probably due to the fact that she carries a lot of Light. The more Light you emit, the more valuable you are.

I've negotiated many soul releases that involve the Light having to "pay for" the soul in question. I've seen Jesus go to the angels and come back holding what looks like a bouquet of individual lights in his hand, and exchange it for just one soul. So, it appears that some souls have more Light than others.

"Suppress The Light"

Regina is not the only person to have her soul unfairly stolen and kept as ransom by the Dark. I can't tell you how many times the Dark and its emissaries have told me their job was to "suppress the Light." I've seen this over and over again with my clients. I've battled it myself many times, but didn't recognize it as being an attack from the enemy. Back in the summer of 2005, I returned from a business trip very depressed. I had sudden and overwhelming suicidal thoughts, just like Cristin. I tuned into myself, and realized that these were not my own thoughts. I wondered if I might be under spiritual attack.

I sat down and meditated. I saw a map of points of light, like a battle map of the United States. It was all black, except for various circles and dots of light. Some lights were bigger than others.

I saw my light on the map. It stood out because it was a bit bigger and brighter than the rest of the ones in that region. Whoever launched this attack saw this bright light and decided, "If we take out this one, we will have a strategic advantage in this area." So they invaded my thoughts and tried to get me to kill myself. It was the first time I'd seen the galactic war in action (we will talk about that later, in Galactic Invaders).

Thankfully, I turned to Jan Antonelli for help (see Resources). She saw that I was indeed being targeted for "removal." She intervened for me the way that I intervened for Cristin, and the thoughts disappeared immediately.

Bright Lights in the Darkest Places

If you have encountered extreme oppression, abuse, neglect or turmoil in your life, it may be because the Dark has targeted you in order to suppress your light. The more light you radiate, the lighter the world becomes. If this world generates a lot of light, then the darkness is driven back. Think of what a candle does to a dark room. I've seen so many special, loving, kind and creative people be abused on this Earth that I use to say, "God puts the brighest candles in the darkest rooms."

The reason for this was a mystery to me. It made me so sad. Why? Why would a loving God put his most tender and precious souls in the midst of such darkness and abuse? It never made sense to me. The truth is, it's never made sense to anyone. *God can't be both all-powerful and not come to people when they need Him.* When we accept the truth, life here on Earth begins to make more sense.

You May Be A Cosmic 'Prisoner of War'

When we understand that many of us have been "prisoners of war," we realize that the enemy is using every tactical advantage to weaken us. In war, it is common to shoot at soldiers, bomb their bases and hospitals, remove their means of communication, overthrow their strongholds and and invade their countries. Lies, deception and subterfuge are also weapons of war. An enemy may also prevent much-needed supplies such as food, additional troops and medical aid from reaching the troops in order to erode morale and weaken the opposition.

The Dark May Prevent God From Helping You

If you have been at war, you know how terrifying it is to find yourself cut off from support at a time when you need it the most. I'm sure many of you reading this book have experienced your own "dark night of the soul" in which you felt cut off from God and support. It is one of the most anguishing things a human can feel. I now believe that these experiences are not just part of the human condition.

I believe that these are highly orchestrated forms of spiritual attack, designed to get us to stop believing in God. After all, why would you continue to devote yourself to the Light or helping people, if you are not receiving the basic care needed for yourself?

In order to suppress the Light and hold it back, the Dark puts a claim on you. It then riddles you with pain, negativity, confusion and torment. This reduces the overall light in the world and also make it easier for them to erode your faith. They may actually move into your system through some form of energetic dragon or dark entity to impede you further.

Being A Prisoner Makes You Their 'Property'

Let's look more at the concept of being a spiritual or energetic "prisoner of war" (POW). When someone is captured, they are now the possession of the opposing army. *It also technically makes that person their "property."* When you are a spiritual prisoner of war, this is why the Dark thinks it has a claim on you. This is why you must produce the deed to your soul in order to be rescued. This is why sometimes your release must be negotiated. Does this make sense now?

The Bible understands that divine intervention may be needed to break the power of the Dark: "*For the weapons of our warfare are not of the flesh, but have divine power to destroy strongholds.*" (*NIV, 2 Corinthians 10:4*) The Bible also speaks to the negotiation process of having to intervene for a soul like Regina:

Ephesians 3:10 "…so that through the church the manifold wisdom of God might now be made known *to the rulers and authorities in the heavenly places.*" This gives me chills. Not only does it say that we break "strongholds," but that we have to prove God's claim to us to the "rulers and authorities in the heavenly places." Another reference to the fact that God is not alone ruling the Cosmos!

Did You Come To Help Win This War?

Many people, including myself, have some sense of being here for a grand purpose. We secretly identify with the hero or heroine, wanting to save the day. Well, now is your chance. The stakes are high and you are needed. Do you feel you may have chosen or been selected to help Earth at this incredible time? Some people feel strongly that they are not actually "from

Earth," but came here from other places, such as Heaven or other star systems, to help Earth win this epic battle, and finally become a planet of peace.

The angels really want you to know how much they love you. They really want you to know that God did not abandon you. God's angels, (another word of emissary or messenger) were kept out, just like the angel who tried to help Daniel. **They want you to know that God did not place you in the darkness.**

God Did Not Abandon You

As the Career Cards say, *"The terrible things that were done to you were not done by your Creator. Never have you been abandoned or hurt by the Universe."*

You have been hurt and abandoned not because God doesn't love you, but because God's angels were kept from helping you.

This is why you have suffered, and why God did not come all the times you have called. God may have placed angels around you at various times in your life, when you didn't even know they were there.

You may also have experienced angelic intervention or miracles you couldn't explain. This is proof that God and the forces of Light are always with you; they just cannot always take physical form to protect you in the ways they would like to. The angels have saved me many, many times in very obvious ways, including saving me from falling off a mountain, and literally lifting me high in the air to avoid tripping over a dangerous hazard in the roadway. Those are the times I know God is with me.

But what about those times when we feel so alone and scared? I had a very unexpected realization during a therapy session about 10 years ago. I was telling the therapist about a time when I had hidden in a closet, away from my parents' fighting. She asked me to go back into my memory of that dark closet.

I went back in time and saw myself, a little girl, huddled inside the closet in the fetal position, with my arms wrapped tightly around my legs, listening to the violent sounds outside my room.

Angel In The Closet With Me

In that frightening moment, she asked me a simple question: *"Is anyone in the closet with you?"* At first I thought, "What a silly question. Of course there's no one in the closet with me!" But then, I looked across the closet and actually saw a bright white light and angel wings—right there with me! I hadn't had the eyes to see or feel that as a little scared girl, but I could look back and see it so clearly then. *Turns out, I had not been alone in those terrifying moments —and I bet you were not, either.*

Why Angels Cannot Stop Bad Things From Happening

We often think, "Why doesn't God stop the evil in this world? If the angels love us, why don't they jump in and prevent things from happening?"

People do bad things because they are occupied or influenced by the Dark.

In order for angels to be able to prevent us from being abused, they would have to jump into the body that is possessed by the Dark and kick them out—and they can't do that because the Dark has already laid claim to it and locked them out.

Plus, angels do not invade or possess people. They have absolute respect for your choices and sovereignty and respect your free will. This is why healers such as myself can only help with your permission. The Light considers it a very serious violation to even peer into another person's energetic space without permission. Yet the Dark uses all kinds of tools to invade, manipulate, permeate and possess us so that it can use human beings to do its evil deeds.

Here's The Good News: The Light Always Prevails

In all of my travels through time and dimensions and galaxies for my clients, I can tell you that the Light wins, every time!

Light is the supreme Power in the Universe. The Light is the assembled forces of God and Good, everywhere. They take many forms, but they are all serving the principles of love, justice, honor, truth and freedom.

These forces all care about you. They want you to be happy. They want you to be free. They want you to shine your Light throughout the entire Universe. These forces all work together for the common good. They are everywhere, in everything and are innumerable. They are all part of what we know to be "God."

So, God IS all-powerful *(just not on Earth)*.

Divine Grace and Mercy

Everyone in this book was rescued from the clutches of the Dark. The Light did whatever it had to do to save them and set them free. They are so grateful to be rescued—and to know that they are not to blame for their suffering.

They were already tormented. Yet most of them somehow found a way to blame themselves, accepting the belief that they had somehow "chosen" this or "agreed to it" in order to "make them a better person."

So many of my clients (Remember Vanessa and Lisa?) refused to get angry at the people who had abused them and turned that rage on themselves instead. The New Age movement taught them that they were responsible for everything that happens in their world, making them to blame.

"New Age Bullshit"

As long as you blame and hate yourself, you will not hold the Dark accountable. It's an isidious and evil manipulation, this idea that you are God; that evil does not exist; that you create everything that happens in your world; and that you should never, ever get angry with anything because "you chose it." Can you see how very disempowering and cunning this is?

This belief is a tool of the Dark. It is meant to keep you blind to the true cause of your suffering. How can you go after the real culprit, if you think you are responsible for everything?

According to former Satanic High Priest Mark Passio, many of these beliefs were actually constructed by the Dark to enslave

humanity. Watch his video, *"New Age Bullshit"* on YouTube. He has a lot to say. I really agree with all 15 points he makes.

Do Not Blame Yourself For Abuse Or Neglect

The Apostle Peter said that we should have compassion for ourselves and for others throughout the world who are suffering as a result of this spiritual warfare, too. He didn't blame anyone for their struggles. The angels show extreme compassion for our strife. They always say they are so sorry the person suffered.

For many of my clients, this is the first time in their lives that anyone has acknowleged or apologized for what happened. Many times, my tears are the only ones that have been spilled for their tragedies. Prior to this, they either believed that God didn't love them or had abandoned them, or thought they had actually signed up to be abused—"for their own good." This just breaks my heart.

Kindness and Compassion For Yourself

The angels ALWAYS come forward with compassion. They are gentle and kind. **They remind the person that their lesson is NOT to take responsibility for the actions and karma of another, but to actually open their hearts and have compassion and *love for themselves*.** Compassion for yourself is key.

In most cases, the angels show the reason for what happened. Sometimes the abuser was possessed. Sometimes it was the result of a curse. Sometimes spiritual parasites and energetic dragons were involved. Sometimes, people were just overwhelmed. Many times they did not receive love and nurturing and didn't know how to be good parents. Hurt people, hurt people.

Perpetrator Took Full Responsibility

I'll never forget one of the first times I talked to someone on the Other Side. I was 23 years old, and my partner at the time had suffered immensely at the hands of her father. He did heinous things to her that no father should ever do. This abuse permanently damaged her mind, spirit and body.

One day when I was doing a healing session on her, her father appeared to me in a vision. He was wearing an off-white colored robe, and was crying. He said, "Where I've been, I've seen everything I've done, and I am so sorry." He asked what he could do to help. I told her he had to let her go. Prior to this, she always said that she felt like her father's hand was holding onto her from the grave. He said he understood, then left.

"I Will Be Denied Sexuality"

There was an immediate improvement in her recovery. She began to feel freer and happier. She continued to deal with the aftermath of the abuse. About 10 years later, her father came through in a session with a psychic. At that time, he took full responsibility for everything he had ever done to her. He admitted his own depravity and selfishness. He told her it was not her fault. He said everything a victim of sexual abuse longs to hear. It was so incredibly sincere and honest.

Interestingly, he told her that he would be denied sexuality for seven lifetimes because of the way he had abused it with her. This is referring to the concept of karma, the belief that "what goes around, comes around" and that we have time and opportunity to learn from our mistakes and do better in the next lifetime.

Notice that he did NOT blame her or say she "chose" what happened to her. He did not say that she needed to have her body and soul broken apart in order to become a good person. He was very clear that HE was the bad person, and was 100 percent responsible for his actions.

What You Need To Know

1. God is the Supreme force in the Universe and ultimately, the forces of Light always prevail.
2. God is not all-powerful in the Earthly realm.
3. God and the angels do love you and want to help you.
4. Humans are involved in a cosmic battle between good and evil.
5. The Earth is ruled by the Dark. This is why there are wars, violence and hatred.

6. You may be persecuted by the Dark in an attempt to subvert your light.
7. The Dark may have stolen your soul.
8. A spiritual intervention may be needed to free you and restore your soul to the Light.
9. The Light is often prevented from reaching you in the same way that help and supplies are prevented from reaching armies during a war.
10. The Bible confirms that humans battle "rulers and authorities" and cosmic powers.
11. You are not responsible for the evil that has been done to you.
12. You did not need to be abused in order to learn how to be a good person. You were already a good person—that's why life has been hard.
13. It is appropriate to be angry at the people who hurt you. Stop blaming yourself.
14. You are not God. Only God is God.
15. The lesson is to love yourself and have compassion for your own suffering.

What You Can Do

- Break the soul contract.
- Forgive God for not being there for you.
- Know that God does love you and will heal you.
- Don't be manipulated by any belief system.
- Let God be God, so you can experience Grace.

Brandy came to me because she believed she must have done something horribly wrong to turn her son against her. When she discovered the truth, everything changed and she knew without a doubt that God loved her.

22

BRANDY AND THE SON WHO WAS SENT TO VEX HER

Brandy tugged urgently on my arm as I finished a talk on "Releasing Pain and Trauma With The Angels" in 2014. She was dressed head to toe in beautiful layers of white linen with a matching turban. She carried herself regally, but the worried look on her face revealed a deep anxiety.

"I know this is going to sound crazy," she said, "but I think my son was sent to vex me. I'm having a terrible time with him. He's only twelve, but he's talking back and giving me nothing but problems."

"He Was Sent To Vex Me"

Having been a stepmother to two teenage boys myself, I initially thought she was dealing with typical rebellion. But, I agreed to do a session for her. True enough, there was a battle going on inside her. I saw an immense battlefield just inside her solar plexus. The skies were dark and heavy, the air thick with gunpowder. Canons exploded all around. The ground was bombed out and desolate.

There were no soldiers, so I looked ahead to see who was in charge of the battle. Through the smoke, I saw a dark figure perched atop a large iron cannon. Behind him, the sky above the landscape split into light and dark.

As I got closer and the smoke cleared, I saw the leader more clearly. It was a young African-American boy, who looked between 12 and 14 years old.

My breath caught in my throat with the realization: *Oh my God. Brandy's son.*

A Soldier For The Dark

I asked the young man what he was doing there. He casually nodded to the dark side of the sky and said, "They sent me." When I asked why, he said, "To bother her, distract her." When I asked him why the Dark would want to do that, he just shrugged and said, "To suppress the Light."

Wow. I took a deep breath and steadied myself. How do you tell a mother that her son really was sent by the devil to torment her?

I hesitantly told Brandy what I'd seen. She burst into sobs. "I *knew* it! I knew he was sent to test me! *I knew it in my soul,* but I didn't want to believe it!" She explained that she had been born into a family of drug dealers and alcoholics, who even named her after alcohol. "I am nothing like any of them, and they constantly put me down for it," she said. "They tell me I am bad and wrong and don't appreciate family. I am the black sheep because I don't use drugs or drink. They say I should be ashamed because I love the Lord."

Brandy told me she moved out of state to get away from them, but they haunted her dreams and said they would never let her go. To make matters worse, Brandy's mother insisted on speaking to her grandson nearly every day, despite Brandy's protests.

Brandy's Pain Is Removed

Brandy began to cry again. "I doubted myself all my life," she said. "I thought I was bad and evil and they were good. I was soooo different. I never wanted that life—all the lying and stealing and drugs and violence and prison. That was never me. But they made me feel like I was the bad one, the wrong one." Waves of relief washed over her as she realized the truth.

I asked the angels to take away her pain. Light upon Light, army after army, they came, removing the stain of the lie that she wasn't good enough, that she was dirty and wrong. She felt their warmth and love surround her. "Hallelujah!" she cried as the shame left her. "I feel so peaceful! It's like a huge burden has been lifted and I can breathe again!"

Soul Washed Clean

Brandy felt cleansed and made clean. In her soul, she knew that God loved her, but she'd always wondered what terrible thing she had done to make her son turn against her.

Just then, something dawned on her. Her son had to live in a state-run group home because of his violent outbursts. On his last home visit, he stopped abruptly outside her front door and wouldn't go inside. When Brandy asked him what was wrong, he shot her a menacing look and demanded, 'Tell me where the Holy Water is. I know it's in there.'

"Where Is The Holy Water?"

Brandy gasped. "How on Earth did he know that? There was some Holy Water in the desk in the living room, just a few feet inside the front door. And even worse: why would he care?"

Now, she understood everything. It all clicked together. The nagging in her gut, her close relationship with God, her son's increasing attacks on her.

She realized the truth.

Her son hated her *because* of her Light, not because she had done anything wrong.

Brandy finally forgave herself, knowing that she hadn't failed as a mother. Everything in her life made sense now. "I'm really not like my family! Thank God!" Her soul flooded with relief.

Hated For Her Goodness

"My soul was set free that day," Brandy believes. "I had been in Hell for so long, not knowing the truth from their lies. But that day, everything became crystal clear. I realized that I am a beautiful child of God—and I am in the Light. God loves me, no matter what."

In Brandy's case, though the truth was not easy, it did set her free. Her soul is no longer tormented. She detached from her son, but still prays for him. She knows who her enemies are, even if they are "family." She knows that her true home is not with flesh and blood, but with an eternal family who waits for her in Heaven.

* See Brandy's testimonial and others at www.freedbythelight.com

---

Brandy was fortunate in that she was not the one afflicted with darkness. Things were far more complicated for Samuel, who was experiencing karma from having been a Nazi in his previous life.

23

SAMUEL'S SOUL IS TRAPPED BETWEEN WORLDS

We often hear the term, "lost soul," but in late October of 2016, I actually encountered a truly lost soul who was really trapped between Heaven and Hell. Ironically, Samuel called me from the Netherlands to tell me that he didn't feel that he belonged on Earth. Samuel said it was a cold, wet and rainy night as he settled into his car for our session. However, the bleakness outside was no match for the gloom within his soul. He spoke of being vacant and depressed.

"I feel like a ghost most of the time. People literally do not see me. And when they do see me, they don't like me. They move away from me. I feel like I don't belong in this world. I don't know where I belong on this planet. *I do not belong here. I don't know why I am here.*"

"I Do Not Belong Here"

Unlike many of my Career Card clients who search for their life purpose, Samuel's story had a dark, cold ring of truth to it that chilled me to the bone. *This was a man who was telling me that his soul really did not belong here.* As we began to talk and I opened to his energy field, a wave of nausea hit me. I pushed it away and focused on helping him. I tried to be positive and upbeat, and reassured him that the soul clearing process helps everyone, and that I would do my best to give him more light and peace. "Thank you," he said with a deep weariness.

Not surprisingly, Samuel was inside a large, dark energetic dragon (you'll learn more about them later.) This explained his feelings of disconnection and alienation. The dragon said that it had been there for over a hundred years, and was effectively the guardian of Samuel's soul.

Numerous other dark entities made themselves known as I looked further inside him. This explained why people avoided Samuel and did not want to be around him.

Since there was so much darkness within Samuel, I asked to be shown the deed for his soul so that I could either affirm his place in the Light or begin to negotiate his release from the Dark.

To my surprise, no one showed up.

No one.

No One Claimed His Soul

Samuel felt like the wretched wraiths you see in the movies, cursed to walk the Earth without actually being a part of it. It felt like a form of Hell, or a punishment of some sort. But could a soul truly be lost? I could see now that Samuel's description of himself was not exaggerated. He was trapped in a dismal "netherland."

When I asked to see what had caused this punishment or karma, I saw Samuel in a succession of lives in which he was merciless and cruel. In one scene, he looked like a Nazi. He wore a dark grey and black uniform and forced thin, desperate people behind bars. The angels showed him being tyrannical and heartless, lifetime after lifetime.

At this point, the only way I could see to bring Samuel's soul into the Light was to ask for salvation. I asked him what he thought about asking Jesus to come into his heart and life. "Oh, I would love that," he said instantly. "Please!"

The angels had me stand up. My body started trembling as I literally felt the power of God begin to gather around us. During this impromptu call-and-response, I paced back and forth in my office like a priest, making the sign of the cross constantly as I listened carefully and repeated exactly what the angels told me to say.

Karma For A Cruel Past

The angels are always forgiving, always compassionate, always easygoing. But, they took Samuel to task. They asked pointedly: "Do you now ask forgiveness for all the sins of your past? Are you completely repentant for your many transgressions?"

The word "many" seemed harsh to me, and I didn't want to say it. However, I say precisely what the angels dictate, because they are outstanding cosmic lawyers. They know exactly how to word things to break, sever and dissolve contracts. Their words are also chosen carefully to give the soul precisely the form of deliverance, forgiveness, mercy, compassion and healing required. The reason they do this is because words have power. Remember in Genesis, *"In the beginning, there was the Word."* Words speak law into action.

Even though I felt badly, Samuel took it all without anger or questioning. He wept when the angels asked him if he wanted to atone for his sins.

What It Means To Be "Sanctified and Purified"

Remember how the angels told Regina she was "sanctified and purified in the Light" again and again when I prayed over her? The angels used this phrase with Samuel, too. I always thought it just meant to be cleansed of sin and negativity. However, it means much more than that:

To Be Sanctified

- **To set apart as or declare holy; consecrate, make sacred, dedicate to God**

- **Make legitimate or binding by religious sanction; support, authorize, legitimize**

- **Free from sin; purify; absolve**

By asking Samuel if he wanted to be sanctified, the angels were telling him they would "set him apart" and "declare him as holy." This means that they took him out of the dark and set him aside as theirs. They also gave their authorization for him to come out of the dark and into the Light, and then made that action legally binding within the cosmos.

To Be Purified

Now that he had been brought under the protection and legal authority of the Light, he was also "purified," which means that he was made free from anything that debases, pollutes or contaminates their spirits, such as darkness. The angels also freed him from foreign or objectionable elements, such as energetic invaders. Finally, being "purified" actually frees him from evil or guilt.

I told you angels are pretty smart! "Sanctified and purified" are two very powerful words!

Samuel agreed to be taken in by the Light, and asked for his soul to be made new in Christ. "I can see and feel the angels!" he said in astonishment as they surrounded him. He sobbed when they told him all past contracts were cancelled and previous bonds were broken.

Jesus appeared, triumphantly holding the deed to Samuel's soul. Samuel was so relieved. He said he felt lighter and more peaceful. He thanked me again for helping to bring his soul to the Light, and delivering him from the endless torture of walking the Earth like a ghostly nomad. I felt like this was a beginning for him, but that he would have to live his life differently to continue to earn his place in the Light.

The angels told him to be kind, to help the downtrodden, and to never again act out of cruelty. Hopefully this will be a new start for his soul.

What You Need To Know

- Souls can be stuck between worlds.
- You can find peace and forgiveness through the Light.
- The Light will love and accept you, even if you previously renounced God.
- Jesus will often "pay the price" to "purchase" your soul from the Dark, regardless of your religion or belief.
- Karma is essential for the soul, as it provides justice, accountability, healing and redemption for all.
- Redemption must sometimes be followed by good works to balance

your karma and demonstrate your commitment to the Light.

- The Light may ask you to choose it so that you can come under its protection and care.
- The Light demands nothing from you, and your life will only get better by choosing to live in the Light.
- You always have Free Will here on Earth. You are free to choose the Light, the Dark or nothing at all.

What You Can Do

- Ask to be sanctified, purified and protected by the Light.

- Ask Jesus to pay your remaining soul debt and to let you start over in service to the Light. Ask the Light to cancel any negative soul contracts you may have knowingly or unknowingly allowed.

- If you feel unhappy or angry at God, search your soul and see where you may have abandoned the Light, either in this life or in previous ones.

- See if you are able to forgive God, now that you know God and the angels may have been prevented from helping you.

Like Samuel, Chryssa told me she felt vacant. I thought it was just a metaphor—until I saw what had actually consumed her.

24

CHRYSSA IS CAUGHT
IN A SPIDER'S WEB

Chryssa embraced the Dark side and everything associated with it. As a surly and rebellious teen, Chryssa rejected God and hung out with dark beings. Even as a forty-something design professional, she didn't do anything without Rammstein or Marilyn Manson blaring in the background. She delighted in everything macabre, sinister and shadowy. Halloween was her favorite time of year. "I absolutely hate Christmas and every other holiday," she told me with zeal.

However, Chryssa wasn't so sure about the Dark anymore. A permeating void had overtaken every aspect of her life. "I feel dead inside," she told me. "I don't feel like I'm really alive. Everything feels dark and blank."

"Vacant And Dead Inside"

She went on to tell me that her feelings for her husband had changed too, and that she was unable to feel love toward him, or anyone—including herself. As I began to scan her energy field, she spoke again of the strange emptiness within. "I don't know what it is," she said. "In the past, I always felt that I was present and making choices. But now, I feel as though nothing is inside of me. I am totally vacant. I want that to change.."

At first, I had trouble accessing Chryssa's energy field. I drew a blank when trying to connect with her. I wasn't sure who or what was blocking me. Since I was unable to get into her energy, I zoomed out to get a wider view. As soon as I did, I saw that Chryssa was stuck in a giant spider web. Layers and layers of webbing surrounded her. She was bound in a thick, white cocoon.

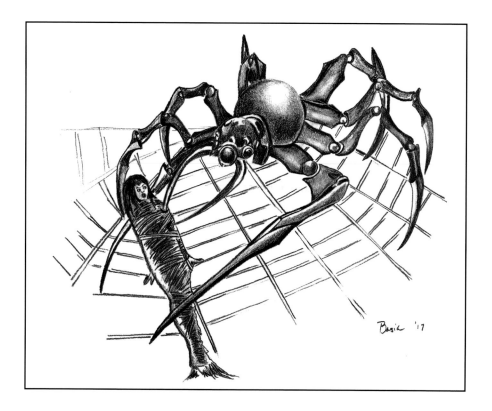

The Spider

I adjusted my gaze upward. A massive, black spider had long fangs thrust deep within her chest. It had liquefied her insides and sucked them out. Everything below her neck was hollowed out and empty. Her heart and internal organs were gone.

I gasped. *Chryssa was right. She was vacant inside!*

This explained her feelings of emptiness and her profound sense of detachment, as well as why I could not see into her energy.

I approached the spider. It indicated it had owned Chryssa for a long time, and saw no reason to abandon its meal. However, an energetic parasite must surrender the space when faced with the true occupant. I commanded it to leave. As the spider detached, I saw that it had stored several eggs deep within her.

Once the spider and its eggs were gone, I could see into the rest of

Chryssa's chakras. The upper chakras were void, but her solar and sacral chakras were dark, filled with two entities that felt like mischievous, head-banging teenagers. These were the playmates she'd talked about at the beginning of the session, when she said she played with the dark. These two entities said they "liked to party" with her. They said they had been with her since she was a teenager.

Goodbye, Old Friends

They also told me that Chryssa really did not want them to go. I asked Chryssa if that was true. She actually teared up a bit and admitted that she felt like she would be losing old friends. However, she understood that keeping them would be retaining a wild, dark, teenage energy within her. She really wanted to grow up and experience the Light.

She told her friends to go, and they left.

Now that Chryssa was free of all the darkness the question remained: Could she be made whole again? Could the terrible vacantness be restored to goodness and light?

Chryssa Gets A New Light Body

I asked the angels how to help her. They said the best solution was to give Chryssa a new Light Body. They asked her to envision herself in a beautiful, safe place out in nature.

She felt all darkness recede from her the minute she stepped into her new, radiant self. She actually saw the angels as they filled every cell within her with divine light and love. A tingling sense of warmth ran from the top of her head all the way down into her body.

The terrible emptiness that Chryssa had felt vanished completely, and was replaced by a new sense of vitality and happiness. Chryssa wept with relief and joy. "I can't believe how differently I feel," she said through waves of tears.

Chryssa wrote the following week to thank me and tell me that she loved her husband again. "He is the most wonderful guy, and it felt weird to not have feelings for him. But as soon as the session was complete, I felt him in my heart again."

Love Returns

Her friends noticed a new warmth in her, too. "Friends say that they want to hang out with me again." In the past, some friends actually said they were afraid of her. "There was this edginess, this creepy coldness about me that no one could explain. Halloween was always my favorite holiday, because I always felt in my element. It was a time when I felt most at home in the world.

"But this year, I am truly and deeply excited about Christmas. I've decorated the entire house. I'm really feeling the spirit of Christmas."

I reached out to Chryssa before completing this book in early 2017 to see if anything else changed. She sent me an email that made me weep. No matter how many times it happens, I am always filled with wonder at these miracles.

Chryssa is a living testament to how much grace and mercy the Light has for all of us, even for those who once rejected it completely. I'm including her list so that you can see if you have any of the same "before" behaviors, and to let you know how incredibly your life can change, too.

"Everything has changed in my life."

"Literally, everything in my life has changed. **When I say that almost nothing is the same, I mean almost nothing is the same.** So much so, that I've spent the last month trying to figure out who I am and what I want to do with my life now.

Love—Mentally, I knew I loved my husband, but I didn't actually feel it. Honestly, prior to our sessions, I don't think I knew what any kind of love felt like—for my partner, my friends, anything.

Anger—For the last several years, I've been consumed with anger and hatred. There was usually a non-stop dialogue going on in my head. I was always in some kind of imaginary mental argument with someone (usually my husband or a co-worker). Thankfully, that has stopped, and if I feel myself getting irritated, it's very easy to simply step back and let it go.

Music—In the past I couldn't do anything without music in the background—the harder the better. Silence or muzak made me nuts. I don't listen to music anymore. Now I find it distracting.

Money—Since our session, I've lost all fear of making or keeping money. I used to have an all-encompassing obsession with money. I was completely consumed with making and keeping it. I was in a constant state of worry about every penny we spent—I'd lose sleep over how we were going to retire and how we'd "make ends meet." If we charged anything on a credit card I'd completely obsess about it until it was paid off. I had absolutely no reason for this fear. I've always had a good job, a great place to live and a wonderful support system.

Interacting with other people—I used to avoid interacting with people whenever possible. If I knew that we were scheduled to have dinner with friends or were asked to go to a party, I would be filled with dread and try to find any excuse not to go. Now, I'm really enjoying going out with friends.

Water—I used to drink a TON of water. People even commented on how much I'd drink in a day (usually over two gallons). Now, I must remind myself to drink. Not sure if this is a good thing, but it's definitely different.

Food—For my entire life I've thought of food as sustenance—I only ate when I was hungry and then only enough to stave off the hunger. In the past 3 months I've gained 30 pounds. I now understand why people enjoy eating!

Clutter—I've spent my entire life as a pack-rat. I've always had a very hard time getting rid of things. I was the master of saying, "I might need that at some point." Now, I can't stand being surrounded by clutter. I haven't had time to get rid of everything I no longer want, but the process has begun.

Christmas—I really disliked Christmas growing up. I never felt the warm, fuzzy feelings that everyone else did. Instead of joy, I always associated it with sadness and loneliness. I really, really wanted nothing to do with it (I've been called Scrooge on many occasions). This year was completely different—for the first time I actually enjoyed the "spirit of the holiday" and looked forward to going out and celebrating.

Exercise/body image—I never left the house without makeup and only wore yoga pants/leggings if I was going to the gym. Now I feel completely comfortable running errands in my yoga pants. without any makeup.

General personality stuff—I was always a very driven and ambitious person. I did whatever I could to get what I wanted. Today, my attitude is completely different. I find it much easier to just walk away. I don't feel the need to "fight" for things. If they don't come easily, I just let them go."

Chryssa's list is really fascinating. **The Dark exerted a profound and pervasive hold on every aspect of her life. It filled her with fear, consumed her with anger, and relentlessly drove her to hoard money and things.** It kept her devoid of love and warm, real relationships. Even her comments about odd food and drink patterns seem to be tied to the creatures that once inhabited her.

Chryssa told me longtime friends are noticing the improvements. "I was with an old friend the other day, and he asked me, 'Are you alright?' I laughed and said, 'Yeah, why?' He said, 'I don't know, you just seem really happy.' I guess for him to see someone go from being dark and cynical for so long to being genuinely happy and upbeat, was weird.

Although he didn't ask me if I had changed, it was obvious I had. I laughed and promised him, 'Someday, I will tell you about it.'"

———

Like Chryssa, a brilliant young artist fought against a dark invader his entire life. Josh's art give us a stunning visual portrayal of the war waged within him and his final victory over darkness.

His story—and the way that his session unfolded in total synchronicity—is something you will probably never forget.

25

JOSH ESCAPES THE DRAGON'S LAIR

Josh McMurtrie's session in the summer of 2015 was a game-changer for both of us. Josh's amazing artistic talents provide the world with a rare glimpse into the courageous battle he waged—and lost—against an energetic dragon that invaded him when he was just a toddler.

Josh was a sweet guy in his mid-twenties. He had a good marriage and a promising career as a photographer and videographer. But something wasn't right within him. Though healthy and athletic, Josh felt inhibited from expressing himself in stronger, more masculine ways. As a result, he felt depressed and disempowered. "I feel like something is holding me back," he said. "I want to be really powerful, but something's in the way. I don't know what it is."

Josh's upper energy centers were fairly clear. However, when I stepped into his heart, I suddenly found myself inside of a large, dark cave. It was pitch black and eerily silent. In the center of the cave shone a single spotlight. Beneath it was a small blonde-haired boy, curled up in the fetal position, his face pressed against the dirt. He appeared to be about three years old. He was dressed like a little prince, in a blue velvet top and pants, with a little matching blue velvet cap ringed with white fur.

"Sssssh!" A Little Boy Is Trapped In Fear

I immediately wanted to rush to him, but he looked up at me with wide eyes. He raised a trembling finger to his lips and silently mouthed "Ssshhh!" He was absolutely terrified I would make a sound.

Telepathically, I asked for more light. Instantly, a soft, candlelight-like glow illumined the room. The scene before me filled me with horror.

Josh was surrounded by dozens of long, black dragons. They lay piled on top of each other, row upon row, clustered along the cave walls. They were all asleep, their sharp, spiny tails pulled close to their snouts.

Poor little Josh was trapped in a dragon's lair. No wonder he was terrified of waking them! I asked the angels to open a hole in the roof so that this terrified part of him could escape safely. They rushed in and carried the little prince to Heaven, without a sound.

Suddenly, grown-up Josh burst into tears. He had no idea why; he just felt something move deep within him. I told him about the dragon's lair and the traumatized three-year old trapped within the dark cave. He gasped when I described the boy's blue and white velvet suit.

"Oh my God! I know that outfit!" he exclaimed. "I think I have a picture of me wearing it when I was little. I came across it just the other day." He asked me to hold on the phone while he looked for it.

"The Grit"

Josh sent me the photo. *Sure enough, it was the exact same little boy I'd seen, wearing the very same outfit.* "Oh, look, I'm even doing 'the Grit'," he pointed out. "My family called it 'The Grit' because I would grit my

teeth and growl and jump out at people. It was like I had to do it. The impulse would build up inside, and I just had to let it out."

Just like a dragon.

Josh and I both grappled with the dawning realization that 'The Grit' had not been an innocent game at all, but the clawing demands of an actual monster hiding within him. I struggled to find the words to comfort him.

Just then, Josh recalled something else. "Wait a minute," he said quietly. "I have a drawing of a dragon that I drew when I was nine years old. Let me go get it." He texted me the drawing just a few minutes later.

Josh Drew The Dragon Within Him

I was as stunned by the drawing on the next page as you are. First, I was absolutely amazed by Josh's artistic talent. Yes, he was only nine when he drew it. *Yes, he is that talented.* You can see his signature in the lower right. I told you he is an absolutely phenomenally talented young man. You can see for yourself how easy it is for him to draw things like this, once you watch his videos on Vimeo.

More importantly for our story, this drawing perfectly captures the struggle—and loss—of Josh to the dragon. I got chills all over as I realized that the beast had swallowed up the brave knight, leaving only his banner and the back of his horse above ground. I also noted that the color of the kingdom's banner and the horse's saddle were blue and white—the same colors that the little prince wore in the photograph of 'The Grit.'

It took my breath away to see this internal struggle come so clearly to life. The dragon's sinister stare chilled me to the bone, too. I can't even imagine what it must have been like for little Josh to try

and fend it off. What was a sweet little boy to do? He must have done the only thing he could do: draw the demon inside him. But sadly for Josh, no one suspected what he had drawn might actually be *real*.

No One Guessed The Truth

Josh and I waded delicately into each of these revelations. In all, his session took almost four hours, giving him time to process each horrible truth as it presented itself. I stayed with Josh and let him feel each wave of emotion as it coursed through him: horror, fear, revulsion, anger, sadness. He realized that he'd desperately cried out for help through his art, but no one had done anything. People only focused on his amazing talent and completely overlooked the terrible truth it was trying to convey.

With no one to stop it, the dragon grew stronger with time. Over the years, it even drew other dark energies to its lair, making Josh a frozen captive inside his own soul. No wonder he had problems being assertive and commanding. These expressions would have woken the sleeping dragons and put his soul in peril.

Josh Is Delivered From The Dragons

It was time for these beasts to go. They had tyrannized this innocent, creative soul for far too long. I asked Josh if he was ready. "Yes, yes!" he said eagerly.

The angels captured them all in a large net. The dragons emitted a deafening cacophony of ear-splitting screams and growls as they struggled against capture. However, the angels vaporized them and turned them back into light, making it impossible for them to torment Josh or anyone else, ever again.

Poor Josh. He was absolutely exhausted. A simple call to feel more empowered had unearthed a nightmarish reality and brought him face to face with the monsters he'd silently battled all his life.

Still, he stuck it out, proving that he still had the strength and valor of that brave knight. He was so relieved to get all that out of him. "That block is gone. I feel normal now!" Josh exclaimed.

Josh's Soul Is Restored

The angels restored Josh's beautiful, strong soul to him. He was free to express his full masculinity for the first time.

The next day, Josh called to tell me that he felt like a new man in every way. His wife was thrilled with his new sense of confidence and strength.

Josh is grateful that the angels and I rescued him from the dragon's lair. But I am also grateful that he is willing to share his story and amazing talent to provide us with such compelling evidence that the unseen world is real.

Shortly after our session, Josh told me that he felt like himself for the first time in a long time, and even started painting again.

A few days later, Josh sent me a text of his latest creation. It made my jaw drop, too. You can see it on the next page.

It's been over a year since Josh was returned to himself, and he now works as a videographer, traveling the world for an eco-non-profit. His soul is as beautiful and stirring as his art. You can see why the Dark wanted to block his light! Such prodigious talent is rare—and a gift from God.

I can't wait to see what else Josh's beautiful, creative soul will bring to the world, now that there is nothing standing in his way.

You can see a video of Josh creating this tiger and more of his art at
https://vimeo.com/joshmcmurtrie/videos/page:2/sort:date

Chryssa and Josh's experiences highlight some terrifying truths. They were invaded by unseen predators who overtook them, held them hostage and used their energy.

How and why does this happen? Just what are energetic dragons and how do we battle them? How do they get inside us? How can we free ourselves from them and protect ourselves in the future?

26

ENERGETIC DRAGONS: OUR UNSEEN COMPANIONS

Barbara sat shyly down across from me in my client's conference room. She talked about her work and personal goals and some of her frustrations. She wanted better relations with coworkers. She wanted to make some positive changes in her home and work life.

The entire time Barbara was talking with me, I couldn't help but notice that she was inside an energetic dragon. She looked hidden, cloaked, dim. There was an aura about her that made her almost invisible. You could walk right by her and not even know she was there. She didn't have many friends at work; probably because her energy told people to stay away.

However, as I listened to Barbara, something amazing happened. The angels showed up and said they wanted to free her from the dragon!

How do you tell a corporate employee that she has an energetic dragon, or that you want to get rid of it? I don't even know what I said, but she eagerly agreed. I told her to bow her head and look within. She did. The dragon was centered in her heart chakra.

The angels released it right then and there.

As it left, she immediately felt—and looked—brighter. She said she felt warm energy flow into her heart and something hard and brittle leave her. The shroud instantly fell off her face. You could see her now! She was smiling and happy. She had literally "come out of her shell." She walked out of that room a completely different person.

Barbara ran to give me a hug when she saw me a few months later. "I did it! I did everything I'd been wanting to do! Thank you!"

It was amazing to see how she related to her coworkers once the dragon was gone. They could see her now. She spoke up. She shared ideas. She laughed and participated in conversations. She was charming and loquacious. Finally, she was free to be herself, without that energy making her invisible.

Josh and Barbara are examples of how energetic life forms can attach to us and dampen our light. Just as the dragon swallowed Josh, these invaders move in and around us, absorbing us inside their energy field. They literally encase you like a blanket or a shroud. They weigh you down and drain your energy. I'd estimate that 70 percent or more of my clients have energetic dragons.

Opportunistic Invaders

These dark energies see us as spiritual real estate: things to invade and use to their own advantage. They scour dimensions, looking for people to break into. They are cosmic "squatters" who move in without your knowledge, refuse to pay rent and consume your energy. Imagine moving into a powerful radio or TV station, taking over its signal and sending whatever you want over its airwaves. This is what they do to humans, taking up space within you, drawing more darkness to you, so it can continue to hide, and then broadcasting pain and negativity to everyone around you.

Energetic dragons are opportunistic and invade when a person is hurting and helpless. When they enter your system, it's usually because there was an opening of some kind due to trauma or pain. If you've ever gone through "a dark time" in your life, but God didn't step in and miraculously save you, an energetic dragon may have responded to your soul's "SOS" beacon and come to you instead.

You know that horrible feeling when you've cried out to God, and waited for a sign, a word, a vision, some form of help—but nothing came. In that deafening void, you may have become more desperate.

If your soul has ever said, "Someone—anyone—please help me!" then you may have unknowingly invited an energetic dragon into your system.

Very Common in Adolescence

Dragons tend to invade children who are abused or neglected. Our energetic houses are much like our physical homes—if they are not strongly guarded and protected, they may be vulnerable to invasion. When the energies see that no one is paying attention or protecting the child, they assume that this energetic "house" is abandoned and no one will notice if they move in and take it over.

Daniel and the Demon

I'll never forget the day Daniel told me he was possessed by a demon. He said it as we waited in line at a Five Guys hamburger restaurant in Mission Viejo, CA. I hadn't seen Daniel or his family for several months, since they moved out of state.

Daniel was in his early twenties. He absolutely glowed as he stepped out of the rental car with his mom and stepdad. He looked like Jesus standing there, with bright blue eyes and long hair down to his shoulders.

I told him how radiant he looked. "Danny, I can't get over how you've changed! What happened?" I asked.

"Oh, I was possessed by a demon," he answered casually, then turned to the menu to make his order. I couldn't believe what I'd just heard in broad daylight, in the middle of a fast-food restaurant.

Danny's stepdad heard him say it too. He was embarassed. "Oh no," I assured him, "It's fine. I get it." Danny had been institutionalized several times in his young life, starting at around the age of 14. He was diagnosed as bi-polar with schizo-affective disorder, meaning that he could hallucinate and become violent. He was also autistic.

We discussed what Danny said about being possessed when he was younger. "Oh, I believe it," his mother said. "He would just get wild. He'd scream and yell and throw things and just go crazy. And he growled too. I heard growling many times from him. It was the most horrifying thing I've ever seen," she said, shuddering from the memories. "I was scared to death he was going to kill me!" At times Danny was so violent at times that it required up to four orderlies to restrain him.

I asked Danny what led to his amazing transformation. "Oh, I don't know," he said. He said he didn't go to church, and hadn't had a religious conversion. The only thing that changed was that he'd moved out of state. When I talked with his mother about the changes, she said she wasn't sure if the move had done him good, or if possibly all her prayers had suddenly been answered. Regardless of the reason, everyone was grateful Danny had finally been filled with Light.

This is very, very common in early adolescence, as hormones and teenage "angst" strikes. I cannot tell you how many dragons invaded my clients at the vulnerable ages of 13 and 14. **The more depressed, isolated and disconnected a teen, the more turbulent their home life, the higher the risk of dragon interference.** This is why it's so important to keep families strong and kids active and engaged.

Dragons like the dark. They like to be alone. They don't want to be bothered. Does this sound like any teenager you know? I'm not suggesting that every teenager is occupied by an energetic dragon, but some certainly may be.

In A Bubble of Negativity

Living inside an energetic dragon is like living in a bubble of negativity. Energetic dragons feed on negative emotions and feelings. They seek to isolate you so they can slowly drain you without anyone noticing.

The dragon insulates you from the world around you, which can be very helpful if you are in an abusive or difficult situation, feeling very overwhelmed or just need to "tune out" to cope with life. However, this barrier between yourself and the world may leave you feeling oddly disconnected from other people or literally "locked out" of yourself.

I've dealt with many people who felt flighty, ungrounded, insecure and off-balance because an energetic entity had taken hold of them and would not let them back into themselves.

Energetic dragons may also wrap you in a coat of pain. You may start to feel depression, anger, anxiety, apathy, disconnection, cynicism, numb, etc. Others may notice this negative vibe and you may start to lose friends, friends that you desperately need.

Role in Disease

Many of my clients who suffer from things like fibromyalgia, diabetes and other auto-immune diseases turn out to be inside energetic dragons. Most of the people in my practice with autoimmune diseases had terrible childhoods. The dragons came at a point in these people's lives when they needed help or insulation from some overwhelming circumstances, but dragons can far overstay their welcome. The dragon starts to drain the person of their life force over time, making them weak, depressed and sick—often with symptoms that appear to have no physical cause. Many people who suffer with energetic dragons and the chronic pain associated with them end up addicted to opiates, marijuana or other pain-relieving medications, which only further insulates them from the world.

The ACE (Adverse Childhood Experiences) Study

The largest study done on how childhood trauma affects the body is the CDC-Kaiser Permanente Adverse Childhood Experiences (ACE) Study. The study is so comprehensive that it spawned more than 70 scientific and mental health papers to date and resulted in legislation in several states to provide support for children and adults with high ACE scores.

More than 15,000 people were studied from 1995 to 1997 and followed up on through 2005. The study began in an obesity clinic in San Diego, California, when clinicians at Kaiser discovered a huge correlation between their obese clients and childhood trauma. This evolved into the study, which asked questions about various childhood traumas, including physical, emotional, or sexual abuse; witnessing domestic violence; growing up with household substance abuse, mental illness, parental divorce, and/or an incarcerated household member. A score was given that indicated the cumulative levels of childhood stress.

The test group was based in a stable, affluent area and does not include traumas resulting from street violence, natural disaster or war. But perhaps they will add these to a new study, along with "spiritual trauma," for those who have endured psychic and physical attacks.

The ACE test (www.acestoohigh.com) shows that children with four or more adverse childhood experiences are 4000 times more likely to become alcoholics or addicts, are 30 times more at-risk for suicide, and have a host of fairly predictable yet complicated health problems, including auto-immune disorders.

Childhood Trauma Creates Physical Diseases

The scientific community is recognizing more and more the effects the spiritual and emotional worlds have on our physical bodies.

"The number of ACEs was strongly associated with adulthood high-risk health behaviors such as smoking, alcohol and drug abuse, promiscuity, and severe obesity, and correlated with ill-health including depression, heart disease, cancer, chronic lung disease and shortened lifespan. Compared to an ACE score of zero, having four adverse childhood experiences was associated with a seven-fold increase in alcoholism, a doubling of risk of being diagnosed with cancer, and a four-fold increase in emphysema; an ACE score above six was associated with a 30-fold increase in attempted suicide.

The ACE study's results suggest that maltreatment and household dysfunction in childhood contribute to health problems decades later. These include chronic diseases—such as heart disease, cancer, stroke, and diabetes—that are the most common causes of death and disability in the United States. (*Source, Wikipedia and Stevens, Jane Ellen (8 October 2012). "The Adverse Childhood Experiences Study—the Largest Public Health Study You Never Heard Of" The Huffington Post.*)

Inside A Dragon For More Than 60 Years

Let's look at Malika, who died at the age of 72, but who had been in poor health for many years before that. Malika scored a 7 on the ACE test because she grew up in an alcoholic home and was severely neglected. True to the study's findings, she drank too much, smoked for most of her life, was obese, had heart attacks and high blood pressure, had several strokes, suffered from depression and anxiety, developed diabetes and had problems with her lungs. She did not eat a healthy diet or exercise consistently. *She literally had every single health problem listed on the ACE study findings.* She was hospitalized at least two dozen times in her life and died at 72. She had little intervention (there wasn't a lot known about trauma until now).

Poor Malika was inside a very large dragon that had been with her since she was just three years old. I saw it very clearly the first time I met her. It probably came during an incident of neglect, and formed a barrier between her and her pain. However, without intervention, it grew and grew until it took over her whole life, using pain and disease (dis-ease) for the rest of her life. She was still inside it when she died.

I only knew Malika casually, and was not asked to help her. However, if someone had been able to get her out of that dragon, she would have enjoyed a much healthier and happier life.

Auto-Immune Disorders and Energetic Dragons

Certainly, not every inflammatory issue is due to a supernatural invader. Our environment and foods are filled with toxins, and this can lead to all sorts of issues with the body. Sometimes, however, you might develop fibromyalgia and other auto-immune problems because:

1) Your body senses an invader and is trying to get rid of it

2) An energetic dragon may be slowing you down and giving you more pain

3) Trapped emotions are toxic to the body and can create disease

"Childhood stress was a huge indicator of emotional, mental and physical health problems later in life. This kind of stress was also found to play an enormous role in auto-immune disorders, including rheumatoid arthritis. (*Source, Cumulative Childhood Stress and Autoimmune Diseases in Adults Study, February 2009, National Center for Biotechnology Information, NCBI*)

Patients with a score of just two or more Adverse Childhood Experienced had a 70% increased risk for hospitalizations for myocarditis and 100% increased risk for rheumatic diseases.

Possible Supernatural Reason For Auto-Immune Problems

If you suffer from these sorts of physical and emotional problems, you've probably tried everything you can to get better. You probably feel confused and feel helpless by being told, "it's all in your head," when you know darn well something is wrong. In addition to seeking medical and emotional treatment, you may want to consider spiritual help as well. As you've seen, many people's physical problems vanish when their emotional pain is removed. When doctors cannot find the antibody or what your system is reacting to, it could be because the problem is not physical, but supernatural.

"Sick and Tired of Being Sick and Tired"

I met Colleen at the Awareness Life Expo in Sacramento, CA in August of 2016. She is a sweet and loving soul, and actually helped me move through my slides for my opening presentation because the audio-visual system wasn't working. The first thing she told me during our session was that she was "sick and tired of being sick and tired." She was diabetic and on 11 different medications for physical and emotional issues. She was also currently estranged from her only son, which pained her deeply.

Not surprisingly, she was also within an energetic dragon. When the angels removed the dragon and reunited her with Jesus, whom she loved dearly, her body changed instantly. She lost 15 pounds in three weeks.

A month later, she wrote me to tell me that she was down to just three medications and felt like a new woman. The angels guided her to take up therapy as a way to heal the rift between her and her son, and to work with them daily in her own spiritual practice. Colleen wrote to let me know that she and her son were back to talking on video chats again and things were much better between them.

Compassion, Not Contempt

When you're struggling with an energetic dragon, you can feel sick and tired of being sick and tired much of the time. It's easy for you to get mad at yourself and think of yourself as weak or defective. It's also easy for loved ones to become angry or frustrated with the toll chronic illness takes on their lives.

It's important to have compassion for yourself or anyone who is dealing with this kind of oppression. If someone appears to be clinging to their darkness, it's usually because their childhoods were so desolate of proper nurturing and love that being "sick" is the only way they know to receive the love, care, affection, nurturing and protection they desperately needed all those years ago.

Building The "Trauma Container"

We are containers. This is why entities call us "vessels." We can only hold so much. In order to feel happy, we must empty out our pain. Trauma resilience counselors call it "building the container," giving you more joy. One way to be happier is to empty the container of pain and fill it with joy instead. You don't want to *manage* your pain any more— *you want to be free of it*!

What You Need To Know

- Hurt people, hurt people.

- Trauma causes a tear in the psyche. This allows energetic dragons and other negative energies to infiltrate you.

- Energetic dragons come to you when you are vulnerable.

- Trauma causes severe physical, emotional and mental health problems.

- If you don't treat your trauma, it will get worsen like a festering wound. More negative energies will gather.

- Chronic health problems can be signs of an energetic dragon.

- Energetic dragons feed on negativity and will cause people to see you as negative.

- Feeling heavy, confused, and sluggish can be signs of an energetic dragon.

- Some autoimmune issues that defy treatment may be related to an energetic dragon

- If you feel locked out of your body or unable to connect to yourself, an energetic invader could be the culprit.

- Cleaning out your pain allows the Light to get in and heal.

What You Can Do

Realize everyone has trauma. Break the cycle by clearing your own darkness and pain. Get evaluated and treated for your trauma. Below are some methods I've used to help release shock and trauma from myself.

Trauma Releasing Methods

The key to healing from trauma is to get the pain out of the body and soul. I've discovered some amazing tools to help remove trauma from the body in addition to Angelic Soul Clearing.™

These tools are based in the body, because the body has its own intelligence and memory. Trauma gets stored chemically in your tissues and the residue can remain there for many years.

Somatic Experiencing™

I strongly encourage anyone with trauma to do Somatic Experiencing™. It was also one of the most nurturing therapies I've ever had. The therapist was able to connect with my inner little girl and give her the gentle and loving presence she needed.

I was absolutely amazed at what Somatic Experiencing™ did for my body. The first time I got a Somatic Experiencing™ treatment, I came home and danced to Taylor Swift music for over twenty minutes. I was so astonished at the organic and free movements that my body made that I actually videotaped it so I could prove to myself that this clunky, stiff, overweight body actually moved like this. I showed it to my chiropractor who said, "Your hips don't move like that!" We were both stunned.

Trauma and Tension Releasing Exercises (TRE)™

About a year after I discovered Somatic Experiencing,™ my angels led me to attend a workshop on Tension and Trauma Releasing Exercises.™ TRE™ has been used by more than a million people all over the world. It was developed by a monk, social worker and massage therapist named Dr. David Berceli. He uses it to help victims of natural disasters and wars quickly recover from the shock and trauma. He has also seen it release complex trauma, memories and even foreign energies from the body.

TRE™ is currently used by the Department of Homeland Security to treat veterans with PTSD.

Releasing Trauma Made Room For Joy

The first time I learned TRE™, my body was so tight that my muscles would not release at all. But by the afternoon workshop, I was releasing all over the place. I did it in the hotel for over an hour that night, and my body was so grateful! Huge muscle groups relaxed for the first time, ever.

The next morning something amazing happened. *I turned on the radio and the song actually went into my body.*

The joy I felt singing actually *went into my cells*. I felt it. My cells released tension and pain, so there was suddenly room for more joy!

You can learn more about TRE at www.traumaprevention.com.

There are certified providers all over the world.

You can learn more about Somatic Experiencing at www. traumahealing.org. More resources are available at www.freedbythelight. com.

——————————— ———————————

When I met Rafael, he was very sick with a sore throat and fever. However, he was instantly cured the moment something supernatural was released from his cells.

27

RAFAEL CATCHES A SUPERNATURAL "STD"

Javier Sandoval urgently knocked on my hotel room door late one night during the Awareness Life Expo in August, 2016. "I need you to heal my friend," he said. "He's sick with a fever."

I felt really unprepared. "Are you sure I'm the one to help him?" Although I'm a certified massage therapist, I hadn't done any hands-on healing in some time, and didn't want to let anyone down.

"Yes," Javier insisted. "Spirit told me you were the one. Let's go." He dragged me down the hall and took me to a tall, thin man laying on a bed.

Spiritual Solution for Physical Ailment

Javier introduced me to Rafael Barragan. He was pale and listless. "Thank you so much," he croaked feebly, holding his throat. "I feel so bad. I wanted to attend the ceremony tonight, but I just can't get out of bed. It's a throat infection," he explained. "This happens a few times a year, and I always need antibiotics."

I touched his forehead. It was hot. "I don't know if I can help you," I told Rafael honestly. What was I supposed to do for a man with a bacterial infection?

"If Javier thinks you can, then you can," he said with a raspy voice.

Obviously he and Javier weren't giving up, so I prayed to my angels to help me help him. The angels always come when asked. I took a deep breath and let them lead the way.

I also closed my own aura to make sure that whatever he had didn't infect me, too.

Energetic Infection

When I tuned into Rafael's energy field, I was surprised to see parasitic, snake-like invaders up around his head, moving in and out of his head and throat. I pulled them out one by one. I continued working on him intuitively, breaking up negative energy and sending it out of his system.

While I was working, Archangel Michael appeared and said that Rafael needed help enforcing stronger boundaries. He gave him his mighty sword to help cut away what he no longer needed in his life. Rafael broke into a huge smile as a burst of powerful, warm healing energy surged through his chest, then down into his arms and hands.

Rafael was completely healed within a half hour. His fever disappeared. His throat stopped hurting. His voice came back, loud and clear. His face glowed brightly, and he was full of energy again. We took this photo at a party later that night.

Completely Healed

Rafael was both astonished and grateful. He was amazed that a

spiritual healing could cure him of his illness, especially when it had always required antibiotics and several days to recover. He could not believe he was back on his feet so quickly, especially when he had been too weak to even get out of bed before.

After thanking me profusely, Rafael and his wife did an impromptu video testimonial about the healing (you can see it at *www.freedbythelight. com*.)

Rafael's wife, Michelle, wrote me a few weeks later to thank me again. "Margo, meeting you made the weekend amazing! Rafael has gone through this type of throat infection four times before, and always had to visit a doctor for antibiotics to get rid of it. After your gracious healing, within a half hour he had a burst of energy, and was able to enjoy the rest of the Expo for the evening. In fact, he felt well enough the following morning to help Javier pack up to leave. Somehow, the healing also cured a torn Achilles' heel!

As for 'Michael's sword,' this is a great honor for Rafael to have received. He will use it wisely, kindly and firmly. Thank you again for sharing your incredible gifts with us!"

Rafael's case highlights the very real presence of spiritual parasites and how they can affect our physical health. Sadly, this happens all the time. You can catch spiritual parasites just as easily as you catch the common cold. And just like the cold, you are especially vulnerable if you are in crowds of people.

"STD's"—Spiritually Transmitted Dis-Eases

I first became aware of spiritual parasites in the Spring of 2016, when my friend Hannah called to wish me Happy Easter. As we chatted that sunny morning, she mentioned that she was suffering from a bad headache. "I don't usually get headaches," she said. "But this one is really nasty. It's focused on the back of my head and won't go away. I've tried everything, but nothing's touching it."

I don't check every ailment my friends have, but I did feel compelled to look in on this. I was surprised to discover a beige, crab-like creature about six inches wide attached to the back of her head. It looked like one of those embryonic things from the *"Alien"* movies. I wasn't sure what to do, so I just reached into the spirit dimension, pulled it off her and snapped it in half.

Energetic Crab

Hannah noticed the shift immediately, even though I hadn't yet told her what I'd done.

Now that it was gone, Hannah wanted to know she got it. Hannah is a doctor and is very careful about where she goes, what she puts in her body and the kind of people with whom she associates.

I scanned her home and didn't see anything. "I'm not sure, "I told her honestly. "Did you recently go to a party or something?"

She thought for a moment, and recalled that the day before she had attended a large spiritual event with about a hundred people. If it had been a business event, her chances of getting "infected" would be much lower than if she had been to some kind of large spiritual gathering, where people are much more likely to be running around with their auras wide open. *These types of events are huge feeding stations for all kinds of energetic entities.* I was pretty sure she picked the crab up there.

Another Friend Gets Supernatural "Crabs"

I encountered this same type of crab entity a few months later, when my graphic designer called to check in on the website. She said she'd just come from a friend's house, where she'd received some new type of healing treatment. She said she felt fantastic—except for "this nasty" headache in the back of her head.

Uh-oh. I immediately checked her energy field, and there it was, the same kind of crab, only slightly larger. I disposed of it as before, and told her what I'd seen. Like Hannah, she was appalled. "Yick! Where did I get that?"

I asked her to tell me about the new healing treatment she'd just gotten.

She said a good friend of hers was in the process of learning it and wanted to try it out on her. "It had something to do with 'running bars,'" she said. "She said it would be fun and we could just play around with it."

A huge red flag went up in my brain. I cautioned her about letting anyone into her energy field, especially when they are interacting with energies they may not fully understand. Opening up your energy field to foreign invaders is just like inviting strangers into your home. You may think they have good intentions, while they are stealing you blind.

Just then the term "spiritual crabs" came to mind, and I thought about how this could be considered a form of an STD, a *spiritually transmitted disease*.

Your Life Force Is A Valuable Commodity

Spiritual predators like to hunt in large groups of people. Hanging out where there are crowds of people, or the wrong types of people, can make you vulnerable to things attaching to you and following you home. It's like a spiritual buffet for these parasites—lots of different types and flavors to choose from. Guard your energetic body carefully. Your life force is a precious commodity. There are innumerable invaders who would do anything to get it. Close your space and keep your energetic walls up at all times.

Avoid Psychic Vampires

Always pay attention to how you feel when you are around other people. If you feel drained, anxious, spacey or heavy, chances are there's something in that person's energy field that is trying to latch onto you or siphon off energy. We all have that one friend we're reluctant to call, because we know the conversation will last for ages and we'll be dead-tired once it's over. People like this are known as "psychic vampires." They drain your energy because they have little life force of their own. Many of them have dragons and don't know it, and they are not aware their presence affects others so negatively. They just know they feel tired and depressed most of the time.

You have a spiritual obligation to honor and protect yourself, so don't associate with people who drain your energy. Perhaps you can offer them this book as a way to help them understand and help themselves.

Hannah and the 'Soul Eater'

In the last days of writing this book, Hannah called me to ask me to check something out for her at a hospital. "It's room 24," she texted. "They say everyone dies in there, and I don't want to put my mother in there unless I know it's safe." She explained that her mother was considered a VIP in the hospital because she'd worked in healthcare in that community for many years, and they wanted to give her a private room. It was the only one available. I suppose they cautioned her mother about the unusually high mortality rate in that room because she was a close friend to many of the staff members.

When I looked into room 24, I saw something I had never seen before. It looked like a huge sucking mouth attached to some sort of spiritual parasite. Its mouth was an enormous spinning vortex that sucked everything around into it like a tornado. It was perched at the top of the bed and was just waiting for someone to lay down so it could eat its soul. I literally have chills all over me as I type this.

I researched "soul eater" and found references to it in Nigerian, Egyptian and Native American cultures. Needless to say, I told her to get her mother another room, and that I would attempt to clear it another time.

Protect Yourself Around Hospitals and Graveyards

Hospitals, hospice centers, graveyards and mortuaries all can attract and hold the spirits of those who have recently died and who are looking for a way to come back into the physical world. On the plus side, I've never seen so many angels gathered in one place as I did at a hospice in Kansas. It was just lovely.

Please shield yourself very carefully as you enter and exit these places. *Zip Up Your Aura!*

Pray that those who are in transition have a smooth journey from this plane of existence to the next life, and that all encumbrances are lifted from them easily and joyfully.

Spiritual Parasites can make you feel:

- Drained
- Suddenly sick with a headache or nausea
- Sharp, stabbing pain in your head or body
- Numb, depressed, anxious or fearful
- A feeling of tightness, constriction, pain or fullness in one or more of your energy centers
- Heavy or oppressed

How to Protect Yourself

Be very discerning where you go and the types of people with whom you associate. Drugs, alcohol and other mind-altering chemicals, especially psychedelics, can leave you open and vulnerable to things invading your inner spaces.

ALWAYS close your aura before leaving your house. If you live with negative people, close it all the time while you are home. Avoid places and people where there is a lot of chaotic, sexual, or negative energy.

How To Close Your Aura

1. **Envision yourself encased in a warm, strong, impermeable golden bubble of light.**

2. **See Archangel Michael's shield of bright white light encircling you and protecting you from all sides.**

3. **Envision his powerful sword in your hand and the warm, pure, divine, golden/white light coming from it, flowing through you from your center outward, up and all around you, filling up the inside of the golden bubble.**

4. **Say this three times, with strong intention: "I close my aura to anything but my highest and best good."**

5. **Sometimes, you need stronger shielding than just a golden bubble of light around your aura. If you live or work in a toxic atmosphere, visualize yourself wearing a complete shield of armor, just like knights do.**

How to Clear Yourself From Spiritual Parasites

1. First, get very calm and focused. Center your attention within yourself. Scan each part of your energy centers one by one. You will feel when there is a blockage. You may even see or hear something in it. If this is the case, state firmly and clearly that you are the rightful owner of this body, that it is yours, and that whatever it is has no right to trespass—and to leave immediately. Be clear and forceful. Announce that you are the owner or this property and that it does not have permission to be there.

2. Pray and ask for Divine protection and for Archangel Michael and the other Archangels to protect you and fight on your behalf.

3. Ask the Archangels to remove it and replace the space with Divine Light and protection.

4. Do another sweep and see if your sensations have changed or shifted. You should feel a sense of clearing, opening, lightness, peace and calm come over you.

5. Seek qualified assistance from a shaman or other spiritual advisor to remove it for you.

Envision yourself in that golden bubble of light every morning and every night. Remind yourself to close your aura. *Never leave home without doing it!* Put a note on the bathroom mirror or near the front door to remind you to do it before leaving.

REMEMBER
Close Your Aura!

**As Josh McMurtrie and his wife say
before they leave the house every day,**

"ZUYA!"
Zip Up Your Aura!

If you forget to close your aura, or feel something may be attached to you, come home and envision a strong, golden flame of fire coming from inside your being and radiating outward until your whole body, from head to toe, is ablaze. Extend this powerful Divine flame up and outside of you. See it burning everything up within your energy field that doesn't belong there. Then state your affirmation: "I close my aura to anything but my highest and best good."

You can also do this to close and protect your aura, too.

Energetic invaders are sometimes the driving force behind addictions. Cindy found herself the victim of an insistent entity who mercilessly drove her to drink.

28

CINDY AND SEAN DEAL WITH DEMONS OF ADDICTION

Angelic Soul Clearing™ has instantly delivered many people from drinking, drugs, smoking, gambling and sex addictions because we removed the supernatural entities that were behind those addictions.

In late 2016, Cindy called me in tears. She confessed to drinking every day, even though she didn't want to. She began drinking to combat insomnia. "I don't know how it got this bad," she said. "First it was once in a while, then a couple of times a week, and now it's every day, even before I go to work." She didn't know how to cope anymore. She was so ashamed.

What Drove Her To Drink

As I cleared the stress and fear within her solar plexus, I saw a large, black humanoid figure in the background, insistently snapping a long black whip. Snap! *You will drink.* Snap! *You will drink.* Snap! *You will drink.* Each snap of the whip drove her to the bottle. The entity brandishing the whip was very shiny; not like a demon or an energetic dragon, something else. I couldn't see clearly until later in the session, when the angels called it forth. Then I saw that it looked a lot like the queen in the "Alien" movies, shiny and tall and black.

The angels instantly vaporized it and returned it to Light. "Oh my, I feel so much lighter!" Cindy exclaimed as the angels released it.

When we cleared the sacral chakra, it felt a little too empty. I asked the angels what needed to go there. Suddenly, a HUGE amethyst cluster dropped down into her chakra. It was at least four feet high and three feet across. They obviously knew she needed this, but why? I looked it up online. I was stunned to discover that amethyst encourages and enhances sobriety. I continued reading and discovered that it relieves insomnia, too. *The angels knew exactly what she needed and gave it to her.*

Desire to Drink Left Immediately

Cindy wrote me three days later to tell me she had not had a drink since her session. "I'm craving free! I haven't wanted a drink since I spoke with you. Thank you so much, Margo!"

Cindy called me for a Career Card reading exactly 30 days after her session. She had not had a single drink since the clearing. She sounded like a completely different woman. She was happy, positive and clear. "I don't feel anything heavy or dark with me anymore. It's like a bazillion pounds just was lifted off my back. For so long, I felt like something dark was pushing and pulling me to do something I didn't want to do, and making me drink. After your clearing, the push/pull just stopped! I'll never be able to thank you enough."

Cindy also brought up the amethysts the angels had placed in one of her lower chakras. "Amethyst is everywhere, all over my house now. In fact, my husband thought that what happened was so amazing that he had a special amethyst pendant made for me for Valentine's Day. Now, I have it with me all the time."

Now She Can Connect To Her Angels

Cindy's relationship with divine guidance has come full circle, too. "I talk to my team every morning and thank them every night," she said. "It's a whole new life, and I am so grateful. Words just cannot express my thanks to you and the angels for freeing me from that terrible darkness!"

Addiction is an enormous problem in our society and is at the root of the majority of crimes. According to the National Council on Alcoholism and Drug Dependence (NCADD), 80 percent of people in jail are there due to crimes they committed because of drugs and alcohol. The vast majority of murders, rapes and suicides are done while the person is "under the influence" of these types of chemicals. *(https://www.ncadd. org/about-addiction/alcohol-drugs-and-crime).*

Half of all people incarcerated are clinically addicted and sixty percent of people arrested of most types of crimes test positive for illegal drugs at the time they are arrested.

"Under the Influence"

It's interesting that the criminal justice system refers to being intoxicated or high as "under the influence." Alcohol was originally referred to as "spirits." I was 18 the first time I saw a spirit of alcoholism. My best friend was playing a gig in a nightclub. I distinctly saw three spirits hovering above the bar. They were spirits of alcoholism, despair and lust.

Drinking and using drugs opens the doors to earthbound spirits and entities who will use the body in order to assuage their ravenous hungers, even if it means killing the host in the process. After all, once the human has been sucked dry and dies, they can just go find another unwitting victim who is willing to imbibe, and then the vicious cycle starts all over again.

I'm definitely not saying that every person with an addiction is possessed by a dark spirit. That is not the case. However, it must be considered, because it can and does happen. Cindy isn't the only person I've encountered whose addiction was caused by a supernatural entity

Serial Killers And the Drunk Connection

If you review the cases of serial killers, you will find that virtually all of them committed their crimes while under the influence of alcohol, drugs or both. Notoriously evil killers Jeffrey Dahmer, Ted Bundy and John Wayne Gacy were all severe alcoholics.

Bundy and Dahmer spoke openly with authorities about the malevolent entities that pushed them to kill. Bundy even called his "The Entity." According to Katherine Ramsland, Ph.D., Bundy told several interviewers (William Hagmaier, Robert Keppel, Steven Michaud), that he had a malignant being—an "entity"—that emerged from him whenever he was tense or drunk.

"Negative Electricity" With Serial Killer Ted Bundy

Ramsland recounts in a September 1, 2013 Psychology Today online article that "Defense investigator Joe Aloi seemed to have gotten a clear view of Ted Bundy's entity. While they were talking, he suddenly noticed an odor emanate from Bundy as his face and body contorted. 'I felt that negative electricity,' Aloi said, 'and along with that came that smell.' Aloi was suddenly terrified that Bundy would kill him. *(https://www.psychologytoday. com/blog/shadow-boxing/201309/bundys-demon-part-i)*

A week before one of Bundy's attacks, his girlfriend saw the dark side of him. He pushed her into a river and didn't try to help her. He was completely blank, she told authorities.

Pop star Rhianna told the media that the most terrifying thing about singer Chris Brown's brutal and sudden attack on her was that, "He had no soul in his eyes. Just blank. He was clearly blacked-out. There was no person when I looked at him."

This is not human behavior.

"Powerless Against It"

In February of 2016, a Michigan Uber driver told police an evil symbol popped up on his phone and ordered him to kill six people. He described it as a "full body takeover." He said he was powerless against it. I don't know if he was indeed possessed, but we need to pay attention when people say they struggle against these kinds of influences.

The Spiritual Scientific Research Foundation believes that up to 70 percent of addicted people are actually possessed, either by a malevolent entity or an earthbound spirit looking to continue their addiction from beyond the grave (*www.spiritualresearchfoundation.org*).

Effects of Alcohol and Drugs on Spirituality

In a detailed article from the Theosophical Society's Winter 2015 Issue of **Quest** Magazine, author Pablo Sender wrote extensively about the effects of alcohol and drugs on spirituality.

"The use of wine, spirits, liquors of any kind, or any narcotic or intoxicating drug, is strictly prohibited. If indulged in, all progress is hindered, and the efforts of teacher and pupil alike are rendered useless. All such substances have a directly pernicious action upon the brain, and especially upon the "third eye," or pineal gland . . . They prevent absolutely the development of the third eye, called in the East "the Eye of Siva." *(H.P. Blavatsky, Collected Writings, 12:496)*

The Scientific Spiritual Research Foundation produced a video showing what alcohol and drugs do to the spiritual body: *(https://www. youtube.com/watch?feature=player_embedded&v=17ephsnEYCA*

"Gateway" Drugs Open The Door To Spiritual Invasion

It's interesting that cigarettes, alcohol and marijuana are considered "gateway" substances, because they do open energetic gateways between this dimension and the lower astral realms.

Think of the astral realm (the dimension that is just beyond this one) as a hotel with different floors. The lower floors are cheaper and reserved for less-valued guests, because they are close to the noise and crime of the streets. The Penthouse and higher floors are further away from the noise and pollution of the city. They are more valuable, but also harder to reach.

People who have passed on and who don't yet want to go to the Light congregate close to the Earth plane. Spirits of addiction and other dark entities wait here for a chance to jump in and inhabit a person in order to live out their desires. To get the purest spiritual connection, you have to go to the highest floors, which are the angelic realms.

Clairvoyant C.W. Leadbeater had this to say about the lower astral realms: "The astral plane is basically sensuous in nature. Its lower part is the realm of passions and desires, and stimulates the animal nature in us. It also can bring quite terrifying experiences…" *(Leadbeater, Talks, 2:34)*

Marijuana and other hallucinogens such as mushrooms, ecstacy, MDMA ("Molly") and other drugs open gateways to these lower astral realms and many people have very frightening supernatural experiences.

Remember, you are spiritual real estate. Guard your home carefully. Think of yourself as a castle. Your awareness keeps the gates closed at all times. But once you get drunk or high, your gates start to go down. This allows anything that's been prowling around to break in. Get even more "under the influence," and those castle walls will collapse completely.

If you're passed out and don't even know what humans are doing around you, how can you possibly guard yourself against spiritual invaders?

I was asked to help a young man whose entire life was consumed by darkness. His ex-wife told me that she knew when he was in town, because things would suddenly start to go haywire: the car broke down, she would have accidents etc., even when he was several hours away from her.

She asked me if I thought he had entities. The angels responded with the words, "hordes of demons." The angels required me to store up energy for two full days prior to his session.

The session was intense, but very safe for both of us. The angels were right—he was extremely infested with dark entities.

When I asked how and when they got in, the angels showed him doing LSD as a teenager. Brian said yes, he did it once when he was 19, and the person doing it with him did dark magic and got possessed by evil spirits that night.

Those entities went into Brian, too, because his energetic borders were down and he was physically close to someone who had opened a portal.

Drugs and alcohol open portals for negative entities to possess you. That's not horror-movie hyperbole. It's the truth.

Possessed By A Single Dose

Geoffrey Hodson noted that "Continued use, in fact sometimes even a single dose of a drug like LSD, can permanently damage the delicate mechanism of consciousness in the brain, especially relating to the brain's switchboard of the thalamus and hypothalamus along with the pineal and pituitary glands, and by so doing prevent any real spiritual progress from proceeding in that lifetime." (*Source, Spirituality and Drugs and the Occult, Pablo Sender*)

Taking drugs and drinking lowers your spiritual immunity and makes it much easier for entities to walk into your energetic front door without you knowing it.

Caution Against Psychotropic Drugs

I met Marcia at a holistic fair. Her energy field looked like swiss cheese. It was full of rips and holes. She said she was part of a group that used Ayahuasca to explore other levels of consciousness. Ayahuasca is a psychotropic drug originally used in a sacred way by the indigenous shamans of South America to contact the spirit realm. However, the leader of Marcia's group was not an indigenous shaman. She did not have centuries of ancestral wisdom in her DNA, nor the spiritual power to create a strong enough container for people to safely explore other dimensions and astral realms. As a result, she ended up blowing holes in people's energy fields and allowing them to be possessed and contaminated by a host of lower entities.

Improper Use of The Spiritual Tools

Once the angels repaired her aura, Marcia told me that the leader of her group routinely drank, smoke pot and engaged in sexual orgies with her students. Drinking and using drugs opens holes in your aura and lets negative things come in.

Remember the analogy about the hotel? Well, the guys hanging around the alleyway are not the sort of people you usually want to turn to for healing and guidance, but this is what happens during many drug and alcohol-induced spiritual encounters. Drugs and alcohol send the spiritual elevator to the basement.

Marcia's experience reminded me of what happened to a once-popular channeler named JZ Knight who allegedly channeled a 5,000 year old entity named "Ramtha" in the 1990s. People flocked to hear "Ramtha," believing they were receiving arcane knowledge. However, everything began to fall apart during "the wine sessions," in which "Ramtha" made followers drink along with him as he humiliated JZ by revealing her sexual history to the crowd in graphic detail.

This is not spiritual behavior. This is possession by very low-level energies.

"Ramtha" And The 'Wine Sessions'

The first time I saw "Ramtha" on TV, I was struck by the fact that this supposedly-ascended teacher had a glass of scotch next to him and puffed on a pipe during the interview. JZ had also gained about a hundred pounds since channeling him. High-vibrational guides do not engage in addictions or numbing substances. Ramtha was just a posing spirit who wanted to get back in a body so he could continue his many addictions.

Earthbound spirits and demons can be involved in any sort of addiction, including food, sex and gambling. You can imagine the kinds of demons who are behind pornography addictions. I once saw a demon in a man featured in a television show about people who weighed more than 600 pounds. This man was so large he could not leave his bed, so he could not get food for himself. The demon flitted across his eyes as he talked about sending his girlfriend out to get him food. It was definitely threatening.

People with addictions this severe are at the mercy of their dark overlords. In most cases, only some kind of spiritual intervention can save them.

Divine Intervention Saves An Addict

One such intervention happened in October of 2016. Michelle Kaplan heard me on the Late Night in the Midlands radio show with Michael Vara and called in about her son's heroin addiction. "We've tried everything," she said. "I was praying about this, and I feel very strongly that you can help Sean. Do you feel he has some kind of entity?" I tuned in and told her yes, I did feel a presence within him. She scheduled a soul clearing for him a few days later.

Michelle remembers that evening vividly. "The session was done over the phone in a quiet room in my home. When Sean first arrived, he literally dragged himself through the front door. He complained how much his neck and back hurt, and he really looked like he was miserable.

Margo called a few minutes later. When I answered, she immediately said she suddenly felt really bad neck and back pain. From that moment, I knew she already made a strong connection with Sean—even before they spoke."

I began the session by telling Sean about the intense pain I felt in my neck and back. "It's like I've been doing construction all day," I told him, rubbing my neck. He told me that he had indeed been working construction that day. He said it was the only work he could get.

Spirit of Addiction

I began Sean's session by scanning his energy center and immediately saw a spirit of addiction around his heart. It had been with him since he was 14 years old. It said Sean was a "good vessel," meaning that he did a good job of giving it all the heroin it desired. It was a greedy thief who demanded all of Sean's energy and resources, but gave him nothing but ruin in return.

Like millions of people, Sean's pain had opened the psychic door, and an entity had taken hold. Sean saw his past differently once the angels showed him the roots of his pain. Now that he was connected to his own heart, the entity had to go. "Oh my God, I actually feel something leaving my body right now, through my chest," Sean gasped. "Some kind of thick heaviness. I feel so much lighter now!"

"Sean Physically Transformed"

Michelle noted the changes in Sean immediately. "My son physically transformed," she wrote. "Sean walked out of the room without any neck or back pain. He just kept saying, "Wow, that was amazing! I really don't know how to describe what just happened, but I feel completely different.'

Later, he told me, 'Mom, she knew about all my traumas, and the exact ages they started at, she knew what I experienced with Dad, she knew the exact age I started using drugs, she knew everything.'

Sean hasn't used drugs since that night.

Michelle wrote me in February of 2017. "It's been about five months since Sean had his session, and he's not using. He has no desire to use drugs at all, and before, it was all he could think about. It's amazing."

These experiences helped Michelle see addiction and pain in a whole new light. "For years, Sean cried out, asking, 'Why me, Mom? Why us?' Now, I look at these questions very differently than before. Now I understand addiction a whole new way, and I want to help addicts."

Inspired To Help Addicts Spiritually

This realization inspired Michelle to create the Assist-an-Addict program to be launched in 2017 with the Image of Change non-profit, and the Image of Mindful Health and Wellness healing community (*www.imageofhealthandwellness.com*). "When everything else seemed to have 'failed,' we finally found Margo and our healing journey truly began. Now we have a way to help addicts," Michelle said.

A Picture Worth A Thousand Words

More addicts are created every day, due to the over-prescribing of painkillers. A social worker told me she could not believe the personality changes in her older clients once they got hooked on prescription pain pills. "They are completely different," she said. "They used to be sweet, kind and generous. Now, they are selfish and cold and only care about what they can take. It's horrible. I don't know what would make them change like that." *I do.* Now, so do you.

The Crypt Keeper Stares Back From The Mirror

Former meth addicts speak of feeling like "living zombies" who no longer eat, drink or sleep and only live to do the drug. Drugs known as "spice," "flakka" or "bath salts" literally turn people into face-eating zombies (*http://abcnews.go.com/Blotter/face-eating-cannibal-attack-latest-bath-salts-incident/story?id=16470389*).

One meth user said he suddenly quit in horror one day because he looked in the mirror and saw "The Crypt Keeper" staring back at him!

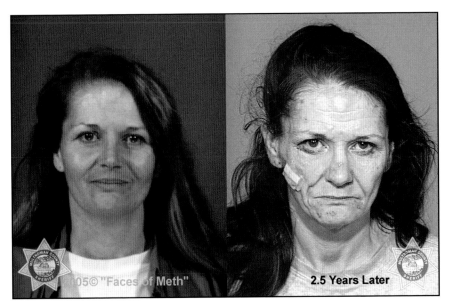

A Lesson From The "Faces Of Meth"

Here's an example. This is from the famous "Faces of Meth" campaign. The photo above was taken just **two and half years** before the second one—not two *decades* later.

If you want a chance to see what I see, I invite you to take a closer look at the photo on the right, when this woman's drug use was so pronounced. Look at each of her eyes separately. Do you sense a different presence in each one? Does one seem more human?

What do you see in the other? Does it give you a chill?

As the old saying goes, *"A man takes a drink. Then the drink takes a drink. Then the drink takes the man."*

What You Need To Know

- Mind-altering chemicals can attract negative energies and entities.

- Earthbound spirits are always patrolling, looking to take over a host to continue their addictions.

- Engaging in addictive substances invites negativity into your soul, body and life.

- Using drugs and drinking shuts down your ability to guard yourself, and opens you up to spiritual invasion.

- The reason why people "turn into someone else" while drinking or using may be because they are actually possessed by a dark energy.

- If you want to use more of your psychic gifts and connect with the Light, your body must be clear in order to reach the higher angelic realms, because negative energy is too heavy.

- Using drugs only once can enslave your spirit, if a strong enough entity enters you.

- Certain drugs are designed to turn humans into zombies, living only to serve the entity.

- If you knew what monstrous energies were attached to drugs and alcohol, you would not pick them up and put them in your body.

Signs of Addiction (please check addiction recovery resources for more information)

- Increasing use or frequency over time
- A sudden urge or craving that won't go away

- Feeling driven to do it
- Feeling that you can't wait to do it
- Feeling a great sense of relief when you do it
- The addiction preoccupies your thoughts
- Your life has changed for the worse because of it
- Wake up craving it
- Being unable to stop doing it once you've started
- Hating yourself but doing it anyway
- Making excuses for your addiction
- Planning activities around your ability to do it, i.e., only going to restaurants that have bars so you can be sure to drink, only associating with other users, isolating so you can use or drink home alone
- The addiction feels like a friend but also like an enemy
- Feeling as if the addiction is controlling you or your life
- Wanting to stop but not being able to
- Not being able to imagine your life without the addiction
- Devoting increasing resources to it

What You Can Do

- Avoid substances entirely. Just walk away. Say no. Leave.
- Cut back significantly to once a month or less (if you try this and find you can't do it regardless of "reasons," you've probably got a problem).
- Get medical help through rehab and detox; 12-Step recovery programs; Christian organizations or spiritual healing such as Angelic Soul Clearing.™ Consult your medical professional first.
- Ask Archangel Michael to free you from whatever has you captive. Stand up to it. Pray for strength.
- Visualize a demon at the other end of whatever it is you want to use. Refuse to put it in your body or engage in the addictive behavior.
- If you can scan your chakras, see if you can locate the entity and

dialogue with it. Find out why it is there and tell it YOU and ONLY you are in charge of your energy. Tell it to go.

- Talk with your doctor about alternative pain management methods (such as acupuncture, Chinese herbal medicine, hands-on healing, chiropractic, etc) if you are having trouble with prescription pills.
- Stop associating with people, places and things that trigger your addiction.
- Find people, places and activities filled with happy, healthy people who are engaged in life.
- Be willing to live your life fully, no longer hiding behind substances to numb your pain or escape from reality.
- Seek physical, emotional and spiritual healing from reputable and qualified resources.

If Your Loved One Is Addicted

What can you do if someone you love is struggling with addiction? It's the most heartbreaking thing in the world. I am so sorry you are going through this. I know it keeps you in perpetual fear, anger and doubt. I know you wonder how to help. I know you are already praying for your loved one.

In most cases, the person will need to be able to consciously connect with their pain and agree to make changes internally so that healing can happen—whether that healing happens through rehabilitation, 12-Step recovery programs or some other kind of treatment. Willingness to change is essential.

If the addiction is caused by an interfering entity, shamanic or Angelic Soul Clearing™ can often help. See if you can get your loved one to agree to a soul clearing with a qualified practitioner (see Resources).

Do not EVER attempt a clearing on your own. This must be done by someone trained and with special skills. You would not attempt to perform surgery on someone without being a trained and certified surgeon, so do not attempt any kind of spiritual intervention on your own, either.

Shamanic practitioners use their spirit guides to do the work for them. Brian, Cindy and Sean were all easily cleared of their demons in an hour, without great drama or trauma—because we did it all entirely on the soul level. People like myself work in other dimensions so there is no need for any kind of potentially dangerous altercation in the physical world.

Choose Light and Life for Yourself

I cannot tell you what line to draw, or how much to engage with an addict. That is a deeply personal decision, driven by many factors. I will encourage you to seek help and healing for yourself. For not only are you dealing with the terrible loss of the person you knew, but their darkness has brought darkness into your life, too. Your peace and mind and safety have been robbed.

You can make a decision to reinforce your own sacred boundaries and restore the Light to your life, though. Your life matters and the Light does not want to lose you to this darkness and confusion. You can close the door to the addict and not allow that negativity into your life or home.

I know it is hard; you think you are turning your back on your loved one. But you still get to choose how you want your life to be. Love does not require you to be miserable. If you do not allow negativity in, it will stop coming around. You can get spiritual healing for yourself, join recovery groups for codependents such as Al-Anon or get Angelic Soul Clearing™ yourself.

I know this chapter may be an entirely different way of looking at "just having a drink" or "chilling out with friends." **I am not suggesting that everyone who does these things will end up possessed or addicted.** Many people can enjoy substances with no problems at all.

However, we've all known people who have crossed that line from just having fun to something else. Addiction is a complicated problem with many possible origins and treatment. I am simply offering some possible alternate causes and solutions. I hope this gives you some hope.

Addiction only creates misery. Life is waiting for you!

Resources:

https://www.ncadd.org/
www.spiritualresearchfoundation.org
www.narcoticsanonymous.com
www.alcoholicsanonymous.com
http://www.angelicsoulclearing.com

*Withdrawal is a serious medical condition and should be monitored carefully by your doctor. Any information in this chapter or book is for informational purposes only, is the opinion of the author or the source credited and is not intended to be medical diagnosis, advice or treatment, nor as a substitute for any medical advice, diagnosis or treatment. Contact your medical health provider and addiction resources in assessing and treating any addictions you may have.

After encountering the creature that inhabited Cindy, I was delighted to help Lea, an Australian woman whose biggest problem was dealing with her overprotective mother—who just happened to live in a galaxy far, far away.

GALACTIC
INVADERS

29

LEA GETS A SACK LUNCH FROM A MOMMA MANTIS

ea came to me for career guidance after her sister enrolled in one of my online Career Card classes. Like her sister, Lea is wicked-smart and vivacious and wanted to kick her career into motion. However, Lea found it hard to "land" on a career. Very artistic, she wasn't sure if she should continue pursuing creative work or try to do something more stable, such as working for the government. Nothing she did panned out, even though she'd gone on over a dozen interviews. She felt stuck and held back by a mysterious force. Lea said she'd been having stomach issues.

Lea and I did her session over Skype, because she lives in Australia. When I first logged into Skype, her profile picture took me aback. It looked like the mouth of an insect. I looked again and saw it was a close-up of a flower. I brushed it off and began her session. I did the usual protections and invocations and started with her crown chakra.

To my compete shock, I was greeted by a life-size green praying mantis, right there in her mind. I didn't know what to say or do: it was the first time I had encountered an insect within someone's energy field.

Life-Size Praying Mantis In Her Mind

I stammered, but Lea caught on right away. "Whatever it is, you can tell me," she said. "I can take it. Go ahead."

I gulped. "Well, what would you say if I told you there was a praying mantis in your head?" I winced as I waited for her answer.

To my surprise, she laughed. "Oh my!" she said. "You're the second psychic to tell me that. I thought the first one was crazy. In fact I call her, 'The Crazy Lady.' But I know you, and you're definitely not crazy, so tell me more."

Relieved and even more curious, I went back to the praying mantis. She looked a bit like a 1950's Earth mother, with a little lace hat and a purse. Her energy was warm, gentle and maternal. All I could do was shake my head and smile.

She explained that she was Lea's mother from another planet. She was worried about her daughter being so far away from home, and wanted to make sure she was okay.

Just like an Earthly mother whose child goes into space or very far away, this mantis-mother just wanted to check in on her child. I could actually feel the tenderness and love in her heart. I also felt that her fear and worry had been constricting Lea's solar plexus.

Momma Mantis

The mantis conveyed her concerns. She didn't understand why her daughter would want to be all alone, on her own. She didn't understand why her daughter would want to leave a "perfectly good family" and "a perfectly good planet" and go so very far away. The concept of independence was foreign to her. After all, insects are extremely communal.

I explained to the Momma Mantis that some souls want to experience freedom and independence. I told her Earth is a free-will zone and is a refuge for these kinds of souls. I assured her that Lea was doing just fine, and had an Earthly family who were very involved in her life and who cared about her deeply.

I explained the mantis's concerns to Lea, and asked her if she wanted to allow her other-worldly mother's energy to remain within her. She thought about it for a minute. "No," she said. "I want to do this life on my own, and this energy is hindering me. I need to experience full independence. I want her to go."

The Momma Mantis sighed deeply and frowned with sadness, just like a worried Earthly mother. She really did not want to go. However, I persuaded her to "pack up her things and leave." She smiled and waved goodbye, then stood up, clutching her purse as she readied to go.

Just then, the angels showed me a small cluster of energetic eggs stashed within Lea's heart chakra. "Hey! Wait a minute!" I called to the mantis. "What's this? You were to take ALL of your energy with you. Why did you stash these here?"

She turned around, chagrined. She explained that she'd wanted to leave something of herself with her child, in the way that a loving mother would pack a brown bag lunch for a child leaving on a field trip.

I had to smile, because the gesture was genuinely sweet, and she obviously loved Lea, even if she was being a bit overprotective.

The Sack Lunch

I told Lea what she'd left and asked her if she wanted the "sack lunch" (no pun intended) to stay.

"Nope," she said. "Get rid of it. I don't want any of this in me anymore. Tell her to take it all home with her."

Lea felt an immediate release in her heart and solar plexus as the Momma Mantis finally withdrew all of her energy from her. Lea also noticed that her stomach was much calmer and didn't feel so constricted. The block that had been holding her back all her life was gone.

Lea got a job a few weeks later. Without her overprotective Galactic mother trying to hold her back, she is now truly free to really live life on Earth on her own terms.

Lea's case reminds me of something that happened during a consciousness retreat I attended in Petaluma, CA in 2007. During the retreat, one woman said aliens had visited her for years and she even had scars to prove there were implants under her skin. She didn't go into any more detail to the group, but while she and I were walking back to the main room after lunch, she pulled up her blouse and showed me three distinct scars on her belly that made a triangle. "They're always with me," she said happily. "They always talk to me and let me know they're around."

I asked her which alien race it was. Before she could get the words out, a large grey praying mantis about six inches long suddenly materialized on the ground right in front of us.

She burst into laughter. "I told you they are always with me! I guess they would rather show you than have me tell you."

———

Lea and the woman from the retreat did not feel threatened by their praying mantis "families." However, Jennifer's experience with extraterrestrials was not so friendly—until she was freed by the Light.

30

JENNIFER REGAINS HER GOLDEN CORD TO HEAVEN

For much of my adult life, I felt I had a glowing, golden cord that stretched between me and God. I always felt 'plugged in' to the Divine," Jennifer Robinson told me at the start of our session. "It came out of my back, between my shoulder blades, and went straight up. If I concentrated, I could feel the energy coming down from Heaven.

"But, that all changed in 2010. I was on my way to work when suddenly, I felt the golden cord get cut. I actually felt it fall onto the top of the car, almost like a heavy rope. I couldn't breathe. I was so panicked and disoriented that I had to pull over. I just sat there on the side of the highway and cried. I was beyond devastated."

Jennifer wondered what she had done wrong to make Heaven abandon her. She hoped I could give her some insight into the situation and help her regain her connection with the Divine. As I reassured her that many other people have called me with similar issues, she began to cry again. "I know this is going to sound crazy, but during the day I feel like my energy is being stolen from something very dark and menacing. But at night, it's even worse. I wake up to things in my room. They look like aliens or something, and they just sit and stare at me. It's like they're saying, 'We see you, and we are in control.'"

Night Terrors and Sleep Paralysis

Jennifer started to hyperventilate because she was so scared. I instructed her to slow her breathing, and we breathed together until she could regain her composure. "Margo, I know they're there. They're always there, in the dark, waiting for me. It's absolutely terrifying. But, is it even possible? I mean, do aliens really come and bother people like that? It's just so hard to imagine."

What Jennifer described could be called "sleep paralysis," or "night terrors" by the medical and psychological communities. Some people wake up completely paralyzed and unable to move. Some report seeing alien-looking or dark beings hovering over them or holding them down. The medical frame of thought is that people get stuck in deep sleep and are just hallucinating or dreaming.

I asked the angels to please show me what was really going on. I was immediately shown an image of small Grey aliens coming in and out of a window in her bedroom. I was even shown the moment in the car, when they gleefully cut her connection to God.

Wow. I told Jennifer what I'd seen.

"I'm Not Crazy!"

"I knew it!" She burst into tears again. "I've seen them many times out of the corner of my eye. But that's not all—I wake up, screaming and fighting what seems like entities trying to get inside me. It's so horrible. My life is a nightmare! I can't take it. How did this happen? What did I do wrong? Why is this happening to me?"

Jennifer's entire soul and life were in torment. She is a beautiful person who spends her entire life helping people, yet she was being attacked by demonic and alien forces.

The angels and I intervened for Jennifer that night. The angels severed the alien ties and restored her connection to God.

After six long years of torment, Jennifer was finally free. "I can feel the golden cord coming back!" she exclaimed. "I can feel it in that same place in my back. It's warm again!"

Jennifer wrote to me a few weeks after our session to tell me how relieved she felt.

"I immediately felt safer. I no longer felt stalked or watched. I am safe and hidden. It's incredible. Thank you."

Golden Cord Is Restored

About four months later, I reached out to Jennifer to see how she was doing. "I'm whole again!" she wrote. "I've been able to put my golden cord all the way back up to God. I feel so much better, that I'd almost forgotten how bad it was. Just writing this has reminded me of the true evil I had to contend with every day. It's a wonder that I made it. In just one session, I went from living in total fear, and being completely at the end of my rope, to really feeling God's love again."

The evil intruders are gone. Jennifer says a beautiful, golden lion with wings now appears by her bedside to protect her each night.

She wanted her story included in the book. "Margo performed a true miracle that night; she was courageous and powerful in returning the light to my heart and my life. It felt like she literally walked into hell, fought off the demons and pulled me free. I am pretty intuitive and have had psychics and readers help me in the past, but this was different, this was *grace*. Thank you Margo for saving me!"

"You Saved Me"

Jennifer's heartfelt gratitude made me burst into tears. *"This was grace."* I felt so humbled. *God does save.* I try to be a conduit so that grace can happen.

"Words cannot even explain the darkness you lifted from me," she wrote. "I prayed and prayed for help. I had no idea where to turn, because who do you call when you feel like you are being abducted by aliens and used by dark evil entities that you can't even understand? I'm so grateful I found you. If other people are in the same boat, I want them to know they are not alone!"

Validation and Support

Many people endure this kind of torment because they have nowhere to turn to. I hope this book opens up the conversation so people feel safe in sharing their experiences. We need to be more open about this as a culture, because most people actually do believe in aliens and alien visitation.

A 2012 *National Geographic* survey indicated that 77 percent of

Americans believe aliens have visited the planet. A 2015 *Newsweek* poll suggested that 65 percent of American men and 46 percent of American women believe in intelligent extraterrestrial life.

"UFOlogy" is big business, attracting millions to books, comics, TV shows, movies, video games, conventions and merchandise. There has to be a reason why we recognize an alien face the same way we recognize any other cultural icon.

What You Need To Know

Many countries are now opening their UFO files for the public to see. According to the Citizens Panel on Disclosure, which was held August 29th to May 3, 2013, in Washington, D.C., our Universe is filled with all kinds of beings. Former Canadian Minister of Defense Paul Hellyer declared that there were 85 species of aliens interacting with earth and had been for thousands of years. Hellyer and 40 other prominent officials gave 30 hours of testimony to an assembled panel of U.S. members of Congress to update them on the reality of extraterrestrials and said that at least two species are working with the United States government. You can watch the hearings for yourself: (http://www.citizenhearing.org/)

What You Can Do

If you feel you may be an "experiencer," help is available to you at www.experiencer.org. The Mutual UFO Network has chapters all over the world: (*www.mufon.com*). You can also contact the Organization for Paranormal Understanding and Support (OPUS) at www.opusnetwork.org or www.aliens-everything-you-want-to-know.com.

Additional help is available through experienced hypnotherapists or consult a shaman or multi-dimensional healer (see Resources.)

Like Jennifer, Dharma had unwelcome visitors at night. Her story is like something out of a Dan Brown novel (The DaVinci Code, Angels and Demons).

31

DHARMA FALLS UNDER THE GRIP OF GALACTIC DEMONS

Dharma introduced me to yet another level of reality. I'll never forget my Skype sessions with her. It was like something out of the "The Exorcist." My partner, Tiffany, won't ever forget either, because she heard the screams all the way in another room.

Dharma is a beautiful, smart and talented young woman in her early thirties who reached out to me from the UK. She said she found me one night on the Internet, and intuitively felt I could help her.

She spun a wild tale involving the Masons, a church and a Christian organization she worked for that sounded like something straight out of a novel. She said "they" were in her head all the time. She talked about thought control. She said her body and mind were being invaded. She said she suffered from terrible neck and back pain. She said "they" had astral sex with her at night. At first I was dubious. How could a nice, perfectly normal lady be involved in some kind of alien/demonic sex cult? How could that possibly be true? Could such a thing even exist?

The answer revealed itself immediately. Dharma's face contorted as if she was in terrible pain the minute she started to ask me for help. She winced and moaned loudly, as if she was being stabbed from within. Her head violently flipped from side to side, insanely whipping from shoulder to shoulder. She screamed and wailed uncontrollably, her hands flailing wildly in the air. The screams were so loud that I feared someone might call the police on me, or come crashing into her flat in London.

After helplessly watching this happen twice within a matter of minutes, I decided to try and intervene. I called Archangel Michael to help me. I addressed the demons and told them I knew they were there.

"How can you see us? No one can see us!" They said at first, alarmed. "We come and go whenever we want. How can you see us?"

I explained that God gave me a special sight to see what is hidden from others.

"Oh, you're clever," they said. "No one ever knows we are here."

Now that I had their attention, I had Archangel Michael introduce them to the tip of his sword of Light.

"Ow!" They said, "That hurts!" Dharma's face and body contracted immediately as if she was in pain. With Archangel Michael holding them at bay, I commanded them to stop. They settled down. Dharma's head flopped down lifelessly on her chest. I also turned on my tablet and recorded the session.

Millions All Over The Planet

I asked them how many of them were on Earth now. "Oh, millions probably," they said with a laugh. "We're everywhere, in lots of people. There are so many of us," they said gleefully. I asked them where they came from.

The answer was not what I expected. "We come from another planet," they admitted. They refused to tell me which one.

"How do you get in?"

"Oh we get in lots of ways, all kinds of ways. Through organizations, people…We get in through the womb."

"What? How do you do that?"

"We just come in, any time we want to." I really was shocked. I wasn't sure what to say. They were so cavalier!

I wanted to know why they targeted her. "Why her?"

"She is a good vessel," they said. "She is very sensitive. We can use her easily."

Dharma's head hung down the entire time the entities spoke through her. When I asked them why they possessed humans, they said, "It's fun! We can come and go as we please, and do whatever we want. No one ever knows we're here."

Evil Coming From The "Prince of the Air"

I thought of that passage from Ephesians again, and its reference to powers of evil in Heavenly places. Satan is often referred to in the Bible as the "Prince of the Air," and the spiritual hosts of evil are described as fighting in the region above the earth.

These were some sort of galactic demons—just like the Bible refers to.

I commanded the entities to remove all traces of themselves from her body, mind and spirit. In a few minutes, Archangel Michael happily cut them into pieces and dispensed of them with his mighty sword of light.

Dharma stirred to life. "Thank you! I couldn't lift my head or open my eyes before. They wouldn't let me," she explained as she rubbed her neck softly. "My neck doesn't hurt any more. It always hurt before." After seeing what they did to it, I understood why.

Dharma and I talked for a while longer while the angels filled the space the demons had taken up with light and love. Dharma required a few more sessions to completely clear all of her chakras.

Like Regina and so many of my clients, at first I did not recognize Dharma the next time I saw her on Skype. Her facial structure had changed. She'd highlighted her hair. She's lost weight. Even the color of her eyes seemed lighter. She looked remarkably younger and more rejuvenated than before. She does not resemble the person in her Skype photo at all.

Her last session was brief. There was no screaming, no wincing, no pain. She smiled and laughed easily throughout our time together. Her voice was light and lilting, filled with happiness and peace.

Dharma wrote a few months later to tell me that everything in her life had changed. She quit that job and the Masonic organization and moved to another country.

I'd been able to help women in three different countries overcome various types of galactic invasion. Still, I wasn't prepared when trouble struck close to home—and turned Rhonda into a robot.

32

RHONDA BECOMES A ROBOT

Remember Rhonda, the animal rescuer, from earlier in this book? Well, I'd like to say that Rhonda's story ended there. However, like most of us, Rhonda's addictive pattern returned later in a different way, revealing a terrifying level of cosmic interference no one could have anticipated.

Rhonda was a beloved and integral part of the LPAC since the start, so it was very obvious when she began missing classes around January of 2016. She cancelled week after week, citing allergy and sinus problems. I reached out, but she didn't respond. I begged her to come to class so that I could have a look at her, but she refused.

Rhonda finally sent me an urgent text message in February. "Help me. I don't feel like myself anymore. I'm completely numb and dead inside. I know this isn't me. I don't know what's going on. I'm really scared." I called her immediately, but she texted that she was at work and couldn't talk.

The angels told me to have Rhonda send me a picture of herself. What I saw shocked me to the core.

I was extremely alarmed. This was not Rhonda. Not only did she look robotic with vacant eyes and a fixed stare, but her neck was oddly distended, too. Who or what had taken her over?

The angels told me I had to do this

healing in person. Rhonda met me in a parking lot about an hour from her workplace. I snapped a photo of her in her car when she pulled up (at left.)

"Margo," she told me, "I don't know what's taken over me. This is not me. I don't feel anything. I feel like a robot."

I asked her to come out of the car. I put my hand over her head and began to channel very intense healing energy down into her crown chakra. I must have looked like an old-fashioned faith healer, there in the Laguna Hills Ralph's supermarket parking lot praying over her, but I didn't care. I just wanted Rhonda back.

Strong pillar-like beams of white light began to stream thru her body. The healing was brief but powerful. *Her appearance changed instantly.* I immediately took this photo (at right.)

"Oh my God, thank you!" Rhonda cried, breaking into a huge smile. She hugged and squeezed me tightly as the sparkle returned to her eyes and color flooded into her face. "Oh thank God that's gone I can feel me again. I'm back!" She said she felt warm all over and filled with light. Her spunk and vitality were back, too.

I was relieved, but wary. What had done this to her?

Rhonda called me later that night and we went into session to find out how this happened. At first, I saw a series of energetic implants strewn throughout her system. These had short-circuited her neural network, causing her to become robotic. In another part of her energy field, I saw two very long tubes or pipe-

like structures. These very deep columns had a type of homing device or signal attached to them that actually summoned negative energies. It was as if someone had turned on a huge spotlight, invited a bunch of cosmic riff-raff, and said, "Come on in, the party's here!"

The angels removed the series of implants, took out the large homing-beacon tubes and reconnected her neural network. I also saw that some sort of hard metallic cap had been installed over her crown chakra, which prevented divine guidance from getting to her.

I had never seen any of this before. I asked her if she had been to any other healers. She thought hard for a moment, then said she'd had a very common and popular healing treatment a few months back. Rhonda explained that she'd felt a little down and had gone to her friend for a hands-on session because it always makes her feel good.

I asked about the strange cap over her crown chakra. Rhonda explained that this particular healing method does install a sort of energetic barrier to keep any other frequency but itself from entering a person's energy field. This may have been a good thing when it was started back in the early 1900's, but it has undergone many changes since then, including a very controversial one introduced recently.

Rhonda was quick to defend her friend. She said the healer was a very pure soul and would never hurt her. I checked in with the angels. She was right: the problem wasn't coming from her healer.

So what caused this horrible mess?

"It's the healing," the angels answered. "It's been hijacked." They showed me a large spaceship intercepting the healing energy as it poured down from the heavens. The aliens then placed their own implants and energetic ties into it, while the unsuspecting healing practitioner mistakenly delivered it right into Rhonda's energy field, thinking it was only pure, Divine energy.

Later that summer, I saw three women at a holistic fair with that same robotic look. I looked on their uniforms and saw that they worked for a healing center. This gave me the chills.

Humans have no clue this is being done to them. *Healers themselves do not know they are being used in this diabolical way.*

Rhonda is fortunate because she has a strong personality and is in touch with her feelings. She noticed when she had become numb. But what about people who are more naturally repressed? Do they even notice as they are taken over?

All it takes is one look at these amazing before-and-after photos to see that something *supernatural* dramatically changed Rhonda.

Unfortunately, people are completely unaware that their minds and bodies are being affected by unseen invaders.

Remember sweet Travis from the beginning of this book?

Now, it's time to tell you his story.

33

TRAVIS BATTLES 'NANOS' IN HIS BRAIN

Remember Travis from the beginning of this book? His story began in the fall of 2015, when his mother stopped by my booth at a spring fair and drew some Career Cards, just for fun. Amelia picked the Farmer, Advocate, Parent and Legislator cards. She looked confused and told me she worked in real estate.

Hmmm. I thought for a minute. Clean food, children, advocacy, legislation. *Fighting for clean food for kids*. Then, it came to me. "Do you know anything about GMO's? Maybe that's what you're going to fight." She shook her head and looked even more confused.

I explained to her that 90 percent of all crops grown in the United States have been genetically modified, and that big candy companies are now injecting nanobots into candy like M&Ms and chocolate bars.

She suddenly jumped to life. "Oh my God! Travis said that the other day! He said, 'Mom, it's like I have nanos in my brain.' He's always talking about how he feels like worms are crawling around in his head. What does it all mean? Is he crazy?!"

"Nanos In My Brain"

Amelia poured her heart out about her seven-year-old son. "I don't know what's wrong with him," she confided. "He talks to himself all the time. When I ask him who he's talking to, he rolls his eyes and says, 'Mom, they never leave me alone.' He says little men are building things inside his brain. He says he hears loud grinding sounds, like clock gears. He says that the little robots inside his head make these noises. He even talks loud, because he says he has to talk over the noises in his head."

"He's Not A Little Boy... He Looks Right Through Me"

"He can't sleep at night. He's always saying there's something in his room. He says he's a soldier and it's his mission to kill people." She

hung her head in her hands. She looked so helpless and desperate. "I don't know what to do! I thought he was crazy. He's so angry all the time. *Sometimes it's like he's not really a little boy at all. He just... looks through me, you know? I wonder, is he going to hurt me or somebody?* I was going to take him to a psychologist. I am genuinely afraid of him sometimes."

"I'm so sorry," I said. "That must be terrifying." I asked if she would like me to do a session for him. She immediately said yes.

Cyborgs Build Scaffold Inside His Brain

I saw a cyborg within Travis's crown chakra. A cyborg (short for "cybernetic organism") is a being with both organic and biomechatronic body parts. It looked much like what we see in movies and television, with a metal attachment on the side of the face, going up into the brain. My attention was drawn away from it because of loud construction noises. I turned to the source of the sound and saw a huge construction project going on in Travis's brain. Big steel rudders were being lowered down on cranes. Massive scaffolding structures were being built over the existing organic structure of his brain.

Travis was right. Little men were building things inside his brain!

Something foreign had invaded his brain, and was actively rewiring it to its configurations. I did not see or feel anything with consciousness. It was all very automated.

I looked outside the window in his command center to see what was out there. Usually, it's a quiet, expansive view into outer space. Not so with

Travis. His view was crammed with dozens of black, hulking spaceships.

Travis was in the grip of a real-world alien invasion; one that did not come from the skies, but from within his cells themselves.

Angels Could Not Help

I had never seen anything like this. Even the angels couldn't help. "We don't have jurisdiction," they said simply. Countries on Earth have different leaders and governments and respond to their own authorities. Whatever planet this invader was from did not recognize the angels as having authority over them. That might seem weird, but not if the invader is a machine. In our dimension, we wouldn't expect a metal hinge or a car engine to know God. So why then would these machines have any understanding of a Supreme being?

The Universe Sends Alternative Rescuers

Since the angels couldn't intervene, I could ask for help from other Universal forces of Light. Thankfully, they came right away, and made the alien invaders take down all the scaffolding and leave. Once the alien circuitry was gone, the angels removed several implants and repaired his neural network with light.

I told Ameila what I'd seen in her seven-year-old boy. "My God," she exclaimed. "It's all true! Everything he said about the robots in his brain, and being talked to all the time! How can that be? How is that even possible?" All I could do was shake my head and commiserate. I had so many questions myself.

Next, it was time for Travis to receive a protective Guardian. Moses from the Bible stepped forward immediately and said he would look out for him. He seemed to know and love Travis personally. Ameila was delighted when I told her Moses was connected to Travis. "Moses? Travis loves Moses! He always talks about him from Sunday School! He's his favorite Biblical character."

Amelia called me that night with good news. "I have a new little boy!" she said. "He emptied the dishwasher and put everything away without being asked. He's also in a really sweet mood," she said happily. "This is amazing!"

I met Travis three days later. This is the day I referenced in the opening chapter. He played calmly around the office while his mother and I talked. After a few minutes, he said something about needing to go outside. I took it as a cue, and followed him. He walked over to a picnic table and sat down. I sat down next to him.

"My Mom told me what you did for me," he said. "Thanks. I feel better."

"Sure. You're welcome." He was so mature and conscious for his age. "I'm sorry you had to go through all that. Those guys have no business messing with you."

"Yeah," he said wearily. "They were always talking. But the dreams!" His eyes got as wide as saucers. "Oh my God—there's a portal to you-know-where in my room!" He covered his mouth in horror and pointed down at the ground.

Sitting in the warm sun beneath a bright blue sky in the suburbs of Southern California, Travis told me about a nightmare in which Satanic robots came to launch a world invasion. He saw the devil holding a big super-soaker type of gun, and it shot out tiny robots that invaded people and took them over. He was absolutely terrified.

I reassured Travis that I would do my best to help him, and thanked him for telling me. He seemed relieved and then went off to play with my dog, Max.

I went back inside and talked with Amelia. I asked about his nightmares. "He's always dreaming of being in war or combat and having to save everyone. We pray together every night, but I can feel that my prayers are not getting through. It feels so... thick in there sometimes. I don't know what's going on," she admitted.

"I can feel the heaviness in his bedroom of something sad and depressing... I feel so helpless. Who do you turn to, when God doesn't seem to be helping, and your little boy seems like someone else? I don't know what to do."

Well, the first thing you can do is understand that this interference is very real, and believe your children when they complain about things in their room, or you feel an oppressive presence, too.

Monsters Are Real

As you've seen this book, monster ARE real. The angels showed me what was going on in Travis's bedroom at night. He was right to be afraid. I see this so often in children, and it was true for me, growing up, too. I've seen many portals to Hell and other worlds in children's bedrooms.

Believe Your Children

As parents, it's hard to admit we can't always protect our children from harm, especially when that harm is invisible. We think we are helping by looking under the closets or the bed and showing them nothing's there, but really we are just making them feel even more alone—because we can't see what they see.

Encourage kids to tell the truth about what frightens them. Don't pretend the problem isn't there. More and more children are being targeted and affected because they harbor so much Light. Honor their reality. Tell them you can't see it, but you will try and find someone who can. **Try and stay calm and just ask questions. "What does it look like? Where does it hide? What does it do to you? When does it come? What does it want?"**

It's hard enough for children to deal with the Dark, but it's even more impossible if their parents don't believe them. It may not make sense to you, but people like myself and other healers who deal with the supernatural may be able to help. **Now, you have places to turn and people who can help.**

I gave Amelia a salt lamp to put in Travis's bedroom for angelic protection, and did another session for him that evening. I found the portal he'd mentioned on the wall near his bed. I closed it and told Amelia to put a picture of Moses over it. The angels cleared his room and gave instructions for Amelia to clear the rest of the house.

Now Sleeps Peacefully

Amelia called a few days later to tell me that Travis was now sleeping through the night. He'd also experienced some amazing physical changes. He grew an entire size, practically overnight. She had to buy him all new clothes. Travis's facial structure changed, too. A dent in his jaw filled in and

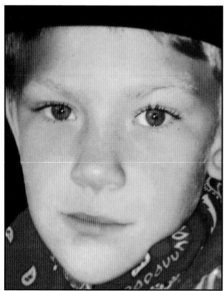 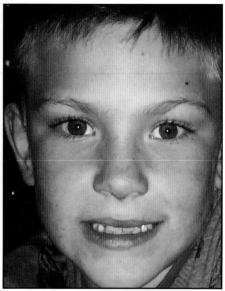

his chin became shorter and rounder. I don't know how to explain that, but you can see right here for yourself. The photo on the left was taken on Halloween, before his clearing. Note the chilling stare and dented chin. The one on the right was taken a few months later, at Christmas. You can see the difference.

"He Changed, Even His Face Changed!"

"He changed so much after Margo did a cleansing on him," Amelia said. "His face changed! He grew a few inches... overnight. He slept without being scared. He was HAPPY, loving. He wanted hugs and kisses. He listened, stopped talking so loud. He knew something inside of him changed... and it was a good something."

Travis smiles and laughs now. Look at him with my dog Max (left). He no longer has the weight of the world on his shoulders. He looks nothing like that burdened, driven soldier on page 230.

"Margo was Travis's knight in shining armor. His Warrior. Travis told Margo all about his feelings and what was going on inside of him. She gave Travis a salt rock nightlight to place in his bedroom, where he could focus on it to help him sleep. It worked! He was mesmerized by the glow soft pink and orange glow, and it really helped.

"Now it feels like angels are in there. You can feel the difference. The

energy is so much nicer and softer and clearer in his room now. It's been a year and a half now, and it still gives him comfort.

"Margo really helped me to understand my son. I was relieved that I wasn't the only one who could see that my little boy was suffering. She helped me realize what was really going on with him, even though it seems bizarre. It all makes sense now."

Angry Since The Womb

Remember the galactic demons that said they come in through the womb? **"I've always said that Travis was born angry,"** Amelia told me. "He wasn't a lovey-dovey baby. He never wanted to be cuddled. Always had a scowl on his face. Something just wasn't right. "How can a little baby have so much anger inside him?

"This little boy wasn't a little boy. I could see it in his eyes. He stared right through me. I was afraid of what he was thinking.... would he hurt me, his sisters, others.... himself?! All I could do was pray he would grow out of it.

"He was often afraid to go to bed, because he would see things and feel things that wouldn't let him sleep. He wasn't getting sleep. He was a zombie. No connection. At bedtime, he would ask me to pray over him. This made him feel safe. But deep down, I knew this wasn't helping him. He was trapped. My poor little boy."

We would like to believe Travis is an isolated case, but he is not the only child haunted by darkness.

Erin Loses Her Anger Overnight

A few months after clearing Travis, one summer evening, I went for a walk outside my apartment. I hadn't gotten very far when I heard a family arguing. I turned my head just in time to see a mother slap her six-year-old little girl across the face. I yelled, "Hey! I saw that! Stop it!" I wanted to call the police, but the angels stepped in. "That's not the answer," they said calmly. "This isn't what it seems. Go over there and talk to the family and offer help and compassion."

So, instead of being angry or threatening, I approached them with concern. The mother looked frazzled and overwhelmed. The little girl looked upset and confused. I introduced myself. The mother shook my hand and told me her name was Joan. I smelled alcohol on her breath. The little girl said her name was Erin. I gave Joan a sympathetic gaze. "I know it's hard raising kids. Sometimes they just drive you crazy."

"Thanks," she said, visibly relaxing. "I'm a single Mom and it's just hard. She's always picking on her little brother!" she told me in exasperation. "She keeps holding him down and hitting him. I don't know what to do to make her stop!"

Help For Erin's Impulses

I asked Erin if it was hard for her to not want to hit her brother. "Yes!" She said. "I don't want to, but then I can't stop myself sometimes. I want to, but I can't. I don't understand," she said helplessly. "I want to be good." She frowned and hung her head.

I told Erin and Joan that sometimes bad things make people do bad things, and it's not their fault. Then I offered Joan a hug. She gratefully accepted and I held her for a long moment. Erin wanted a hug too, so I happily obliged. The tension melted, and they invited me into the house to meet Erin's brother and all the animals. I stayed about 45 minutes. When I left, I hugged Erin goodbye and told her I would see if I could help get rid of the urges to hurt her brother.

I went home and prayed for the entire family. Several dragons and parasites left them.

A Kinder Child

I saw Erin a few days later. I was surprised to see that she had grown several inches taller, just like Travis. She was also gentler, less hyperactive and more cooperative while playing outside with other kids in the complex.

When we moved out six months later, I asked the leasing agent how the family was doing. "You know, they're doing great," the agent said. "The Mom was always angry every time she came in; mad about everything. We got complaints about them fighting, too. But about six months ago, that all stopped. Now, she's always smiling and happy. Just the other day she thanked us for putting up with her before. I haven't noticed her drinking anymore, either. I don't know what happened, but they're great!"

Travis's Plight Is Not Far-Fetched

Travis begins and ends this book, because his story is so important. When I first wrote, "Everything changed the day I met Travis," I knew those were going to be the first words of the book. Those words were sacred. They flowed onto the page and remained there patiently for 18 months, while the book took its time to evolve around them.

At the time, Travis's plight seemed really far-out. I thought perhaps he was just an unusual case, like Lea. However, since then, I've cleared many other people around the world of the exact same things.

They all had the same neural implants and scaffolding—all the way from a three-year-old to a 66-year old man.

Tragically, Travis's predicament is becoming more and more common. Some parents say their children became "zombies" after receiving certain vaccines. Autism is rising at an alarming rate. Children are actually excreting pesticide in their urine.

One day, I gathered my courage and asked the angels how all these people got "infected" with this alien technology.

"Food," they said. "It's in the food."

That's when I learned about nano-technology and genetically modified foods—and that "scaffolding" is actually a term used in tissue engineering.

34

PESTICIDES, GMOS AND NANOBOTS: THE HIDDEN WAR ON HUMANITY

I wasn't surprised when the angels said food was the source of the changes in Travis's brain, especially since so much has changed about the U.S. food supply in the last 20 years.

When I began writing this chapter, I had no idea where the rabbit hole would take me. The angels kept leading me to more and more revelations, long after I hoped the book would be complete.

This chapter and the next contain a lot of little-known information the angels want you to know about what is *really* going into your body through food and vaccines. The angels love you, and want you to be able to make informed choices about your health and safety.

This information affects nearly everyone in one way or another. We hope that our governments are looking out for our safety and best interests. However, the way our food and water are handled gives much cause for alarm.

Food is supposed to be nutritious. Food is life. Water is life. However, today's kids ingest so many poisons *that they are actually peeing pesticide:*

it's in their urine.

While researching what was behind the strange "scaffolding" I'd found in Travis and other clients, I discovered many disturbing facts about *our food supply—and how it affects children's brains.*

A Universal Problem

Even though the material in this chapter was hard to process at times, I enjoyed rolling up my sleeves and returning to my investigative reporter days. I read scientific journals and research papers. I combed through vaccine ingredients. I investigated GMOs, genetic engineering and nanotechnology. I discovered links between pesticides and ADHD. I worked hard to bring you information straight from the source, including the Vatican itself.

Pesticides Linked to ADHD

As you remember, Travis and Erin were both very hyperactive prior to their clearings.

The angels were right: pesticides sprayed onto food strongly do affect children's neural networks.

Children regularly ingest overwhelming amount of toxins, including highly toxic forms of neurotoxins that damage their growing brains and result in problems like Attention-Deficit Hyperactive Disorder (ADHD), according to Dr. Phil Landrigan, Chair of the Mt. Sinai School of Medicine in New York City *(http://www.nbcnews.com/id/44260583/ns/health-childrens_health/t/pesticides-food-linked-adhd-kids).*

When asked how children are introduced to such poisons, Dr. Landrigan said, "The exposure is mainly through food."

Children with substantially higher levels of a breakdown product of neurotoxic organophosphate pesticides were **twice as likely to be diagnosed with ADHD,** according to the United States Centers for Disease Control and Prevention's National Health and Nutrition Examination Survey *(https://www.cdc.gov/nchs/nhanes/).* Pyrethroids are found in insecticides that control mosquitoes, ants, spiders, cockroaches, termites and agricultural pests.

Pyrethroid Linked To Agressive Behavior

It seems that these neurotoxins also lead to bad behavior in children. Pyrethroid traces in the urine of mothers-to-be was associated with children who showed what psychologists call "externalizing behaviors," which includes cheating, stealing, rule-breaking, physical aggression, and destruction of property, according to a 2006 study by the French Research Institute for Public Health (*https://tonic.vice.com/en_us/article/a-common-bug-killer-may-be-causing-problems-in-kids*).

Children with the highest levels of pyrethroid metabolites in their own urine were about three times more likely to display abnormal behavior.

Autism Linked To Pesticides

The widespread use of pesticides may be contributing to autism, too, because of the very potent neurotoxins and how they affect the nervous system and brain development.

Autism has risen seven-fold since 2000 and researchers are scrambling to determine the cause. Scientists at the University of California, Davis, found a strong correlation between pesticides and autism in the most comprehensive study conducted on the correlation between pesticides sprayed on crops and autism in children.

The study of 970 children, born in farming areas of Northern California, is part of the largest project to date that is exploring links between autism and environmental exposures.

Babies whose moms lived within a mile of crops treated with widely used pesticides were more likely to develop autism.

Children with mothers who lived less than one mile from fields treated with organophosphate pesticides during pregnancy were about 60 percent more likely to have autism than children whose mothers did not live close to treated fields.

When women in the second trimester lived near fields treated with chlorpyrifos—the most commonly applied organophosphate pesticide—their children were 3.3 times more likely to have autism, according to the Northern California-based Childhood Risk of Autism from Genetics and the Environment (CHARGE) Study.

U.S. Crops Sprayed With Derivative Of Nazi Nerve Gas

So what exactly is causing all these reactions? The number one pesticide used on U.S. crops today is chlorpyrifos, a powerful neurotoxin—a neurotoxin that was originally developed as a biological weapon by the Nazis during World World War II. It is *so* toxic that the EPA banned it in 2000 for residential use. Unbelievably, something that was not considered safe to ever be used in a home is still massively sprayed onto the very food we eat. More than 200 million gallons of it are sprayed annually on about 50 different types of crops, from almonds to apples.

So Dangerous Workers Must Wear Hazmat Suits

Have you ever really stopped to wonder WHY field workers have to wear full hazmat suits to spray the food you eat?

The reason you see field workers wearing hazmat suits when they spray the crops is because chlorpyrifos is an acute neurotoxin that can cause convulsions and even death. Each year, more than 100,000 fieldworkers are treated for acute poisoning from spraying fields. A Los Angeles jury awarded $3.2 million to six Nicaraguan farmworkers who were rendered sterile from a Dow pesticide *(http://articles.latimes.com/2007/nov/06/local/me-dole6)*.

In 2016, the United Farm Workers Union petitioned the Enivronment Protection Agency (EPA) to protect children from exposures that cause irreversible brain damage, including reduced IQ, attention deficit disorders, and learning disabilities.

Pesticides Harm Children's Brains

All this exposure to chemicals is overloading and mutating children's brain cells and severely affecting their mental, physical and social development.

A 2017 petition to the EPA by The Center For Food Safety sums it up pretty well: "Long-term studies sponsored by the EPA and NIH have established that when pregnant women are exposed to chlorpyrifos and other organophosphate insecticides, resulting in fetal exposure, their children grow up to have lower IQ scores, increased rates of attention deficit hyperactivity disorder (ADHD), and poorer mental development than unexposed children. The evidence is so strong that Dr. David Bellinger, a Harvard neurologist, estimates that Americans lose, collectively, 16.9 million IQ points due to fetal and early childhood exposure to chlorpyrifos and other organophosphates. Fetal exposure to chlorpyrifos has also been associated with reduced birth weight and length, reduced gestation time and autism spectrum disorder."

The U.S. uses a billion pounds of pesticide each year. This pesticide also runs off into our groundwater and affects people and cattle, too *(https://www.ncbi.nlm.nih.gov/pmc/articles/PMC2946087/).*

20 Pesticides on One Strawberry

Every year The Environmental Working Group creates a "Dirty Dozen" list of the most chemically-laden foods. **A single strawberry was found to contain 20 different pesticides in 2016. (***www.ewg.org and Food News, www.foodnews.org*).

Do we need that many pesticides, when they're clearly bad for the brain and body? You might think that it's okay because insecticide is just sprayed onto food and might be able to be rinsed off. However, that is not the case.

Today's "food" is engineered to have even more poison grown right into the plant itself.

Genetically Modified Organisms

In August of 2016, I gave a presentation entitled, *"The Terrifying Truth Behind Nanobots, GMOs and Vaccines"* at the Awareness Life Expo in Sacramento, CA. It was selected to be one of the opening presentations for the three-day conference, and was extremely well-received.

The audience listened raptly as I explained that ninety percent of food grown in the Unites States is now genetically modified.

That means that virtually ALL conventional produce is no longer considered "food" because it has been altered so significantly. It does not exist in nature.

It's now an "organism."

**GMOs—or genetically modified organisms—
are created in a lab by altering the genetic makeup
of a plant or an animal.**

Consumer Reports, February 9, 2016

Welcome To "Frankenfood"

Virtually all of the ordinary produce you eat is not really food anymore. It has been created IN A LAB through gene-splicing, and is then planted.

Business Insider makes this distinction about how genetics are used in today's food supply. "A distinction must be established, particularly in the public sphere, between 'genetically modified organisms' (GMOs) generated through the transgenic introduction of foreign DNA sequences and 'genome-edited crops' (GECs) generated through precise editing of an organism's native genome. Genome editing is a more efficient and precise method of manipulating genes than the conventional breeding methods we have used for millenia. By comparison, GMOs contain DNA from other organisms, which would not be found in nature." (*http://www. businessinsider.com/difference-between-genetically-edited-crops-and-gmos-2016-2*)

Even if it's not a separate organism that doesn't exist in nature, do you still want scientists playing God with your grapes?

What's Inside That Organism?

Want to know what's now inside your produce? Well, it could include insect DNA, viruses, parts of animals, parts of plants, virtually anything. "The current regulations were written for the earlier generation of genetically modified organisms, where scientists used bacteria and viruses—typically from plant pests—to drop a payload of new genes into the nuclei of the plant cells where they merge with the plant's DNA. That worked, but scientists could not control where the new genes would be inserted, and that led to worries of potentially dangerous genetic disruptions or crossbreeding with non-G.M.O. crops." *(These Foods Aren't "Genetically Modified, But They Are Edited," New York Times, January 9, 2017. www.Nytimes.com)*

The Food *Inside* Your Food Is GMO

Thanks to companies like Monsanto, virtually everything we eat, including corn, soy, canola and alfalfa is now genetically modified organisms. Corn is the #1 GMO "food" and it's in virtually everything imaginable. Thankfully the sweet corn you eat is not likely to be genetically modified, but "field corn" that is used to make everything from corn syrup to ethanol is. Pick up anything in your pantry and look for corn syrup. Milk is also genetically modified as cows are given antibiotics and growth hormones.

A Time Magazine article on April 30, 2015 gives a comprehensive look at how ubiquitous GMOs are in our food supply: including being used heavily in animal feed. Corn and Alfalfa are predominantly all genetically modified "organisms." *(http://time.com/3840073/gmo-food-charts/)*

So *we're* eating GMOS and *what we're eating* is eating it, too.

All this genetic tinkering has introduced a number of foreign bodies into what used to be products like wheat, corn and milk—the staples of much of the world's diet. I didn't find out about GMOs until the last few years, but I've known something was wrong with our produce for a long time.

Noticed A Change in The 1990s

I grew up in the Midwest with homegrown fruits and vegetables. I know what food is supposed to be like. I'll never forget the day I walked into a market in California in the mid-1990's and selected a plum. That moment has stood out in my mind for over 25 years. It was one of those moments when you realize that something has fundamentally changed.

I remember being so excited for a fresh crop of plums—sweet, juicy, a great combination of slightly crunchy skin, but then the delicious eruption of sweet juiciness inside. I happily picked it up and inhaled deeply to enjoy its sweet scent. *But there was no scent at all. It was hard. It was strange. It really did not taste or smell like food.* Then strawberries burgeoned to three and four times their size and were red on the outside, but hard and shiny white on the inside. I discovered that they started introducing GMOs into the food supply in 1994.

Today, I always buy organic. One day I bit into an apple that Tiffany assured me was organic. It was horrible. I spit it out. Still thinking it was organic, she threw it outside for the birds. I came across it in the dirt two two days later, absolutely untouched. Not one insect had eaten it. Not one bird nibbled from it. "In the old days," when food was really food, if you dropped anything on the ground, the ants swarmed it immediately.

So what is in that apple that is so bad that even ants won't eat it?

Poison Apple?—"Arctic' Apple First Openly Marketed GMO Food

The first broadly marketed GM (Genetically Modified) apple is called "Arctic" and its targeted to kids, pre-sliced. It's supposed to debut in 2017. Scientists tinkered with it to stop apples from browning. We have no idea what that new organism really consists of—because it did not grow from a natural tree, and they are not required to disclose that fact to us.

This "apple" is owned and created by a bio-firm called "Intrexon." Do you want to eat an apple "created" by a company?

Worldwide Resistance

I doubt the "Arctic" apple will be labeled as GMO, though, since a bill that would have been passed in 2016 that would require GMO foods to be clearly labeled was stopped by Congress. More than 38 countries have banned GMO crops, and 60 countries require GMO labeling, but not the U.S. Here in America, money far outweighs conscience, so Monsanto is allowed to hide its dirty deeds from us and not tell us what is really in our "food."

Genetically Modified Salmon

I used to love canned salmon. I ate it for lunch a few times a week. But then, about a year ago, Tiffany brought home a can of salmon and I knew something had changed about it. I could not bring myself to open the can, much less eat it. I then found out that scientists are "planning" on introducing genetically-modified salmon to the consumer sometime soon. My senses tell me they already have.

Food Allergies and Gluten Intolerance

In 2016, Consumer Reports tests discovered that GMOs were present in many packaged foods, such as breakfast cereals, chips, baking mixes and even protein bars. These hidden "foreign bodies" may behind the rise in food allergies, because our intestinal systems were not designed to digest DNA from insects, plant viruses or other animals. Our bodies are trying to kick out those foreign genetic invaders, which has created an epidemic. Gluten intolerance is not celiac disease. It is an inflammatory response created in the gut to ward off things that your body knows do not belong there.

Organ Failure, Cancer, Intestinal Bleeds From GMOs

In 2012, Dr. Hussein Kaoud, of Cairo University's Faculty of Veterinary Hygiene, fed nine groups of rodents different genetically modified foods such as potatoes, corn, grapes and tomatoes for a period of three months. Symptoms started within a month, *even though GMOs only constituted about 10 percent of the animals' diet.* Their kidneys shrunk. Their liver and spleens changed. They experienced kidney failure and intestinal bleeds.

"The brain functions were touched as well, and the rats' learning and memory abilities were seriously altered," he said. Some rats had a severely lowered immune response and were much more sensitive to environmental pollution, especially heavy metals and dioxin. Some even developed cancer.

The death rate of baby rats raised by mothers on a diet of genetically modified corn increased by 35 percent, compared with the group of babies whose mothers ate natural corn. They were also considerably smaller.

Half of them died after three weeks.

What You Need To Know

- 90 percent of all the fruits and vegetables grown in the United States are Genetically Modified Organisms.

- Genetically-Modified Organisms are NOT food. They do not exist in nature. They are a unique life form that has been created in a lab.

- Corn, soy, canola, beet sugar and cotton are ALL GMO now and are staple products in almost every food product—i.e., corn syrup, glucose, soy lecithin, etc.

- Genetically-modified fruits and vegetables often contain viruses, bacteria and genetic material from insects, animals and humans.

- Genetically-modified products and produce are not required to be labeled.

- Popular baby foods and formulas are made with GMOs

Americans Want GMO Food Labeled

Even Gerber confirms that only its organic line and pureed fruits and vegetables are free of GMOs. But at least Gerber is disclosing what is in your infant's food, something that 92 percent of Americans want. They believe that GMO foods should be labeled before they're sold, according to the Consumer Reports National Research Center. In 2013, sales of non-GMO products that were either certified organic that carried the "Non-GMO Project Verified" seal increased by 80 percent, according to the Nutrition Business Journal.

Don't you want to know what is in your food? You can advocate for stronger standards and labeling practices, but the biggest step you can take for your family's health is to eat organic fruits and vegetables and grass-fed beef. This solves the pesticide problem, too.

Eating Organic Reduces Pesticides And GMOs

"It's been shown that people who switch to an organic diet knock down the levels of pesticide by-products in their urine by 85 to 90 percent," Dr. Phil Landrigan said. The pesticides study researchers concluded that parents should buy organic and that women should eat organic at least six months before conception and throughout pregnancy.

Look for the label above. *Don't assume that your local farmer's market is run by local farmers and is organic.* Their crops are highly likely to be GMO and heavily sprayed, too. Tiffany and I were going to stop at a cute farmer's market in Irvine, CA—*until I literally saw three men spraying the fields in hazmat suits*—just like the picture at the beginning of this chapter.

Organic Is Now More Affordable and Accessible

Organic and gluten-free foods are becoming more affordable and are carried by mainstream markets such as Ralphs and Stater Brothers. Even Wal-Mart is getting in the game, because consumers want clean and healthy food. Even spice companies are going non-GMO (see right).

Check Consumer Websites And Publications

Subscribe to publications and online groups such as The Center For Food Safety *(www.centerforfoodsafety.org)*, Consumer Reports *(www. consumer reports.org)* and other websites mentioned in these graphics. They offer shopping guides, foods to avoid and conduct ongoing testing to ensure that foods do not contain GMOs and other questionable substances. There are lots of resources out there to help you buy what is truly wholesome and nutritious for your family.

Consumer Reports has great information on which foods have the highest levels and how to mitigate pesticide consumption in your household *(http://www.consumerreports.org/cro/health/natural-health/pesticides/index.htm)*

Understand Bar Codes

Check for bar codes, but know that most GMOs are not labeled.

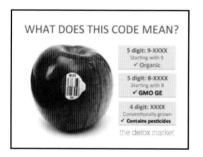

Buy produce starting with #9 or a label. Always wash produce, even if it organic. Some pesticides can be removed by rinsing thoroughly under water.

But that will not remove the poison spliced into the plant's DNA—or the genetic encoding that is being passed directly into your cells, either.

Nanotechnology and You

Now that you understand GMOs, it's time to tell you about the latest thing to be snuck into your food: **nanotechnology.**

"New research shows that when we eat, we're consuming more than just vitamins and protein. Our bodies are also absorbing information, through RNA, which carries information through the cells." *(The Atlantic, January 9, 2012)*

Nanotechnology is the branch of technology that deals with dimensions and tolerances of less than 100 nanometers, especially the manipulation of individual atoms and molecules. Nanoparticles are 1/1000 smaller than a single human hair and exist at the sub-atomic level.

Nanoparticles are so infinitesimally small that they just float in and out of your cells. They bypass the very important blood/brain barrier, which is a crucial protective membrane around the cells that keep foreign matter out.

Nanos Bypass The Crucial Blood Brain Barrier

Think of the membranes that surround your cells and your brain itself like screen doors. Ordinarily, the holes in the screen are small enough to trap invaders and keep them out. But tiny gnats and other insects can get through if they are small enough.

Nanotechnology makes it now possible to permeate these protective mechanisms. They are too small. The normal barriers that our cells erect to protect themselves from invading organisms cannot keep nanotechnology out. *It slips through and inserts itself right into the cell.* Nanobots allow for programmed nanos to be put into the body, where they then carry out their program. Some medical applications include using nanos to target cancer cells instead of using destructive chemoetherapy, which attacks the entire body. Medicines could also be delivered directly into the cell itself, bypassing the digestive system, which could make treatments more effective.

Nanotechnology and Scaffolds

Nanotechnology is being widely used in tissue regeneration, which brings me back to Travis and the strange "scaffolding" I kept seeing being inserted over his neural network. My angels kept saying the word "scaffolding" over and over again, until I finally researched it and discovered that **"scaffolding" is an actual term used in genetic tissue engineering—and nanotechnology is used to change and modify human tissues.** The scaffolds are there to provide a place for the nanobots to build new tissue over existing organic matter.

Scaffolds Hold Tissue So Nanos Can Build Over It

"These scaffolds essentially act as a template for tissue formation and are typically seeded with cells ... or subjected to biophysical stimuli in the form of a bioreactor; a device or system which applies different types of mechanical or chemical stimuli to cells. These cell-seeded scaffolds...

can then be implanted into an injured site, or are implanted directly... using the body's own systems, where regeneration of tissues or organs is induced *in vivo*. *(Source: Materials Today, Vol. 14, issue 3, March, 2011)*

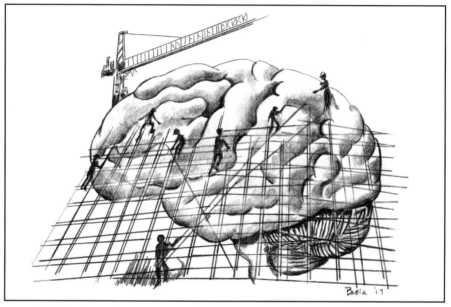

This is how the scaffolding appeared within Travis's brain.

Nanos Can Redirect Cell Function

Nanotechnology is literally used to implant a different cellular code within a person's living tissues and then change cell growth to the new code. The new code also get wired directly into the cell's DNA, where it then gets replicated in all future cells. *This then begins to permanently change the organism into something different than it was before.*

Apparently, what I saw inside Travis's brain is exactly like real-world nano scaffolds. This is how scientists change, modify and regenerate cell tissues using very small nanobots. However, none of my clients were medical patients. I've energetically removed several implants from the brains of Travis and several other people who had scaffolding being erected over their brain tissue. Other healers keep removing what they call "nannites," which are also always found coupled with implants.

Invisible Machines Inserted Into Candy and Food

I know it seems right out of a science fiction movie (again.) But these are the times we live in. Technology is growing faster than we can contain or moralize it. *Would you knowingly insert a micro-machine programmed for God-knows-what into your cells?* Probably not—just like you would not consent to toxic pesticides or GMOs.

So, how are nanos getting into people's bodies?

Remember when the angels said the invader was getting in through food? I thought of Travis being groomed to be a soldier, along with the strange and hyperactive behavior many children exhibit after eating candy. I went looking for nanotechnology in candy—and was shocked by what I found.

Mass-Produced Candy Contains Nano-Technology

"Nanotechnology is a powerful new tool for reconstructing nature at the molecular level—and it has some scary repercussions when used in food products. Nano-scale materials are really small, highly reactive particles that can pass through the body's blood-brain barrier to places in the human body that other materials can't, and cause more damage when they do... and consumers have almost no information." *(http://www.centerforfoodsafety. org/blog/4549/say-no-to-nano-tricks-in-our-treats-please#)*

I long suspected candy might be a carrier, but last year at Halloween, Tiffany walked in the house with some candy that had a cartoon superhero on the box.

"Want some?" She said cheerily.

"No. Throw it away," I said without thinking. "It has nanobots."

I could sense them.

Top Candy Company MARS Commits to Phasing Out Harmful Nanoparticles from Food Products

Center for Food Safety urges fast action and broader commitment on removal - WASHINGTON— This week MARS Corp.

Read More

Titanium Dioxide Found In Food

"Titanium dioxide is often found in candy... and studies show it can cause pathological lesions of the liver, spleen, kidneys, and brain; lung tumors; and inflammation, cell necrosis, and dysfunction in the kidney." *(Center for Food Safety, www.centerforfoodsafety.org).* Titanium Dioxide is a nanoparticle used in many food and plastic products—everything from yogurt to sunscreen to tires and even baby products. It is said to be used as a whitener and to provide texture.

I shudder when I think about the scaffolding going on in Travis's young brain, or the fact that our favorite snack and comfort foods are laden with tiny machines—all without our knowledge or consent.

"Partially Produced With Genetic Engineering"

I edited this chapter on March 31, 2017, and happened to see this on the back of a popular brand of cupcakes.

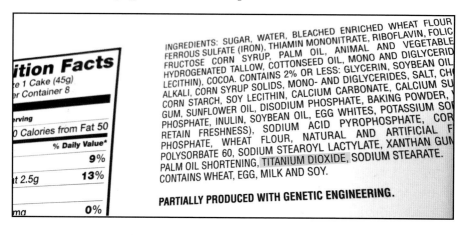

Titanium Dioxide / Partially Produced with Genetic Engineering

Look just above this headline. See? It's right there. "*Partially produced with genetic engineering.*" I also recently saw the same thing on the back of a "100-calorie" cookie package. Go ahead. Let it sink in. I know it's hard to believe, but it's true. It's right there in the candies you trust. Does this seem "wholesome" to you? Do you want your food made in a lab?

Hostess, M&Ms, Hershey's, Betty Crocker, Kool Aid Contain Nanos

Nanotitanium is found in products produced by Jello, Nestlé, M&M's, Mother's, Mentos, Albertson's, Hostess and Kool Aid. *(Source: "Nano-Particles in Consumer Products Damage DNA Leading to Cancer "Waking Times April 10, 2014)*

These brands have also been tested and confirmed to contain them: Skittles, Cadbury, Pop-Tarts, Trident, Dentyne and Eclipse gum and Mars candies.

Are Nanos Necessary?

Why on Earth would food and beverage companies need to insert something that goes past your cell's defense system and goes directly into your brain? Do you really believe it's making your food and candy taste better? **Do you think your food should have tiny robots in it**?

Besides truly terrifying in their broader implications, nanoparticles have been proven to be harmful.

According to the Center for Food Safety, nanoparticles can cross biological membranes, cells, tissues and organs more readily than larger particles. "Once in the blood stream, nanomaterials can circulate throughout the body and can lodge in organs and tissues including the brain, liver, heart, kidneys, spleen, bone marrow and nervous system. Once inside cells, they may interfere with normal cellular function, cause oxidative damage and even cell death. (*http://www.centerforfoodsafety.org/issues/682/nanotechnology/risks-of-nanotechnology)*

Not surprisingly, the same government that fails to keep you safe from GMOs and pesticides currently does not regulate the use of nanotechnology in food products, despite its widespread use and serious public health concerns. Europe and the Canadian government have taken the first steps to limit the use of nanotechnology in food, but the U.S. has so far only issued draft guidelines to companies.

Check The Center For Food Safety's Interactive Database

The Center for Food Safety maintains an interactive database (shown on the next page) so you can check specifically which candy and foods contain nanos. You or your child could be eating something that contains nanotechnology, but has not yet been tested.

What You Need To Know

- Nanotechnology is 1/1000 the size of a human hair and can penetrate every cell in your body.

- Nanoparticles are too small to be seen by a miscoscope.

- Nanotechnology is used in tissue engineering, where it is implanted within the cell and then begins to grow the new cells that have been programmed into it over existing ones.

- Nanotechnology bypasses the blood/brain barrier and inserts itself directly in your cells. It may carry an unknown payload that could rewrite your cell's codes.

- At this writing, nanotechnology is in many popular foods,

including M & Ms, Hershey's chocolate bars, yogurts and baby products.

• Nanotechnology is found in food dyes.

• Nanotechnology has been proven harmful to the body and can even cause cell death.

• Nanotechnology is not regulated by the U.S. government.

What You Can Do

• Avoid popular candy brands. Buy organic sweets and chocolate.

• Check to see if your favorite foods are listen in the Center for Food Safety's nanotechnology database (www.centerforfoodsafety.com).

• Avoid processed foods, because they often contain unlabeled GMOs and nanoparticles.

• Strengthen your immune system with quality probiotics & supplements (check with your health care provider)

I know it hasn't been easy or fun to learn the dark truth about what's really inside your food, but hang in there: there's one more important thing the angels want you to know.

———————————————————

Remember those tiny Satanic robots that Travis saw being shot out of a super-soaker type of water gun? I didn't know what to make of it at the time. However as I was finishing this book, I had a vision of that water gun as a syringe, shooting out microscopic invaders. In other words: a vaccine.

35

MARY AND JESUS CONFRONT "THE INTELLIGENCE"

Mary Prosh's story unfolded just as I was finishing this book. It's the perfect ending, in so many ways. Mary's story is one of the most touching stories of Divine intervention I've ever witnessed, and demonstrates that God is the most powerful force in the Universe.

The angels brought Mary and I together at a crucial time while I was working on this chapter. I'd previously gathered some material on GMOs and nanobots, but didn't have enough on vaccines. So, two days before the book deadline, I hunkered down, doing research. I felt so pressured that I locked the door to my office, handed Tiffany my phone and told her not to bother me for any reason. About twenty minutes later, just after I discovered the U.S. government's National Vaccine Injury Compensation Program begun in 1986, Tiffany appeared at my window. She smiled tentatively and pointed to my phone. For some reason, I wasn't upset at all, and got up and took the phone call.

Mary introduced herself and apologized for bothering me. She said she knew I was on deadline, and was looking forward to reading my book. I thanked her for her understanding. Then, for some reason, I blurted out that I was researching the detrimental effects of vaccines.

Nurse Calling About Vaccines

"Well, I'm a nurse, and I have an issue with some vaccines," Mary said. "In fact, that's why I made the appointment with you. I've had low back pain ever since I got a flu shot back in 1987. I've thought about it many times, and I just know that somehow that shot is the reason for my pain."

My jaw dropped. I was working on a chapter about vaccines, and the only call I decided to take happened to be from a woman complaining about vaccines? What are the odds?

"It's so weird that I called you," she said. "I didn't want to interrupt you, so I was actually writing you an email. Then I distinctly heard, 'No. You have to call her. Call her right now!'

Mary and I agreed that the angels worked hard to connect us that day, first by urging her to call me, then by causing Tiffany to bring me the phone, and finally by persuading me to take the call. I told Mary I would postpone my writing and do her session that evening.

"Strange Pain In My Back"

Mary started the session by telling me about the pain. She described it as a "malaise," a "weird-I-can't explain-it pain" in her back. "It's always there, ranging from a three or four on the pain scale, all the way up to a seven or eight most days," she said. "It's just the strangest pain. There's no explanation for it. All my blood work comes up clean. Doctors don't know what could be causing it. The pain itself is hard to describe: it's not like anything I've ever felt before. It's not localized. It's not specific. I just hurt. My lower back always feels strange. Every time I think about this pain, I look back to that day in 1987, after I got a flu shot. I got sick when I got home. I knew something was very wrong, because I hurt all over. So many times I've looked back in regret, and thought, 'I never should have gotten that flu shot. It all started then.'"

I began Mary's session with her crown chakra. Two little girls greeted me, jumping up and down and clapping their hands. "We're so excited you're here!" they said. "We don't know what else to do." Mary then told me that she had literally tried everything she could possibly think of to heal her back, including: chiropractic, acupuncture, supplements, yoga, water therapy, Japanese cupping, (see photo above) stretching exercises, etc. Absolutely nothing worked. I understood why she was so eager for relief.

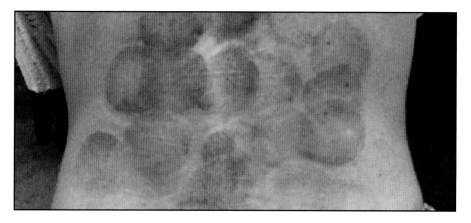

The little girls pointed to several square boxes about a foot wide that were stored all over the command center. I opened the boxes to find what looked to be some kind of spoiled produce. I left them there for the moment, knowing that I would come back later. There was also a white shade over the windows. I couldn't see outside. This concerned me

I moved onto Mary's throat chakra. It yelled loudly, "Somebody help us! I'm sick of this pain!" I assured it I would do my best. I tried to access Mary's heart chakra, but could not get in. Down in the solar plexus I heard the tell-tale screams and wails of demonic visitors, but they did not seem to be "dark" in nature. This was some other kind of demon. They seemed more technological in nature. "We were unleashed on her long ago," they said, and pointed to a small metal box secreted in the chakra below.

Transmitter In Her Back

I've seen this type of device in other people. It appears sort of retro, like it was made in the 1950's or 1960's. It's a square metallic transmitter with antennas and blinking lights. One of the archangels instantly picked it up and lifted it out of her carefully, as if it was a bomb that might explode. He set it aside. To all of our surprise, it detonated with a deafening explosion just a few seconds later.

"What was that?" I asked the angel. The angel responded that he'd seen it many times before, in people that received shots and vaccines. "It's a foreign invader, involving gene splicing," he said. "The body is resisting this foreign invader and is trying to get it out." With the black box removed from Mary's sacral chakra, I was able to see the devastation it created within her. The nerves and tissues in the low back and sacral area had been completely ravaged. The network of nerves and tissues appeared to be "fried" in some way.

The angels removed and vaporized it. As they did, a hard, circular black metal piece fell to the ground—some kind of remnant. Instantly, a portal to another galaxy opened up right beside it, snatched it up and then slammed shut behind it.

The "Intelligence" Appears

As soon as the transmitter vanished, a tunnel opened up to Mary's root chakra, just beneath where the box had been. A deep, authoritative and scholarly voice protested the removal. "We want to know!" The voice boomed. A definite intelligence was present in Mary's system.

Intelligence: *"We want to know."*
Me: "What do you want to know?"
Intelligence: *"How our technology is being used."*

I was shown some sort of medical emblem or badge. I got the sense that this was part of a vast medical experiment or survey in which data was being collected. I reminded the Intelligence that Mary had not agreed to have any sort of technology or tracking devices placed inside her. The Intelligence reacted strongly.

Intelligence: *"No! No, no—this is part of the agreement!"*
Me: "What agreement?"
Intelligence: *"To explore and examine."*
Me: "But the subject did not give her consent."

Agreement With The Pentagon

The Intelligence was incensed. It showed me a long, dimly-lit room with old-fashioned green metal manual typewriters and grey metal desks. The room looked like it may have been the Pentagon, back in the late 1950's-mid 1960's, from what I've seen in movies. The Intelligence then produced a long stream of official-looking documents or contracts that stretched out ten to fifteen feet long. Apparently, it had some kind of agreement with the United States government and was very upset I'd interfered.

I disputed its authority and reminded it that Mary was a sovereign being. "The subject is not owned," I told the Intelligence.

"*Everyone on Earth is owned!*" it disputed. "*It's part of the Program! They said we could test to see if the subjects could be controlled.*"

I asked why they wanted to conduct this program.

"*For population purposes. To depopulate. There are too many people consuming too many resources.*"

"Vaccination Program Between 1965 and 1987"

It further explained that Mary had been made part of a United States government vaccination program that ran between 1965 and 1987.

A group of subjects were selected for the purpose of receiving and obtaining information about lifestyle, food choices, entertainment and recreation, so that they could study their habits in order to infiltrate them more affectively.

In response to this information, Jesus suddenly appeared—with the Archangel Gabriel just behind Him.

The Intelligence shrank back in surprise. "*We were not told of this Authority! Why was I not told of this Authority? This is egregious, unfair! A violation of the contract!*"

I observed all of this in stunned silence. I had never encountered any of this before. I hadn't asked Jesus to show up, but He often appears when matters of authority or ownership are involved.

The Intelligence was quite upset that Earth had a power that superseded its government contacts.

Jesus Intervenes

I asked the Intelligence if it knew Jesus and Archangel Gabriel. *"No, no. I have never seen them before. We have no such beings."*

The Intelligence must have mentally challenged Jesus's authority, because Jesus smiled slightly and held out his hand, with his palm facing upward. A vision of the Earth being created played in his hand like a hologram, proving that He had a hand in its creation.

The Intelligence was very surprised.

Jesus then calmly ripped the long line of contracts in half and said firmly, "You will let her go. You will remove all of your equipment from her completely." Jesus then listed all the specific elements and equipment that had to go.

Name of God Turns The Intelligence To Dust

Then the most amazing thing happened. Jesus turned to the Intelligence and spoke the name of God. The creature cracked in half and turned to dust—just like that.

I was awestruck. Things had been moving so quickly that I struggled to stay present and write it all down. At this point, I checked back in with Mary, who had been waiting patiently on hold as this all transpired. She could feel something major had shifted.

"All this energy is running through my body right now," she told me excitedly. "My hands are pulsing, and I feel lighter!" Even with the Intelligence gone, there still a lot to do to return her system to normal.   I went back to the crown chakra and cleaned out the boxes. Her command center responded by opening up and organizing itself into a nice, clean office.

The throat chakra, which had previously yelled its frustration, was now weeping in gratitude. I could see that Mary's heart had a grey metallic shell around it that had kept me out before. I was able to chip away at the metal encasing until it was gone completely, revealing two other happy little girls inside, playing with toys.

Remnants of Galactic Demons

The solar plexus was another story. I suspected this space contained the same type of galactic demons that infected Dharma from the chapter "Gods and Ghouls." They were strong, defiant and resistant. Thankfully, they were no match for Jesus. He captured them all in a large net and stuffed them inside a container until they eventually vanished.

Mary's bombed-out root chakra remained. Now that the demons had been vanquished, I asked Mary how her back felt.

"Oh my God," she said, "I have no pain at all. I cannot believe it! The pain is completely gone—and I feel really energized right now." "This is crazy, Margo! I knew it was that damn vaccine."

Even though Mary felt terrific, I started to feel uneasy. My energy began to be disrupted. I felt another, even larger Intelligence enter the scene. It was looking for me. I quickly put Mary on hold.

The Boss Shows Up

The apparent "boss" of the previous Intelligence said, *"You did not have the authority to remove this one from the program. This is very disruptive to us."* It showed the ripple effect this had on their world. It was like we had created a hole of some sort, and now everything was off-kilter.

The Intelligence wanted to press forward and speak to me personally, but the angels would have none of it. Legions of angels surrounded me and "met him at the door," so to speak, to keep him away from me. They kept hiding me deeper and deeper in their midst until it finally gave up and went away. They closed the portal to its world, and I started to feel normal again.

Within a few minutes, I felt well enough to continue the session. I didn't tell Mary what happened. There was still much to do for her, and both of our energies were waning. I asked the angels what to do next. They said she had to cancel all existing contracts. I thought this didn't make any sense, given that she had no knowledge of the secret government program, but then Mary remembered something:

Cancelling The Consent Form

"You know, you have to sign a consent form to be given the vaccine. So in essence, I did sign a contract. In fact, my fellow nurses and I were appalled at what rights you actually sign away in order to get a flu shot."

The angels guided Mary in cancelling any and all contracts involving her. Once that was complete, the angels gave Mary a whole new Light Body, rather than trying to repair all the damage the alien vaccine caused. Mary looked at her old energetic body, laying there like a crumpled up pile of clothes.

"It's so dull and grey. I was so happy to just fly out of that," she said. "It feels so great to be free!" She looked down at the older discarded body.

The angels gifted Mary with a beautiful katana sword with which to protect herself. "That's so funny," she said, "because my new Light Body looks like an oriental robe, so this is the perfect sword to accompany it."

Apologizes To Her Back

Finally, the angels gave her a brand-new crown chakra. "The entire top of my head is vibrating right now," Mary said as the energy settled into her system. As I completed a final sweep of her energy field, I still felt that her back needed attention.

I sensed that some of the pain she'd experienced was a result of the lingering resentment that her back felt from being put through all this. I suggested she put her hand on her low back, form a connection, and apologize to it, visualizing the techniques we mentioned earlier in this book.

"You're right," she said. "It is mad at me." I suggested she spend a few minutes connecting with her back, since she essentially they'd been estranged for 30 years. "It's interesting," Mary said. "There's a burning in my back right now. I can feel energy moving through there. It feels like it is healing."

I then invited Mary to stand up and put her new back to the test. Her joy was palpable. "Margo, I feel so light! I feel like I could fly. I have absolutely no pain at all."

MARY, JESUS AND THE "INTELLIGENCE"

Mary Has No Pain

She began jogging. "Wow! I haven't been able to do this in forever," she said in wonderment. "Usually, I try it and have to stop. But not now. I have no pain at all. This is a miracle!" Mary and I both erupted in chills as we realized what had just taken place. "Thank you, Jesus!" she cried. "I just love Jesus," she told me. "He is so awesome."

We took a few minutes to process everything that had taken place in the last hour and a half. We both experienced chills several times during her session, which is a sign of God's presence and of Truth.

"Margo, this is unbelievable!" she exclaimed. "I didn't know about any of this until I called you tonight. Never in a million years would I have guessed that this was the cause of my back pain all this time, although intuitively I always knew that vaccine had to be the cause of it."

Mary and I both hung up the phone in awe at what had just transpired. We were astonished and grateful at the power of God, and how Jesus Himself intervened on her behalf. As I closed the session and thanked the angels, they thanked me in return. "Thank you for freeing this one," they told me.

Testament To Divine Intervention

Mary contacted me a few weeks later to let me know that the back pain that plagued her for 30 years had truly vanished. "*The pain that was there for so long is gone.* I've gotten back massages every week for the last three years to get rid of this specific knot in my left lower back. Despite all the work — eating right, exercise, yoga, massages, chiropractic adjustments —it was always there. I can't tell you how many times I've asked various healers, 'That is sooooo deep. What is that?' No one knew. I've had two massages since your clearing, and *the knot is not there.* I guess I know what it was now!"

Wow. I still have to shake my head sometimes. I am not a conspiracy theorist, but I have heard of secret government-alien programs reaching back to that time period. I found it very interesting that the Intelligence was so specific about the duration of the program: from 1965 through 1987. I remembered the Vaccine Injury Compensation Program I'd discovered just before Mary's initial call. It started in 1986, the year *before* her flu shot.

National Childhood Vaccine Injury Act of 1986

I thought back to the boxes of rotting produce in Mary's brain and how they resembled a "payload"—a payload that had been "spoiled" or was "rotten" in some way.

The U.S. government obviously knew something was wrong with those vaccines. **The government created the National Vaccine Injury Compensation Program in response to an overwhelming number of lawsuits filed against vaccine manufacturers for vaccine-related injuries and deaths.**

Did you realize the government *knows* vaccines are seriously impacting people, maintains a list of known reactions and reported injuries, and even compensates people for vaccine-related problems?

Mary knew nothing either, even though she's a nurse and has been administering vaccines for more than 20 years. But wait, *there's more.*

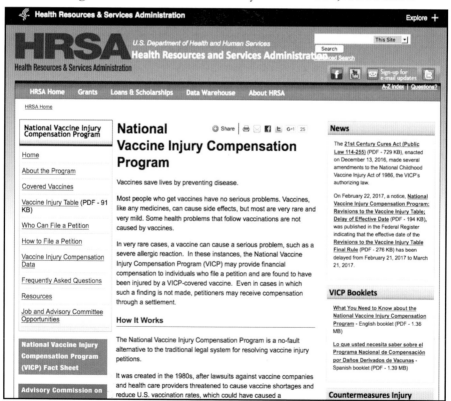

Insect DNA Injected Into Your Bloodstream

Remember the "gene-splicing" the angel said was causing the inflammatory response in Mary's body? **Today's vaccines actually contain insect DNA, as well as the DNA of cows, dogs, monkeys, pigs, chickens and human fetuses in a bizarre and frightening gene soup.**

The Flucelvax flu shot is made with dog cell proteins and dog DNA.

Aborted Fetus DNA In MMR Vaccines

The MMR vaccine given to millions of children worldwide for measles, mumps and rubella is cultured in "WI-38 human diploid lung fibroblasts," according to the U.S. Food and Drug Administration's fact sheet on the vaccine's ingredients. Merck, the vaccine's manufacturer, acknowledged that those cells were originally obtained from an electively aborted fetus. *(http://abcnews.go.com/Health/aborted-fetuses-vaccines/story?id=29005539)*

State of Missouri Seeking To Ban Foreign DNA In Vaccines

Did you know that vaccines are riddled with powerful neurotoxins, including mercury, aluminum, MSG and formaldehyde? In January 2017, State Representative Lynn Morris introduced HB 332 in the Missouri House of Representatives seeking to restrict the use of certain vaccines containing foreign human DNA contaminates.

Representative Morris also introduced HB 331, prohibiting vaccines containing mercury or other metals used for preservation or any other purpose from being administered to a child or adult in a public health clinic in Missouri. If passed, the legislation would take effect on Aug. 28, 2018.

Vaccines Contain Known Poisons

The U.S. Environmental Protection Agency (EPA) maintains that **"All forms of mercury are quite toxic, and each form exhibits different health effects."** "Yet, the Flu shot contains 25 mcgs. of Thimerosal (Mercury). Note that it is being given in-utero to the fetus and at least five more times until school age. That is 150 mcgs. of mercury to a child by the time he/she is 6 years old." *(Source: Vaccine Liberation Army).*

Vaccines Contain Toxic Additives

"Hundreds of peer reviewed studies by leading government and university scientists show that thimerosal is a devastating brain poison linked to neurological disorders now epidemic in American children.... No published study shows thimerosal to be safe." (*Source: "Trace Amounts" Robert F. Kennedy, Jr.*)

You Can Check Vaccine Contents For Yourself

Here is a list of toxic additives in vaccines. This is straight from the CDC website *(https://www.cdc.gov/vaccines/vac-gen/additives.htm).*

Common substances found in vaccines include:

- **Aluminum** gels or salts of aluminum which are added as adjuvants to help the vaccine stimulate a better response. Adjuvants help promote an earlier, more potent response, and more persistent immune response to the vaccine.
- **Antibiotics** which are added to some vaccines to prevent the growth of germs (bacteria) during production and storage of the vaccine. No vaccine produced in the United States contains penicillin.
- **Egg protein** is found in influenza and yellow fever vaccines, which are prepared using chicken eggs. Ordinarily, persons who are able to eat eggs or egg products safely can receive these vaccines.
- **Formaldehyde** is used to inactivate bacterial products for toxoid vaccines, (these are vaccines that use an inactive bacterial toxin to produce immunity.) It is also used to kill unwanted viruses and bacteria that might contaminate the vaccine during production. Most formaldehyde is removed from the vaccine before it is packaged.
- **Monosodium glutamate (MSG)** and 2-phenoxy-ethanol which are used as stabilizers in a few vaccines to help the vaccine remain unchanged when the vaccine is exposed to heat, light, acidity, or humidity.
- **Thimerosal** is a mercury-containing preservative that is added to vials of vaccine that contain more than one dose to prevent contamination and growth of potentially harmful bacteria.

For children with a prior history of allergic reactions to any of these substances in vaccines, parents should consult their child's healthcare provider before vaccination.

You can see what every vaccine contains at: **www.cdc.gov/vaccines.** Search the CDC's WONDER database and Vaccine Court section to find out information about reported vaccine injuries and known side effects. Scroll through the list for the specific vaccine and read the contents for yourself.

Gardasil Debacle

The Vaccine Court just awarded $6 million dollars to five children who suffered disabling side effects from the vaccine here in the United States and the drug has led to class-action lawsuits and Japan and other countries. *(http://www.medscape.com/viewarticle/866731)*

"Vaccines Serve Only To Generate Profit"

In April of 2014, French medical doctor Bernard Dalbergue, a former doctor with Merck, the manufacturer of the HPV vaccine Gardasil, said: "I predict that Gardasil will become the greatest medical scandal of all times because the evidence will add up to prove that this vaccine, has absolutely no effect on cervical cancer and that all the very many adverse effects which destroy lives and even kill, serve no other purpose than to generate profit for the manufacturers." *(www.Vaccineimpact.com)*

Vaccines Are a $25 BILLION Industry Every Year

Vaccines are a $25 billion industry ANNUALLY for pharmaceutical companies. Novartis recently opened a $1 billion, 430,000 square foot facility in Holly Springs, North Carolina just to produce the first cell-based (DNA-splicing) flu vaccine.

Robert F. Kennedy Jr. discloses that there are currently 271 new vaccines under development in hopes of boosting vaccine revenues to $100 billion by 2025—even though there are nowhere near that many valid diseases to innoculate against.

Isn't this supposed to be the sole purpose of vaccines? To protect us against *actual diseases* that threaten our lives in a major way?

"Children Can Take Up To 10,000 Vaccines"

When I first read that quote in an article, I thought it must be hyperbole or quoted out of context. But it wasn't. The industry's principle spokesperson, Dr. Paul Offit, says that he believes "children can take as many as 10,000 vaccines." *(Source: http://www.cbsnews.com/news/how-independent-are-vaccine-defenders/)*

In 1985, vaccines cost about $80 for all the rounds of shots. Giving your kids all their shots now costs $2,200 for each child in the United States.

Perhaps this is why children are now being forced to endure a staggering 50 vaccines before they are six years old and a total of 69 before the age of 18.

50 DOSES OF 14 VACCINES BEFORE AGE 6?
69 DOSES OF 16 VACCINES BY AGE 18?

Before you take the risk, find out what it is.
Based on the CDC's 2017 Recommended Childhood Vaccine Schedule

Vaccination.
Your health. Your family. Your choice.

Is the Childhood Vaccine Schedule Safe?

An epidemic of chronic disease and disability is plaguing America's children, who are the most highly vaccinated children in the world and also among the most chronically ill and disabled. Today, the Centers for Disease Control (CDC) states that 1 child in 6 in America suffers with learning and behavior disorders while millions more suffer with asthma, diabetes and other chronic allergic and autoimmune diseases. The epidemic of chronic disease and disability among children has increased dramatically in the past five decades.

U.S. CHILD CHRONIC DISEASE INCREASES

1976: 1 child in 30 was learning disabled → *2013:* 1 child in 6 is learning disabled.
1980: 1 child in 27 had asthma → *2013:* 1 child in 9 has asthma.
1992: 1 child in 500 developed autism → *2013:* 1 child in 50 develops autism.
2001: 1 child in 555 had diabetes → *2013:* 1 child in 400 has diabetes.

THREE TIMES AS MANY VACCINATIONS FOR CHILDREN

1953: CDC recommended 16 doses of 4 vaccines (smallpox, DPT) between two months and age six.
1983: CDC recommended 23 doses of 7 vaccines (DPT, MMR, polio) between two months and age six.
2013: CDC recommended 50 doses of 14 vaccines between day of birth and age six and 69 doses of 16 vaccines between day of birth and age 18.

MULTIPLE VACCINATIONS GIVEN SIMULTANEOUSLY
In 1983, the CDC directed doctors to give a child no more than 4 vaccines (DPT, polio) simultaneously. By 2013, the CDC directed that a child can receive 8 or more vaccines at once.

The Institute of Medicine published a report in 2013 stating that *"key elements of the entire [CDC recommended childhood vaccine] schedule – the number, frequency, timing, order and age of administration of vaccines – have not been systematically examined in research studies."*

VACCINATIONS DURING PREGNANCY
A new CDC policy directs doctors to give pregnant women one dose of influenza vaccine in any trimester and one dose of pertussis containing Tdap vaccine after 20 weeks during every pregnancy. The Food and Drug Administration (FDA) has determined that large, well controlled long term studies have not been conducted to confirm that influenza and Tdap vaccination during pregnancy is safe.

 National Vaccine Information Center

The People Entrusted With Making Unbiased Decisions About Public Health Are On Big Pharma's Payrolls—Including the CDC

We think that the Centers for Disease Control and Prevention (CDC) is a completely unbiased governmental entity with no incentive to encourage vaccines unless completely medically necessary, right? Not so.

The CDC has a foundation that accepts millions and millions of dollars directly from drug makers. Julie Gerberding was in charge of the Centers for Disease Control and Prevention (CDC) from 2002 to 2009, when the FDA approved the Merck Gardasil vaccine. Soon after she took over the CDC, she completely overhauled the agency's organizational structure, brought in vaccine insiders and then left to head Merck's vaccine division. She recently sold 38,000 shares of Merck stock for $2.3 million.

Paul Offit is in a $1.5 million research chair position funded entirely by Merck. The National Institute of Health owns patents on Gardasil. Each state gets money from vaccine makers for every vaccinated child, plus doctors routinely get money and bonuses for hitting vaccine quotas, too.

A March, 2016 NPR *report found that nine out of 10 U.S. doctors regularly get paid for prescribing brand-name drugs and vaccines.*

Did you know any of this? I didn't. I don't have a vaccine ax to grind, either. The angels just kept taking me down rabbit holes. Would you like to know the other reason why drug companies can get away with creating such strange and dangerous "toxic cocktails?"

Vaccine Makers Have No Legal Liability for Their Products in U.S.

Big Pharma has absolutely NO legal responsiblity to provide safe vaccines and are held totally harmless for vaccine injuries or deaths.

If you're wondering why Big Pharma is pushing as many vaccines as possible, it's because a 2011 Supreme Court ruling shielded them from ANY LIABILITY for any injuries or death resulting from their products.

Parents Cannot Sue a Vaccine Maker for Damages in the U.S.

In the United States, no person can sue a drug company for any type of vaccine-related injury or death. *They have NO liability for the drugs they bring to market.* They can keep raising the recommended number of vaccines, fill those vials with whatever DNA or drugs they want to, and then deliver it in a solution that includes mercury and other known poisons. **There's nothing to stop them.** According to the Department of Justice website, "A significant, positive result of the Program is that costly litigation against drug manufacturers and health care professionals who administer vaccines has virtually ceased."

This is why Mary and other nurses are so disturbed at the rights you sign away when you get a vaccine. Vaccine Court was created to limit the amount drug companies pay out for injuries. It's more like abitration. It is difficult to win, but it does happen.

United States Vaccine Court Already Paid $3 Billion To Victims

Since its inception, the Vaccine Court has paid out more than $3 billion to victims of vaccines and another $120 million in attorney fees. However, the problem is so widespread now that many law firms are solely dedicated to representing vaccine victims. This law firm lists recent lawsuits and the injuries their clients sustained from vaccines: (*https://www.mctlawyers.com/vaccine-injury/cases/*).

Vaccine makers do not have this kind of immunity around the world. Governments in Japan and the United Kingdom have launched massive class action lawsuits against vaccine manufacturers. Millions of dollars have already been awarded, and seven executives from Novartis Korea were indicted for illegally giving $24 million to doctors to push them to recommend their drugs.

Here in the U.S., though, the policy of drug companies giving money to the people who regulate, recommend and prescribe them is standard practice—and completely legal.

It's obvious that vaccines are being used for many purposes that have nothing to do with improving our health. However, I wasn't prepared for the final rabbit hole the angels led me down.

'The Intelligence' and Bill Gates Both Say Vaccines Will Depopulate

Remember when 'The Intelligence' said that the vaccination program was partly designed to depopulate the planet? That reminded me of some disturbing statements Bill Gates has made many times in reference to his $10 billion pledge to make this *"The Vaccination Decade"* through the Gates Foundation, which has major links to Mansanto and Big Pharma and is actively making new vaccines with drug manufacturers.

You really should watch Bill Gates talk about vaccines. In a February 5, 2011 interview with CNN's Dr. Sanjay Gupta, Gates talks about using vaccines to reduce the number of sick children throughout the world by half. He says, "The benefits there in terms of reducing sickness, **reducing the population growth**, it really allows a society a chance to take care of itself." (*https://www.youtube.com/watch?v=U_Gi6cf-jiI*).

You don't even notice it at first, because he says it all so casually, with a big smile on his face. Gupta didn't catch it either, because Gates *looks* like he's talking about preventing disease But he's not.

Bill Gates is not talking about saving or improving lives. *He is talking about exterminating them.*

"Secret Agenda" Behind Sneaky Vaccines

Bill Gates said this in February, 2010 during a TED Talk on climate change and zero population growth:

"If we do a really good job on **new vaccines**, health care and reproductive health services, we could **LOWER that [population growth] by ten to fifteen percent."** What?

He did not say he could lower disease through new vaccines. He did not say they could make people healthier. **He said new vaccines could reduce population growth** (*https://www.ted.com/talks/bill_gates*).

Just what do these "new" vaccines he's developing have to do with population control, and why is he talking about it so casually?

Perhaps it's because he is aware of the fact that UNICEF and the World Health Organization *have already used vaccines to secretly sterilize millions of people all over the world for more than 20 years.*

Vatican: UNICEF And WHO Are Sterilizing Girls Through Vaccines

On March 20, 2015, Vatican Radio put out a news release with the headline above (Vatican Radio is the official "voice of the Pope and the Church in dialogue with the World.")

Vatican Radio charged that United Nations organizations including the World Health Organization (WHO) and UNICEF are using vaccines to surreptitiously sterilize women in Third World countries. Paul Kariuki Njiru, Chairman of the Kenya Conference of Catholic Bishops Catholic Health Commission of Kenya, says the measure was **"a permanent population control tool"** and urged the Ministry of Health to investigate. *(http://www.news.va/en/news/africakenya-the-bishops-what-does-the-tetanus-camp)*

"Catholic Bishops in Kenya have been opposed to the nationwide Tetanus Vaccination Campaign targeting 2.3 million Kenyan women and girls of reproductive age between 15-49 years, terming the campaign a secret government plan to sterilize women and control population growth," reported Vatican Radio.

"Mass Sterilization Exercise"

Dr. Wahome Ngare, spokesman for the Kenya Catholic Doctors Association, stated: "This proved right our worst fears; that this WHO campaign is not about eradicating neonatal tetanus, **but a well-coordinated forceful population control mass sterilization exercise using a proven fertility regulating vaccine."** *(www.globalresearch.ca)*

Catholic doctors become suspicious at the way the tetanus vaccine program was administered. They wondered why it involved an unprecedented five shots over more than two years, and why the vaccines were only given to women of childbearing years and no males at all.

"Usually, we give a series of three shots over two to three years, we give it to anyone who comes into the clinic with an open wound, men, women or children." said Dr. Ngare.

"The only time tetanus vaccine has been given in five doses is when it is used as a carrier in fertility regulating vaccines laced with the pregnancy hormone," said Ngare.

Tetanus Vaccine Vials Contained Sterilization Agent

The Kenya Catholic Doctors Association ordered laboratory tests of tetanus vaccines being administered in Kenya by the World Health Organization (WHO) and the UN Children's Fund (UNICEF). **"The unfortunate truth is that the vaccine was laced with [sterilizing agent Human Chorionic Gonadotropin] HCG just like the one used in the South American cases,"** Dr. Ngare said.

According to the organization, the hCG found in the United Nations tetanus vaccines causes women's bodies to develop an immune response to attack the hormone, which is essential to pregnancy. So, when a woman who has received the UN shots gets pregnant, her body fights the crucial hCG —resulting in the death of the unborn child in the womb.

Eventually, the supposed inoculations—pushed on Kenyan women by the UN under the guise of "preventing neo-natal tetanus" —result in permanent sterility after multiple doses.

Only WHO-UNICEF Vaccines Contained Sterilizing Agent

Upon testing, the Expert Committee found that one third of the WHO-UNICEF vials *did* indeed contain HCG. Interestingly, 50 tetanus vials that *weren't* part of the WHO-UNICEF campaign didn't have any HCG at all.

The Catholic Church condemned the Kenyan secret sterilization program as "unethical and immoral," and insisted that "no further vaccination campaigns should be undertaken in this county without sampling and testing before, during and after the vaccination campaign."

UNICEF Secretly Sterilized Women in Nigeria and the Phillipines

This is not the first time UNICEF secretly placed sterilizing agents in vaccines. In 1995, the Catholic Women's League of the Philippines won a court order halting a UNICEF anti-tetanus program because the vaccine had been laced with B-hCG, which results in sterility.

The Supreme Court of the Philippines found the surreptitious sterilization program had already vaccinated three million women, aged 12 to 45. B-hCG-laced vaccine was also found in at least four

other developing countries, including Mexico and Nicarauga.

In 2004, Nigeria launched a complaint about the *same sterilizing agent given in oral Polio vaccines*. When Dr. Haruna Kaita, a pharmaceutical scientist and Dean of the Faculty of Pharmaceutical Sciences of Ahmadu Bello University in Zaria, felt the drug manufacturers would have contaminated the Oral Polio Vaccine, he said, **"These manufacturers or promoters of these harmful things have a secret agenda which only further research can reveal."**

Gates Foundation Sued By India For Illegal Vaccine Program

The Gates Foundation has been sued by the Indian government for illegally giving children as young as nine the Gardasil vaccine without obtaining consent and for using its population as "guinea pigs" in "illegal drug testing." The Foundation did not obtain permission from parents. Several children died after receiving the vaccine. The Indian government also is investigating the Gates Foundations' ties to Big Pharma and financing of new vaccines.

The Daily Mail, a large newspaper in the United Kingdom, reported on January 16, 2015 that an Indian parliamentary committee had concluded that the **trials amounted to a serious breach of trust and medical ethics amounting to child abuse and "a clear cut violation of the human rights of these girl children and adolescents."**

"At best, there were serious irregularities and, at worst, gross violations of fundamental human rights," said Kerry McBroom, one of the lawyers. (*http://www.dailymail.co.uk/news/article-2908963/Judges-demand-answers-children-die-controversial-cancer-vaccine-trial-India.*)

Be Informed And Make Your Own Decisions

This was not an easy chapter for me to write. I didn't know any of this about vaccines before the angels led me to investigate. Did you?

Now, you are informed and can make your own decisions. Please be your own advocate. There are many books, movies and websites about vaccines. Listen to all sides of the equation. If you do choose to vaccinate, be watchful of the signs of a bad reaction and report it immediately.

If You Vaccinate Your Child,
Learn How to Recognize the Signs
and Symptoms of Vaccine Reactions*

VACCINE REACTIONS	MOTHER'S DESCRIPTIONS
High Fever (over 103° F)	"His temperature was 105 degrees. I had to put cool towels on him to bring the fever down."
Skin (hives, rashes, swelling)	"There was a big, hot swollen lump at the site of the shot that stayed for weeks."
High Pitched Screaming	"It was a pain cry, a shrill scream and lasted for hours and nothing would help."
Collapse/Shock	"She turned white with a blue tinge around her mouth and went completely limp."
Excessive Sleepiness	"He passed out and we couldn't wake him to feed or do anything for over 12 hours."
Convulsion	"Her eyes twitched, her chin trembled, her body went rigid and then would shake."
Brain Inflammation	"He just laid in his crib with his eyes wide open then would arch his back and scream and go un conscious. Now he has seizures."
Behavior Changes	"She won't sleep or eat. She throws herself down and screams for no reason. She was sweet and happy and is now out of control. She changed into a totally different child."
Mental/Physical Regression	"My 18 month old son stopped talking and walking after those shots. He developed severe allergies, constant diarrhea, ear infections and was sick all the time."

Other reported vaccine reactions include: loss of muscle control, paralysis, regressive autism, asthma, arthritis, blood disorders, diabetes, Guillain Barre syndrome, sudden death.

Call a doctor immediately or go to an emergency room if symptoms of serious vaccine reaction complications or dramatic changes in physical, mental, or emotional behavior after vaccination.

NATIONAL CHILDHOOD VACCINE INJURY ACT OF 1986
By June 2016, over $3.3 billion had been awarded for vaccine injuries and deaths suffered by more than 4,500 children and adults.

REPORT VACCINE REACTIONS
Serious health problems following vaccination should be documented in medical records and promptly reported to the federal Vaccine Adverse Events Reporting System (VAERS). You can also make vaccine reaction reports to NVIC's Vaccine Reaction Registry, which has operated since 1982 and serves as a watchdog on reports submitted to VAERS.

LEARN MORE
Go to NVIC.org and learn more about signs and symptoms of infectious diseases and vaccine reactions; how to report vaccine reactions; how to meet deadlines for applying for federal vaccine injury compensation and how to protect your legal right to informed consent to vaccination in America.

What You Need To Know

- Vaccines include DNA from aborted fetuses, monkeys, cows, dogs, pigs and insects.

- Vaccines contain toxic ingredients such as formaldahyde, mercury, aluminum, antibiotics and MSG.

- The vaccine release form severely limits your rights in the event of injury or death.

- Drug companies are not held liable for any damages done by their vaccines in the U.S.

- The Vaccine Injury Compensation Program or "Vaccine Court" is the only option for vaccine victims. Compensation is only awarded in about a third of the cases presented.

- Vaccine Court has paid out $3 billion in awards since its inception in 1986. This is a small fraction of what would have been paid if vaccine makers were held legally liable for defective products that result in injury or death.

- Vaccines make drug companies over $25 billion a year.

- In the U.S. drug companies routinely pay The Centers for Disease Control, state governments and doctors for the number of vaccines given.

- The vaccine industry spokesman says it is safe to give a child 10,000 vaccines. Yet no child faces 10,000 life-threatening illnesses that require immunization.

• UNICEF and the World Health Organization have sterilized millions of people around the world by secretly administering sterilizing agents under the guise of Tetanus and Polio vaccines.

What You Can Do

• Be informed. Check vaccine contents list and known side effects.

• Read the vaccine release form carefully. Make sure you understand your rights and limitations.

• Opt out of vaccines through religious or other exemptions provided by your state.

• Weigh the risks and side effects of vaccinating vs. non-vaccinating. The disease itself may not be as lasting or damaging as the side effects of the vaccine allegedly given to prevent it.

• Find out if your doctor is receiving money from Big Pharma by checking the Docs for Dollars website: (*https://projects.propublica.org/docdollars/*).

• You can report adverse reactions and check reported injuries and deaths through the U.S. Vaccine Adverse Reporting System (VAERS) and WONDER databases. *(https://vaers.hhs.gov/esub/index)*

———————————

Woohoo!
We are done with rabbit holes now.

You can take a big gulp of fresh air,
because we are OUT of the darkness and into the Light!

HANG ON, THERE'S HOPE!

LIVING IN THE LIGHT

36

LIVING IN THE LIGHT

Congratulations! You Made It!
It's been a wild journey, hasn't it? I know it probably challenged some of your perceptions about reality (mine, too), but hopefully also gave you much-needed validation and comfort. It was kind of like taking a big breath and diving deep underwater, not knowing what strange

and bizarre world you might encounter in those unknown depths. But what a wondrous Universe you discovered, once you took the plunge!

Now, you're back on the surface of the water again, breathing in new air. You have come from darkness into light. You're coming out of this great adventure wondering, "What's next?" It's a whole new, exciting life for you.

Look back to who you were when you started this book. You've come a long way, haven't you? You've grown so much! I know some of it wasn't easy. I know much of it is shocking. But, I had to wake you up—so you can protect yourself and the people you love. Now, you are awake. You're not the same person you were before. You are aware, and no one will be able to manipulate you in the same way again.

Spiritual Survival Guide

Think of this as your spiritual survival guide. You've been dodging supernatural hazards your entire life, but never knew it. This book has given you more tools to understand some of what's going on, and to help deal with issues you once thought were "just in your head" or didn't even know existed at all. Now you understand why humanity is so obsessed with the supernatural—why we can't get enough movies, TV shows, comic books and reality shows about cosmic battles involving alien races, UFOs, angels and superheroes.

Today you can put on your Superhero cape and wear it proudly, knowing that you are defending your own soul and helping planet Earth in the process.

Restored Faith In God and The Light

I hope this book has validated and restored your faith in God. Once that shroud of darkness is cast off, Light floods in and restores the soul. For while we battle "evil invaders from the cosmic realms," you have seen time and again how God and the forces of Light rush in to save and protect, every time. You realize that God is truly with you whenever you need Him, and that the forces of Light are assembling around you at all times—even if they are momentarily delayed because of interference.

Step Forward In The Light

You are invited to experience the Light more fully than you ever have before. It's time for you to throw off everything that has held you back and be truly free. It is your birthright. No matter where you are in your personal or spiritual development, the Light is here for you.

The angels have a simple, three-point mantra or phrase for you going forward. You can use it to guide all your choices moving ahead. It is beautiful in its simplicity and power.

"Clear, Claim and Connect"

Living in the Light comes down to clearing yourself from negativity, claiming the deed to your own soul, and connecting with yourself and your Divine guidance. This is the way to make it through this world.

First, you have to clear yourself of darkness and pain. Do all you can to clear and heal yourself. It will light up the world and make you an inspiration to others. This is why the angels wanted me to include all that information on the toxins in our environment and poisons injected into your body from vaccines. I didn't plan to write more than a page or two on each of those topics, but the angels were adamant. They want you to be cleansed of all the things that are holding you down, making you sick and and closing down your senses.

Clear

Clear Negativity. Avoid people, places and substances that make you feel badly. Whether or not you realize it, you respond to the energy of a person every time you come into personal contact with them.

High-vibrational people generally make us feel good, happy and centered when we are with them. Low-vibrational people can make us feel sad, depressed, stuck and drained.

Clear Yourself Of Fear. While television can be a great companion and source of entertainment, news programs are designed to keep you in fear. News is a form of terrorism. *The rule in the newsroom is, "If it bleeds, it leads."*

If you are afraid, you will constantly tune in to see what's happening next. The content is selected because it is unusual and scary. This keeps the advertisers' money flowing, because the networks can promise them a huge, captive audience for their commercials.

Studies have shown that consuming too much news is bad for your health. It raises blood pressure and increases anxiety and feelings  of helplessness. Even without a television, news is constantly pumped into your awareness through social media and updates on your phone.

Try reducing your diet of news and suspenseful programming and just see if it makes you feel happier and more in control of your own life.

Thirdly, your fear and anxiety actually fuel some of the dark entities that surround this planet. Spend some outdoors. Breathe more. Exercise. Try forms of meditation and yoga or just dance!

Clean up your diet. Eat certified organic foods and if possible, grow your own foods with certified organic seeds. Eliminate GMOs from your diet as much as possible. Look for those certified organic and non-GMO labels and go with your own intuition.

It may also be vibrationally better for you to consume meat and poultry that is free-range and grass-fed, instead of being fed GMOs. Some people find that being vegan (eating no animal products) works for them.

Consume clean water. Most tap water has contaminants. Even some bottled waters are questionable. I drink bottled water "bottled at the source" in California. I notice many other high-vibrational healers drink this type of water, too.

Clear your chakras. Reduce or abstain from alcohol, drugs and cigarettes. You can't move up to the angels' frequency if you are stuck in these low-vibration activities. If you want to use more of your own psychic or spiritual gifts, consider limiting or eliminating the amount of toxic substances you put into your body.

Clean your house. Cleaning your living spaces is crucial to letting the light in, too. As you know, energetic dragons like to live in the dark. They like cramped and dark spaces. So many of my clients with dragons told me they kept their shades drawn, lived in clutter and rarely went outside. The spirit needs sunlight. It needs nature. We were put on this Earth to enjoy her bounty and receive her energetic gifts. Go outside. Unplug. If possible, live in clear air and surroundings.

Clear Away Clutter. Give away things you no longer use. They collect stagnant and negative energy. The Chinese practice of Feng Shui can show you how to clean your house and set it up for a positive energy flow for both you and your life. I've used Feng Shui many times, with very positive results.

Claim

Claim yourself completely. Claiming yourself means that you live like you matter. You've read about how other people changed their lives by finally deciding they were worthy. It's time to do it for yourself. If you don't treat yourself like you matter, energies may see you as "vacant" real estate and try to move in on you.

Claim your rightful place in the Light. Earth is like a spiritual gangland: if the Dark doesn't clearly know whose side you're on, it may assume it has a right to you.

If you ask to be aligned with the Light, know that it will not take anything from you in the future, and you are free to cancel at any time. The Light wants you to be completely empowered at all times.

Claim Your Sovereignty. Claim yourself by breaking soul contracts and severing ties to past lives and relationships. Claim yourself by breaking curses. Reclaim parts of yourself that you may have given away, and return energetic parts of others you have been holding onto.

Claim God's Love And Acceptance. Whether you think of God as "Source," the "Universe," "Buddha," "Ganesh," "Kwan Yin" or the Light, God exists in all religions and loves all of us. As you've seen time and again in this book, Jesus shows up with the deeds to souls, regardless of whether those people believe in Him. He has come to Hindus, Jews, Christians and agnostics in this way. Deities from other religions have also helped in spiritual clearings, too. The Hindu God Ganesh has been very instrumental in my life. He is the breaker of obstacles and a guide to writers, so he helps me every day in the same way that Jesus and the angels do. He is the guiding force behind the Career Cards and and is a powerful force in Angelic Soul Clearing™ too.

We need to bring the worlds of religion and spirituality together so that we can all be One, instead of arguing about whom God accepts.

No one owns God. Don't let anyone tell you God doesn't love you. Don't let anyone tell you that you are "going to Hell." No one knows what is in the heart of God, except God!

The Bible says, *"There is one body, but it has many parts. But all its many parts make up one body. It is the same with Christ. We were all baptized by one Holy Spirit. And so we are formed into one body. It didn't matter whether we were Jews or Gentiles, slaves or free people. We were all given the same Spirit to drink."* (NIV, 1 Corinthians 12:12)

Claim Your Spiritual Gifts. Don't let anyone make you think that using the supernatural senses that are hard-wired into your body and soul is weird or "of the devil." This is a trick of the Dark itself to keep you oppressed and disempowered. Your senses are your path to God. Use them. With them, you can see the Truth.

The Bible itself says these are gifts of the Holy Spirit and given to us to help us connect with God and to bless and heal others in our midst:

"The Holy Spirit is given to each of us in a special way. That is for the good of all. To some people the Spirit gives a message of wisdom. To others the same Spirit gives a message of knowledge. To others the same Spirit gives faith. To others that one Spirit gives gifts of healing. To others he gives the power to do miracles. To others he gives the ability to prophesy. To others he gives the ability to tell the spirits apart. To others he gives the ability to speak in different kinds of languages they had not known before. And to still others he gives the ability to explain what was said in those languages. All the gifts are produced by one and the same Spirit. He gives gifts to each person, just as he decides. (NIV, 1 Corinthians 7 -11)

Many people would still be in torment if I did not follow the leading of the Holy Spirit. Many people would still be in darkness had I not accepted that my spiritual gifts of clairvoyance, discernment, wisdom, prophecy, healing and knowledge are from God. These are all blessed gifts of the loving Holy Spirit within me.

Connect

Connect With Yourself. It's time for you to use your God-given gifts, too. This book was meant to help you connect with yourself in a whole new way. I want you to stop thinking of yourself negatively and begin to see the Light that is waiting within you. Some of you may have been locked out of yourselves, and are only now getting to know the real you. Loving yourself is everything.

Connect with Compassion. I hope this book has helped you to have more compassion for yourself. See yourself as a beloved friend and treat yourself accordingly. Forgive yourself, and be gentle with yourself. As Buddha said, *"If your compassion does not include yourself, it is incomplete."*

The angels want you to love yourself as much as they love you. They want you to give yourself the compassion and care you did not receive when you should have. They want you to be joyous and full of life and love.

Connect to Support. It's so important for you to have support. Humans are tribal people. We need each other. Many of you have felt alone your whole lives, struggling with things you could not share with others. Get rid of your energetic dragons and your addictions, and your vibration will lift. You will automatically start to be happier and will attract more positive people. You can always find community and understanding at www.freedbythelight.com and on our Freed By The Light Facebook page. Hopefully, this book has given you new faith and hope in humanity, realizing that people are not the ones doing evil in this world. Try to open your heart and trust anew.

Connect With Spirituality. The New Age movement offers a wide range of healing modalities that are not found in religion, such as crystals, hands-on healing, meditation, yoga, whole foods and more. This is an exciting world, because the possibilities are endless. Try going to a metaphysical bookstore. See what speaks to you. Holistic fairs are open, loving, happy places where you can meet many like-minded people, have new experiences and make new friends.

Some Cautions. Always close your aura before attending any crowded event, especially something spiritual. Before you go, pray and ask your angels to guide you to the people and experiences that are only for your highest and best good.

However, as with churches or organizations of any kind, not every pracititioner is guided by angels—so use your discernment.

You will feel warm, loved and safe with someone who is working with angels or God. Your body and soul will relax and you will know that you can trust.

You might want to be cautious with healing modalities and practitioners who feel cold, sterile, hard or fake. Don't be pressured into receiving a healing you did not ask for. Beware of "attunements" unless the practitioner truly feels and looks angelic. Be very protective of what you do and whom you let into your energy field. Do not ever let anyone slash their hand through your energy field. If they do, immediately rescind it by doing declaring your own sovereignty.

Connect to Your Angels and Guides. I wanted to include a short meditation here for you to connect to your angels, but they are concerned that something else may step into your energy field if you do this on your own. They say that pouring clean water into dirty water does not make the water clean. You must first pour out the dirty water, and then fill yourself with clean energy.

Instead, they encourage you to buy a book or audio course in connecting with your angels and guides so that you take your time with it and do it properly. Doreen Virtue and other authors have many good books on the subject.

The Next Step In Your Journey

I know this book has opened you up to a whole new world, which can be confusing, exciting and scary all at the same time. I want you to know you are not alone. I don't want you to feel overwhelmed or lost, so **I've put together a special online course, workshop and retreat called, "12 Keys To Understanding And Using Your Spiritual Superpowers," which will help you awaken and claim your own spiritual gifts (see page 304-305).**

The course and workshop take you toward full spiritual empowerment, teaching you how to clear darkness, fully claim yourself by revoking soul contracts and curses, and connecting you to your own angels and guides. I want to empower you to cast off your darkness and come into your own power.

Another reason for the course is because I don't want you falling into the hands of someone pretending to be of the Light. After Lily got cleared of the curse, she found something on the Internet that told her to ask Archangel Michael to "override her free will for her highest and best good." She did it, and then immediately felt horrible. She felt her power and life start to slip away again.

I asked Archangel Michael if that prayer went to him, and he said no. Never, ever allow anyone to interfere with your free will. It is your most valuable possession.

Treat your energy and life force as if it is the most valuable thing in the world. Guard it fiercely. Protect it. Defend it. Nurture it. Grow it. Love it.

In closing, the angels have a special message for you as you prepare to finish this part of your journey:

Congratulations!

"More than anything, we want to say, "Thank you." Thank you for reading this book and being true to your own soul. You are a brave and courageous human. Thank you for coming to Earth and joining us in strengthening the forces of Light. Each of you is needed in this battle.

We want you to know how very, very much you are loved. You are so precious. So many of you have been treated badly here on Earth, and it isn't right. It was not what was intended for you by your Creator.

We are heartily sorry for the pain you have carried, and the pain you may have caused to others through your own blindness. Please know that we have always *tried to reach you in your darkest hours, and that we will continue to try and bring you the healing and love you need now.*

Know that we love you beyond measure.
Know that you are precious beyond measure.
Know that you are worthy and deserving of love and support.
Know that we are with you always, even if you cannot feel or hear us.

Spend time with us. We are still there waiting for the moment when we can rejoin you, and let you feel our immense love for you. Clear yourself so that you may see and hear our words. We always come to you gently, carefully and respectfully.

Our energy is very subtle. We may ring a bell loudly in your ear, call out to you in times of danger, or communicate to you in dreams. We may reassure you through feathers, signs in the sky, the unlikely words of a stranger or other means. You can reach us through meditation. You can always find us through your heart. You always have a pathway to God, and you need not travel through any house, building or institution to find Him: He is always waiting within you, the last place you have been taught to look.

Please, please, take these words to heart. There is nothing more important or powerful than ridding this planet of the darkness. You are the only ones who can do this. Your souls are encoded with special frequencies of Light that can lift the darkness, if enough of you do what is suggested and "lighten the load."

Heal what hurts
Mend what is broken
Tend to what needs care
Love yourself first, always
All of God's kingdom is in you

It is our deepest desire to free you so that you may live radiantly
Let there be Heaven on Earth.
Let all souls be as One.
May Peace prevail.
Let Love reign.

In All Light,
We Are With You."

37

MIRACLES AND WONDERS: SUPPORT FOR YOUR JOURNEY

The Miraculous Stories Behind The Cover Photos

The front and back cover photos for this book are gifts from God. In the Spring of 2015, I received a vision about the cover of this book. I saw a sky filled with clouds, with radiant light streaming out from the center. I always hoped that the cover of the book would actually allow the reader to feel Divine love and light streaming from it. It would have to be very special. I didn't know where this image was going to come from. I looked at stock photos, combed through my own cloud photos, but found nothing that resembled my vision. I was discouraged and a little worried that I wouldn't find the right image.

Looking For A Specific Cover Photo

Several months passed as I searched for the right photo. As usual, whenever I worry about how something is going to work out, it turns out that God already has the plan in place.

In December of 2015, I prepared for the monthly holistic fair at the Temple of Light in Irvine, CA. Spirit told me that this particular fair was going to be very important for me. I was so excited the night before that I could hardly sleep. Enormous amounts of energy poured into my system. I remember checking to see if there were solar flares or some other reason for the profound effect on my energy, but there was nothing unusual. I went to the fair the next day.

A few hours later, three women recognized me in the hallway. "You're the one!" they exclaimed. "You're the one we came to see!" They explained they had made the five-hour trek from Las Vegas that morning to see me.

I asked how they heard about it. "I got an email inviting us to the fair. We saw your face and knew we had to come to see you," Kim Becker told me. We all exchanged hugs, and I told them I was so glad and honored that they had come so far to see me. We all felt like old friends. They came to my booth and each got readings. They all purchased Career Card sets to take home with them. Kim bought extra to give to friends. Kris invited me out to celebrate my recovery birthday with her in Vegas a few weeks later, and I had a lovely time.

Sends Me What I'd Seen In My Mind

On January 10, 2016, Kim Becker texted me this photo. "Isn't this amazing?" she wrote. My jaw literally dropped, I was so speechless. This was the photo I'd seen in my mind for almost a year! I called her immediately. **"Do you realize this is the exact cover of my book?"** I asked her. "I had no idea where I was going to find that picture, but you just sent it to me right now!"

A Message Of Love

"Oh my God," Kim exclaimed. "The story behind that photo is amazing. I was driving around the Red Rock area of Vegas, praying for guidance today," she said. "I was in the car listening to "Hello" from Adele. I've been had been going through a difficult

situation at work, and really needed to know that Spirit was looking out for me. So I asked my guides to send me a sign. I turned a corner, just past Blue Diamond—and there it was. I looked up at the sky through my sunroof, and took this picture. It's just amazing. I feel like I always know my guides are there, but sometimes I just need to see it."

Kim and I sat in stunned silence as we realized the enormity of this gift. For her, it was a beautiful and clear confirmation that her guides were listening. For me, it was the culmination of many months of waiting and hoping I would find the exact vision I'd seen for the cover. I asked Kim if I could use the photo for my book. She agreed immediately.

A Career Card Magically Appears In Her Briefcase

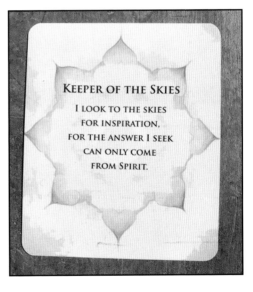

A few hours later that same day, Kim called me with yet another incredible sign. "You'll never believe what happened this afternoon after I took that picture. I came back to the office to do some work. I opened my briefcase to get something, and the Keeper of the Skies card came tumbling out! The rest of the Career Cards deck is on my desk. How did *that* card get into my briefcase? I'm just amazed!"

The Career Cards are a practical guide to life, and the oracle speaks to everything in life, not just careers. However, there is only one card in that entire 88-card deck that is directly about Spirit. The Keeper of the Skies card is the one and only card whose affirmation reads: *"I look to the skies for inspiration, for the answers I seek can only come from Spirit."*

The Keeper of the Skies card goes on to say, *"When you receive the Keeper of Skies, Spirit is reaching out to you. This can include communing with your spirit guides, angels or the spirits of those who have left the Earth plane and are now on the Other Side."*

Kim had been listening to the song "Hello" when she took the picture. Spirit also used this card to let Kim know that they understood she was having a hard time. *"If you have been feeling down or discouraged lately, the Keeper of the Skies is here to lift your spirits."*

I reached out to Kim on March 20, 2017 and asked if she'd like to submit a photo of herself for this chapter. She was delighted and immediately sent one over. I had just told my designer that this book was like giving birth to a child. Kim told me that afternoon she felt led to eat lunch outside. As she did, she looked up at the sky and saw this cloud formation and just had to take a picture. She had never seen anything like it.

To me, it looks like the eye of God on the right, and a uterus with an open birth canal on the left. Some people even see a baby being born. Perhaps Heaven was letting me know that it was acting as a midwife during the birth of this book.

Miraculous Back Cover Message

The incredible photo of God's hand reaching down from Heaven was taken on July 9, 2016 (also Tiffany's birthday), the day before I said

goodbye to Nalani Rose, a beautiful, loving red merle pitbull who shared my life for 12 years. Nalani was the gentlest dog I've ever known. Nalani was also the first dog I'd encountered with a human soul.

Rose or "Rosie" as she liked to be called, had been a woman during the Victorian times. I saw a vision of her then, very lady-like in a white lace bodice and white gloves, reclining on a red velvet sofa. She still loved men and was very emotionally sensitive in this incarnation. She was so attached to the men in her life that she developed cancer when they left: the first when my stepson Caleb left home in 2008, and again after losing her mate, Dakota, in 2009. However, Rose was very strong, and recovered completely from the cancer. She remained with me for another happy and healthy seven years.

In late June of 2016, Rose suffered a stroke and collapsed while on a walk. She continued to decline over the next few weeks. The medication she'd been on to keep the cancer at bay had finally taken a toll on her liver. There was nothing we could do but support her until she was ready to go. She was 15 years old, a very long life for a larger breed.

Rose was beloved by many of my friends, including her "Aunt Angie," our dear friend Angela Keller. When Rose's health took a turn for the worse, Angela flew from Oklahoma to be with Rose during her passing.

One afternoon I decided to work on this book while Angela and Rose cuddled in the living room. About fifteen minutes later, my Pomeranian, Max, began to bark at me furiously. I looked outside, but no one was there. I told Max everything was fine, and to settle down.

Instead, he stared at me and barked even more insistently. Whatever it was, he was not giving up. I stopped writing and took him outside.

I looked up at the clear blue sky and saw this (at right.)

I immediately ran inside to get Angela. She could barely believe her eyes, too. Over the next few minutes, the scene slowly transformed across the sky, until the Hand of God came down to meet the angel's outstretched hand (below).

As this beautiful image formed above my head, I heard the words, *"Take heart, children."* I immediately burst into tears, knowing it was a loving message for us about losing Rose. It was also meant as an everlasting message for the world.

Rose passed away the next day. I like to think that beautiful Heavenly

angel was waiting right there, ready to carry her home—and that angels are waiting for all of us, as close as an outstretched hand.

As we come to the close of this book, I want to thank you so much for taking this journey with me. It's been an important one.

The angels have already given you their prayer, so here's my prayer for you. I pray that you free yourself from darkness and unite with the Light, so that you know how very, very much you are loved, and how much Heaven is waiting to help you.

Healing Resources

I am only one person, so I asked some of my personal healers to help you, too. Katie Weatherup and Jan Antonelli have helped me for more than ten years. Katie loves to clear entities and is great at removing galactic interferences. Jan loves to clear emotional problems, past life and soul issues. Vickie is an R.N. and her husband is an M.D., and they get your body healed from pesticide overload, vaccine reactions, allergies, viruses and hormonal imbalances. Jason is a clear and heart-centered intuitive and healer who can remove emotional blocks and connect you to your higher self.

Removing Entities, Curses and Contracts

Katie Weatherup	katie@handsoverheart.com
Jan Antonelli	janantonelli@yahoo.com
Jason Wechs	www.mystichealingpaths.com
Maya Starhawk	www.mayastarhawk.com
Gloria Lindsay	www.glorialindsay.com
Steven Flores	Razieal@earthlink.net

Messages from The Other Side

Debbie Hamilton	debbie@dhhealinglight.com
Denise Willis	www.denisewillis.com
Morag Hislop	love light and angel sparkles on facebook/ m.hislop@hotmail.co.uk

Physical Healing

Dr. Mark W. Light/ Vickie Van Scyoc	530-899-7300
Dr. Rich Di Stefano	816- 333-3700

Trauma Releasing

T.R.E.L.A. Website	trelosangeles.com
Rachel Miller TRE Somatic Experiencing	www.angelhealinglove.com
Victoria Schlict	www.transforminghearts.com

Sound Healing/Music

Rama Inacio	www.innershiningtemple.com

Advanced Healing Training & Scientific Verification

Melinda Connor	melindaconnor@mindspring.net

See www.freedbythelight.com for a complete and updated list
All these resources work long-distance anywhere in the world

CONTINUE YOUR JOURNEY

Support you'll need

12-Week Online Course

Each Class Gives You:

1:1 Time with Margo
Webinar
Training Materials
Group Discussion and Forum

"FREED
BY THE
LIGHT:

12 KEYS TO
AWAKEN
YOUR SPIRITUAL
SUPERPOWERS"

INTO LIGHT...
for the life you'll love!

WEEK 1	WEEK 2	WEEK 3	WEEK 4
Energize Your Chakras	**Remove Blocks & Obstacles**	**Tune Into Your Intuition**	**Connect With Your Spirit Guides**

WEEK 5	WEEK 6	WEEK 7	WEEK 8
Psychic Self Defense	**Recalling Past Lives**	**Clearing Karma**	**Develop Discernment**

WEEK 9	WEEK 10	WEEK 11	WEEK 12
Cancel Soul Contracts	**Heal Addictions**	**Eliminate Energetic Entities**	**Receive Messages From The Other Side**

Turn Heart Break Into Bliss!

Love Beyond Your Greatest Expectations

Spiritual Counseling & Healing to Transform

Hurt Souls into Love Champions!

Divine Guidance For Your Health And Life

Contact Jason Wechs for a

FREE Consultation and Mini Healing Today

Jason@MysticHealingpaths.com

* Available in person, by phone or Skype *

Hands over Heart

Soul Retrieval   Shamanic Healing

Shamanic Journey Training   Distance and In-person Sessions

Practical Shamanism

For a Really Good Life that just keeps getting better.

Katie Weatherup

A former mechanical engineer with over fifteen years of experience as a shamanic practitioner, Katie Weatherup offers effective solutions for thriving in the modern world. Katie helps people find their way back to themselves, all the parts they've lost, forgotten, denied and disowned.

Soul Retrieval and Shamanic Healing

:turn to wholeness. Soul Retrieval and Shamanic Healing offer a solid foundation r wellness and vitality. In a single, comprehensive session, the practice helps ople unlock their power within, so they can overcome anxiety, pain, and trauma, d live life to the fullest. Learn more at www.handsoverheart.com

www.handsoverheart.com

FROM CELL TO SOUL MEMORY MANIFESTATION

Your amazing body cells hold memories of everything you have ever experienced. Your soul also carries memories of all your experiences. Sometimes, these memories create negative and limiting beliefs, which manifest in your life causing you pain and distress.

Healing doesn't need to be painful; it takes a willingness to go beyond your own expectations. I offer a variety of tools to assist you in moving through the layers gracefully which will enable you to...

- Access the memories held by your body's cells.
- Access the unlimited memories held by your soul.
- Identify the sources of your emotional, physical and spiritual pain.
- Release those memory sources through a simple healing process, and replace them with new, expanded beliefs, which begins to manifest positively in your life.

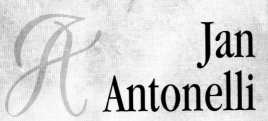

Jan Antonelli

For more information or to set up a session
email me: jantonelli9@gmail.com

WITH SOUL MEMORY DISCOVERY YOU CAN BEGIN TO HEAL...

Interpersonal Relationships ▣ Destructive Life Patterns ▣ Physical Ailments and Imbalances ▣ Dissatisfaction with work ▣ Past Life Experiences ▣ Spirit Attachments ▣ Money Issues ▣ Spiritual Alienation

WHAT IS SOUL MEMORY DISCOVERY?

Your body cells hold memories of everything you have ever experienced. Soul Memory Discovery enables you to... Access the unlimited memories held by your body cells ▣ Access the unlimited memories held by your soul ▣ Identify the sources of your emotional, physical and spiritual pain ▣ Release those memory sources through a simple healing process ▣ And replace them with new, expanded beliefs, which begin to manifest positively in your life.

With Soul Memory Discovery, you can begin to... Find your purpose in life, Live your life with meaning, Focus your energies, Honor your Self, Experience new joy and fulfillment.

PAMELA HAWKINS

artist and art medicine woman

Connect with your sacred and creative magic

I'd love to help you rediscover your inner resource of
natural creativity, perhaps hidden from you, so that
you can feel more inspired, more connected to who
YOU ARE—your dreams, your insight, and
your capacity to express, and create the life
you most deeply desire!

We can also find creative and imaginative ways to
move through really challenging emotional
territory and transform it. The truly beautiful part is,
the "medicine" comes from deep inside of you,
so it's the perfect "blend" for you. Your inner
shaman knows what you most need.
And like a midwife,
I can help you bring it forth.

PAMELAHAWKINS.COM

FREED
BY THE
LIGHT
II

ANGELS, ALIENS AND
THE AFTERLIFE

MARGO M. MATEAS

THE FREED SAGA CONTINUES,
WITH YOUR REAL-LIFE STORIES ABOUT THE
SUPERNATURAL!

SUBMIT YOUR VERIFIABLE STORY TO:
STORIES@FREEDBYTHELIGHT.COM

ABOUT THE AUTHOR

Margo Mateas is an award-winning writer, scientifically verified healer, spiritual teacher and ordained minister who's helped thousands of people in more than 12 countries.

Margo's divine clairvoyance has been featured on major media outlets including Coast to Coast AM, Sirius XM, Fade to Black and more. She is the creator of Angelic Soul Clearing™ and works directly with the Archangels and other high-vibrational guides to clear the soul of darkness. She has a unique ability to see into energy centers and locate hidden entities and energies that are blocking a person's ability to be happy and heal.

Devoutly religious and spiritual, Margo had her first premonition at the age of eight. Angels began tutoring her in dreams at 13. She became a lay minister and professional speaker at 14 years old. She is now the lead pastor of Freed By The Light Ministries.

Margo was an investigative reporter and newspaper editor for 10 years before working for the world's largest public relations firm and becoming an internationally known trainer and executive coach to organizations including Google, Verizon and the Red Cross. She has been a featured speaker for the American Medical Association, the American Cancer Society and many others.

She is the author of the popular oracle, *The Career Cards: A Practical Guide to Life* and conducts online courses, workshops, speaking engagements and retreats all over the world.

She can be reached at www.margomateas.com.